WELSH-ENGLISH
ENGLISH-WELSH
Dictionary & Phrasebook

Hippocrene Dictionary & Phrasebooks

Albanian
Arabic (Eastern Arabic)
Arabic (Modern Standard)
Armenian (Eastern)
Armenian (Western)
Australian
Azerbaijani
Basque
Bosnian
Breton
British
Cajun French
Chechen
Chilenismos
Croatian
Czech
Danish
Dari *Romanized*
Esperanto
Estonian
Finnish
French
Georgian
German
Greek
Hebrew *Romanized*
Hindi
Hungarian
Igbo
Ilocano
Irish
Italian
Japanese *Romanized*
Korean

Lao *Romanized*
Latvian
Lithuanian
Malagasy
Maltese
Mongolian
Nepali *Romanized*
Norwegian
Pashto *Romanized*
Pilipino (Tagalog)
Polish
Portuguese (Brazilian)
Punjabi
Québécois
Romanian
Romansch
Russian
Serbian
Shona
Sicilian
Slovak
Slovene
Somali
Spanish (Latin American)
Swahili
Swedish
Tajik
Tamil *Romanized*
Thai *Romanized*
Turkish
Ukrainan
Urdu *Romanized*
Uzbek
Vietnamese

WELSH – ENGLISH
ENGLISH – WELSH
Dictionary & Phrasebook

Heini Gruffudd

HIPPOCRENE BOOKS, INC.
New York

Copyright © 2005 Heini Gruffudd
All rights reserved.

ISBN 0-7818-1070-1

Publisher: George Blagowidow
Editors: Robert Stanley Martin, Nicholas Williams
Welsh copyeditor: Elin Meek
Typesetting: Susan A. Ahlquist, Perfect Setting, East Hampton, NY
Jacket design: Cynthia Mallard, Cynergie Studio

For information, address:
    Hippocrene Books, Inc.
    171 Madison Avenue
    New York, NY 10016
    www.hippocrenebooks.com

Cataloging-in-Publication data available from the Library of Congress.

Printed in the United States of America.

CONTENTS

INTRODUCTION   vii

THE WELSH ALPHABET   1

PRONUNCIATION GUIDE   3

ABBREVIATIONS   5

A BRIEF GRAMMAR   7

WELSH-ENGLISH DICTIONARY   27

ENGLISH-WELSH DICTIONARY   97

PHRASEBOOK   173

INTRODUCTION
CYFLWYNIAD

Welsh, the language of the people of Wales, is spoken by close to a million people worldwide. According to the 2001 census, more than half a million Welsh residents speak it fluently, while many more have some knowledge and understanding of the language. International speakers congregate in Welsh societies all over the world.

Before the invasions of the Angles and Saxons during the Middle Ages, Welsh was the *lingua franca* of the British Isles. It has a long history and its rich literature extends back almost 1,500 years.

This dictionary and phrasebook concentrates on standard spoken Welsh, which is also used for writing. The phrasebook includes situations which you are likely to encounter in Wales, and the 6,000-entry two-way dictionary will give you basic vocabulary. The grammar section will help you form sentences.

Welsh is the predominant language in many parts of northern and western Wales, but large numbers speak it in cities and towns in the southern portion of the island. If you start a conversation with a Welsh greeting, you will quickly see if the person you're talking to can speak Welsh. If he or she can, you will be made doubly welcome.

Pob hwyl!

THE WELSH ALPHABET

Letter	English pronunciation
a	a (short) or ah (long)
b	b
c	k
ch	ch (as in Scottish 'loch')
d	d
dd	th (as in that)
e	eh (or ee after 'a' and 'o')
f	v
ff	ff
g	g
ng	ng
h	h
i	ee
j	j
l	l
ll	ll (voiceless 'l')
m	m
n	n
o	o
p	p
ph	ff
r	r
rh	rh
s	ss

t	t
th	th (voiceless)
u	ee
w	oo
y	uh *or* ee *or* i

The letters "w" and "y" are vowels in Welsh.

'^' is sometimes used to denote long vowels, e.g.
â (*ah*), ê (*eh*), î (*ee*), ô (*oh*), û (*ee*), ŵ(*oo*), ŷ (*ee*)

PRONUNCIATION GUIDE

Vowels are short or long, but always "flat":

a	as in bad, far
e	as in bed, nee
i	as in pin, seen, yacht
o	as in dog, note
u	as in been, (or French 'u' in northern Wales)
w	as in moon
y	as in pin, cut, been

Diphthongs:

ae	as in ay-o
oe	as in boy
yw	as in cue, or how
au	as in ay-o

When a word ends in "au," it can be pronounced as *ahee* or *eh* (in southern Wales), or *ah* (in northern Wales).

Most Welsh consonants are pronounced as in English. Welsh is much more phonetic than English, so the pronunciation is easier to discern.

The accent on most Welsh words is on the next-to-last syllable.

ABBREVIATIONS

adj.	adjective
adv.	adverb
art.	article
conj.	conjunction
f.	feminine
inter.	interjection
interrog.	interrogatory word
m.	masculine
mf.	masculine and feminine
n.	noun
neg.	negative word
nf.	feminine noun
nm.	masculine noun
npl.	plural noun
num.	numeral
ord.	ordinal
pl.	plural
poss.	possessive
prep.	preposition
pron.	pronoun
rel. pron.	relative pronoun
sing.	singular
v.	verb
vn.	verb-noun
+ S.M.	followed by soft mutation
+ N.M.	followed by nasal mutation
+ SP.M.	followed by spirant mutation
N.W.	North Wales
S.W.	South Wales

A BRIEF GRAMMAR
GRAMADEG BYR

VERBS

Verbs in Welsh can have a short form and a long (periphrastic) form. The easiest to use is the long form, and this is the form mainly presented in this book. Personal forms of the verb "to be" are followed by a pronoun, then a tense marker (*yn* or *wedi*), with the unconjugated verb put at the end.

Let us begin with a simple sentence construction in English, in the present tense:

I am going.   *Rydw i'n mynd.*

In the English, "I" is the subject pronoun, "am" [a conjugation of "to be"] is the auxiliary verb, and "going" is the verb participle.

In Welsh, the order of the subject pronoun and the auxiliary verb are reversed. A tense marker is then put before the verb denoting the action verb. The tense marker for continuing the time of the auxiliary verb is *yn*. The tense marker for indicating a time prior to the auxiliary verb is *wedi*. The verb denoting the action is not, as in English. a participle. It does not change its form from the verb-noun found in dictionary listings.

Therefore, in the Welsh equivalent of the "I am" in "I am going," the auxiliary verb *rydw* comes first and the subject pronoun *i* comes second. The verb-noun *mynd*, the Welsh equivalent of "going," comes after the tense marker *yn* (which changes to *'n* after a vowel).

Other examples:

I am singing.	*Rydw i'n canu.*
I am thinking.	*Rydw i'n meddwl.*

All tenses of a verb are indicated by a tense marker between the subject noun or pronoun and the verb noun.

In the present tense, the tense marker is *yn*. If the subject noun or pronoun ends with a vowel, a contraction is formed by dropping the *y*, leaving only the *'n*, e.g.

I am going.	*Rydw i'n mynd.*

In the perfect tense, the tense marker is *wedi*, e.g.

I have gone.	*Rydw i wedi mynd.*

This is the auxiliary verb in the imperfect and pluperfect tenses:

I was/I had	*Roeddwn i*

In the imperfect tense, the tense marker is the same as in the present, e.g.

I was going.	*Roeddwn i'n mynd.*

The marker in the pluperfect tense is the same as that in the perfect, e.g.

I had gone.	*Roeddwn i wedi mynd.*

The future tense and the future perfect tense are formed using conjugations of the Welsh equivalent of the auxiliary modal verbs *will* and *shall*.

The auxiliary verb in the first-person for the future and future-perfect tenses:

I shall/I shall have   *Bydda i*

This is the future-tense first-person conjugation of "to go". Note the structure: future-tense auxiliary verb + the tense marker *yn* + the verb-noun.

I shall go.   *Bydda i'n mynd.*

This is the future-perfect first-person conjugation. Again, note the structure: future-perfect auxiliary verb + the tense marker *wedi* + the verb-noun.

I shall have gone.   *Bydda i wedi mynd.*

The tense markers, in conjunction with the tense of the auxiliary verb (the equivalent of "to be") indicate the time of occurrence: *yn* maintains the tense of the verb; *wedi* denotes a prior action.

To master verbs in the present, perfect, future, pluperfect, and future perfect tenses, all you need to learn are conjugations of the verb "to be".

Welsh differs from English in that the main verb remains constant regardless of tense. This makes Welsh a very easy language to master.

The forms of *bod* ("to be"):

PRESENT TENSE

English	Welsh	Interrogative form
I am	*rydw i / dw i / w i*	*ydw i?*
you are	*rwyt ti*	*wyt ti?*
he is	*mae e*	*ydy e?*
she is	*mae hi*	*ydy hi?*
we are	*rydyn ni / ryn ni / dyn ni*	*ydyn ni?*
you are	*rydych chi / rych chi / dych chi*	*ydych chi?*
they are	*maen nhw*	*ydyn nhw?*

IMPERFECT TENSE

I was	*roeddwn i / ro'n i*	*oeddwn i? / o'n i?*
you were	*roeddet ti / ro't ti*	*oeddet ti? / o't ti?*
he was	*roedd e*	*oedd e?*
she was	*roedd hi*	*oedd hi?*
we were	*roedden ni / ro'n ni*	*oedden ni? / o'n ni?*
you were	*roeddech chi / ro'ch chi*	*oeddech chi? / o'ch chi?*
they were	*roedden nhw / ro'n nhw*	*oedden nhw? / o'n nhw?*

FUTURE TENSE

I shall	*bydda i*	*fydda i?*
you will	*byddi di*	*fyddi di?*
he will	*bydd e*	*fydd e?*
she will	*bydd hi*	*fydd hi?*

we shall	*byddwn ni*	*fyddwn ni?*
you will	*byddwch chi*	*fyddwch chi?*
they will	*byddan nhw*	*fyddan nhw?*

QUESTIONS

To form a question in the present or imperfect tenses with the first- and second-person conjugations, drop the "r" at the beginning of the auxiliary verb, e.g.

| Was he? | *Oedd e?* |

To form a question in the third-person singular (or with plural nouns), the auxiliary verb *mae* becomes *ydy*. The plural conjugation becomes *ydyn*, e.g.

Does she understand?	*Ydy hi'n deall?*
Are the men drinking?	*Ydy'r dynion yn yfed?*
Do they understand?	*Ydyn nhw yn deall?*

To form a question in the future tense, replace the "b" at the beginning of the auxiliary verb with an "f", e.g.

| Will you? | *Fyddwch chi?* |

ANSWERING QUESTIONS

Na is Welsh for "no".

Ie is one Welsh word for "yes". It is used to answer a question beginning with a noun or pronoun.

The auxiliary verb is used to answer "yes" to questions beginning with a verb, e.g.

Does she understand? – Yes.
Ydy hi'n deall? – Ydy.

Are you coming? – Yes (I am).
Ydych chi'n dod? – Ydw.

Were you there? – Yes (I was).
Oeddech chi yno? – Oeddwn.

Will you be on the train? – Yes (I shall).
Fyddwch chi ar y trên? – Bydda.

NEGATING VERBS

In the first- and second-person conjugations of present-tense verbs, the negative is formed by replacing the "r" at the beginning of the auxiliary verb with a "d" and putting the word *ddim* ("not") before the tense markers *yn* or *wedi*, e.g.

I don't understand.	*Dydw i ddim yn deall.*
She hadn't slept.	*Doedd hi ddim wedi cysgu.*

With the future tense, the negative is formed by replacing the "b" at the beginning of the auxiliary with "f" and placing *ddim* before the tense marker, e.g.

I won't pay /	*Fydda i ddim yn talu.*
I won't be paying.	

THE PAST TENSE

To form the past tense, the following endings are added to the verb stem:

Singular

first-person:	*-es i*
second-person:	*-est ti*
third-person (masculine):	*-odd e*
third-person (feminine):	*-odd hi*

Plural

first-person:	*-on ni*
second-person	*-och chi*
third-person	*-on nhw*

to get up	*codi*
I got up	*codes i*
you got up	*codest ti*
he got up	*cododd e*
she got up	*cododd hi*
we got up	*codon ni*
you got up	*codoch chi*
they got up	*codon nhw*

The following five verbs are irregular:

to go	*mynd*
I went	*es i*
you went	*est ti*
he went	*aeth e*
she went	*aeth hi*
we went	*aethon ni*
you went	*aethoch chi*
they went	*aethon nhw*

to have, to get	*cael*
I had	*ces i*
you had	*cest ti*
he had	*cas e*
she had	*cas hi*
we had	*cawson ni*
you had	*cawsoch chi*
they had	*cawson nhw*

to do, to make	*gwneud*
I did	*gwnes i*
you did	*gwnest ti*
he did	*gwnaeth e*
she did	*gwnaeth hi*
we did	*gwnaethon ni*
you did	*gwnaethoch chi*
they did	*gwnaethon nhw*

to come	*dod*
I came	*des i*
you came	*dest ti*
he came	*daeth e*
she came	*daeth hi*
we came	*daethon ni*
you came	*daethoch chi*
they came	*daethon nhw*

to be	*bod*
I was	*bues i*
you were	*buest ti*
he was	*buodd e*
she was	*buodd hi*
we were	*buon ni*

| you were | *buoch chi* |
| they were | *buon nhw* |

COMMANDS

To form commands, add *-wch* to the verb stem.

English verb	Welsh verb-stem	Welsh command
get up	*codi*	*codwch*
sit down	*eistedd*	*eisteddwch*
read	*darllen*	*darllenwch*
write	*ysgrifennu*	*ysgrifennwch*
talk	*siarad*	*siaradwch*

OTHER USEFUL VERB FORMS

I should	*dylwn i*
may I have	*ga i*
you may	*cewch*
I'll come	*do i*
I'll see	*gwela i*
I can	*galla i*
can you?	*allwch chi?*
will you (do)?	*wnewch chi?*
yes (I will)	*gwnaf*

QUESTION WORDS

The Welsh equivalents of English question words are:

| who | *pwy* |
| what | *beth* |

where	*ble*
when	*pryd*
why	*pam*
how	*sut*
how much	*faint*

These are followed in a sentence by the conjugation of the auxiliary, e.g.

Where does he live?	*Ble mae e'n byw?*
Who is he?	*Pwy ydy e?*
What is he drinking?	*Beth mae e'n yfed?*

The words *pwy* ("who") and *beth* ("what") may be followed with the word *sy* in the present tense, *oedd* in the imperfect tense, and *fydd* in the future tense, e.g.

Who's paying?	*Pwy sy'n talu?*
What was there?	*Beth oedd yno?*
Who will be coming?	*Pwy fydd yn dod?*

All verbs also have short forms, which are conjugated. These are most often used in the past tense.

USING SUB-CLAUSES

The following are some methods used to introduce sub-clauses:

Noun clauses:

| that | *bod* |
| I know that a bus is coming. | *Dwi'n gwybod bod bws yn dod.* |

that	*i*
I know that the bus came.	*Dwi'n gwybod i'r bws ddod.*

Adjectival clauses:

the bus **that is ...**	*y bws **sy'n** ...*
the bus **that has ...**	*y bws **sy wedi** ...*
the bus **that was ...**	*y bws **oedd** ...*
the bus **that will be ...**	*y bws **fydd yn** ...*

Adverbial clauses:

because it is raining	***achos mae** hi'n bwrw glaw*
	***achos ei bod** hi'n bwrw glaw*
as we arrived	***wrth** i ni gyrraedd*
as you know	***fel y** gwyddoch chi*
so that we are early	***fel y** byddwn ni'n gynnar*
if it rains	***os** bydd hi'n bwrw glaw*

ARTICLES

In English, there is a single definite article: *the*. Welsh has three: *y*, *yr*, and *r*.

The definite article *y* is used with nouns that begin with a consonant, e.g.

the cinema	*y cinema*

The definite article *yr* is used with nouns beginning with a vowel or the letter "h", e.g.

the river	*yr afon*
the school	*yr ysgol*
the road	*yr heol*

The definite article *yr* contracts to *'r* when it follows a vowel.

to the cinema	*i'r sinema*
from the school	*o'r ysgol*
to remember the work	*cofio'r gwaith*

There are no words signifying the indefinite article (the equivalent of the English *a* or *an*) in Welsh. It is inferred when a noun stands alone.

NOUNS

Most Welsh nouns are either masculine or feminine.

Examples of masculine nouns:

the man	*y dyn*
the door	*y drws*

Examples of feminine nouns:

the woman	*y fenyw*
the desk	*y ddesg*

Some nouns are both masculine and feminine, e.g.

the minute	*y munud / y funud*

The plural is formed in many ways. Whenever learning a new noun, learn the plural form along with the singular. The most common plural ending is *-au*:

field	*cae*
fields	*caeau*

Plural forms are noted in the Welsh-English and English-Welsh parts of the dictionary.

ADJECTIVES

Most adjectives follow the noun in Welsh, e.g.

a small town	*tref fach*
a small man	*dyn bach*

The following adjectives precede the noun, causing the first letter of the following noun to undergo soft mutation (mutation is explained further down):

main	*prif*
main work	*prif waith*
old	*hen*
an old man	*hen ddyn*

ADVERBS

Adverbs derived from adjectives are formed by placing *yn* before the adjective, e.g.

generous	*hael*
generously	*yn hael*
quick	*cyflym*
quickly	*yn gyflym*

There are several adverbs indicating place and time, e.g.

here	*yma*
then	*wedyn*
there	*yno*
today	*heddiw*
yesterday	*ddoe*

PRONOUNS

Examples of subject pronouns:

I	*i, fi*
you	*ti, di*
he, it, him	*e*
she, it, her	*hi*
we, us	*ni*
you	*chi*
they, them	*nhw*

The "you" equivalent *ti* is used with children, animals, and people you know well. It is always singular. The "you" equivalent *chi* can be either singular or plural.

Subject pronouns are put after the verb forms,. e.g.

I am	*Rydw i*

Examples of possessive pronouns:

my	*fy*
your	*dy*
his, her, its	*ei*
our	*ein*
your	*eich*
their	*eu*

The possessive pronoun is placed before the noun, which is followed by the appropriate subject pronoun, e.g.:

my bag	*fy mag i*
your father	*dy dad di*
his ticket	*ei docyn e*

her hair	*ei gwallt hi*
our lunch	*ein cinio ni*
your tea	*eich te chi*
their hotel	*eu gwesty nhw*

Note that some of these cause initial mutations (see below).

Possessive pronouns may also be used as indirect objects relative to a verb, e.g.

to pay me	*fy nhalu i*
to see you	*dy weld di*
to buy them	*eu prynu nhw*

Note that some of these cause initial mutations (see below).

CONJUNCTIONS

These words link parts of sentences, clauses or nouns, e.g.

and	*a*
because	*achos*
but	*ond*
or	*neu*

MUTATIONS

This is possibly the part of Welsh grammar that causes most concern to learners. The first thing to remember, however, is that most Welsh speakers make mistakes in this area, especially when talking, and that these mistakes have no effect on meaning.

There are nine letters, when used as the initial letter of a word, that can change to other letters in certain circumstances. Three of these letters change in three different ways, six change in two ways, and three others change in one way.

Letter	Soft mutation	Nasal mutation	Spirant mutation
c	g	ngh	ch
p	b	mh	ph
t	d	nh	th
b	f	m	
d	dd	n	
g	[drops off]	ng	
ll	l		
m	f		
rh	r		

Soft mutation occurs in:

1. Feminine singular nouns after the definite article, e.g.

   the mother   *mam → y fam*

2. Nouns after the prepositions *am, ar, gan, heb, i, o, dan, dros, trwy, wrth,* and *hyd,* e.g.

   to Cardiff   *Caerdydd → i Gaerdydd*

3. Nouns after the Welsh equivalents of the English "two," *dau* and *dwy,* e.g.

   two coffees   *goffi → dau goffi*

4. Adjectives after feminine singular nouns, e.g.

a good girl   *merch → merch dda*

5. Singular feminine nouns after *un* (the Welsh equivalent of "one"), e.g.

one chair   *cadair → un gadair*

6. Nouns and adjectives after *yn*, e.g.

it's good   *da* ["good"] → *mae e'n **dda***

it was a pub   *tafarn* ["tavern"] → *roedd hi'n **dafarn***

7. Nouns after the possessive pronouns *ei* ("his") and *dy* ("your"), e.g.

your father   *tad → dy dad*
his mother   *mam → ei fam*

Nasal mutation occurs in:

1. Nouns after *fy*, the Welsh equivalent of "my," e.g.

my brother   *brawd → fy mrawd*

2. Nouns after *yn*, the Welsh equivalent of "in," e.g.

in Cardiff   *Caerdydd → yng Nghaerdydd*

Spirant mutation occurs in:

1. Nouns and adjectives after *a*, the Welsh equivalent of "and," e.g.

pencil and paper   *papur* ["paper"] → *pensil a **phapur***

2. Nouns after *â*, the Welsh equivalent of "with," e.g.

| to visit [with] a castle | *castell* ["castle"] → *ymweld â **chastell*** |

3. Nouns after *ei* ("her"), e.g.

| her chair | *cadair* → *ei chadair* |

PREPOSITIONS

These show the position or direction of a thing or an action. They are often followed by a mutation (see above). In this list, * indicates those followed by a soft mutation, ** indicates those followed by a nasal mutation, and *** indicates those followed by a spirant mutation.

along	*ar hyd*
by [produced by]	*gan**
by [over by]	*ger, wrth**
by the side of	*yn ymyl*
in	*yn ***
for	*am**
from, of	*o**
near	*ger, wrth**
on	*ar**
over	*dros**
through	*trwy**
to	*i**
towards	*at**
under	*dan**
until	*hyd*, tan**
with	*gyda***, â****
without	*heb**

LEARNING WELSH
DYSEGU CYMRAEG

There are many opportunities to learn Welsh in classes. Many summer courses are offered, which include courses for beginners and more advanced students. Some are taught over a weekend, others can last a week or a fortnight, and other are taught over a longer period. Information about many courses is available from the Welsh Language Board, 5-7 St. Mary Street, Cardiff, CF10 1AT. E-mail: ymholiadau@bwrdd-yr-iaith.org.uk.

Information on coursebooks and other books for learners is available from the Welsh Books Council, Castell Brychan, Aberystwyth, Ceredigion, SY23 2JB. E-mail: cllc.marchnata@cllc.org.uk. They also have a website for selling Welsh books: www. Gwales.com.

WELSH–ENGLISH
DICTIONARY

Words are listed according to Welsh, rather than English, alphabetization.

Within the entries, words are alphabetized according to the English alphabet. (In Welsh dictionaries, it is standard practice to use the Welsh alphabet to alphabetize the definitions within entries.)

With noun entries, the plural form is indicated in one of two ways, depending on how it is created. If the plural is created by altering the root spelling of the singular noun, as with the noun *abaty* and its plural form *abatai*, it is indicated like this:

abaty/abatai

If, however, the plural is formed by adding a suffix to the original noun, as with the noun dyn and its plural form "dynion", it is indicated by following the singular noun with the suffix, like this:

dyn/-ion

For abbreviations, please refer to the list on page 7.

A

a *conj.* + *SP.M.* and; *interrog.* + *S.M.*; rel. pron. + *S.M.*
　　who, which, whom, that

â *conj.* + *SP.M.* with; *conj.* + *SP.M.* as

ab *nm.* son of

abaty/abatai *nm.* abbey

aber/-oedd *nm.* estuary

abl *adj.* able

absennol *adj.* absent

absenoldeb *nm.* absence

abwyd/-od *nm.* bait

ac *conj.* and; ~ **eithrio** *prep.* except, apart from

academaidd *adj.* academic

academi/academïau *nf.* academy

acen/-ion *nf.* accent

achlysur/-on *nm.* occasion

achos *conj.* because; *prep.* because of; /-ion *nm.* cause;
　　~ **llys**/achosion llys *nm.* court case

achosi *v.* to cause

achub *v.* to save

achwyn *v.* to complain

act/-au *nf.* act

actio *v.* to act

actor/-ion *nm.* actor

actores/-au *nf.* actress

acw *adv.* yonder, there

adain/adenydd *nf.* wing

adalw *v.* to recall

adar *npl.* birds

ad-daliad/-au *nm.* repayment

addas *adj.* suitable

addasu *v.* to adjust

addewid/-ion *nmf.* promise

addo *v.* to promise; ~ **rhywbeth i rywun** to promise
　　someone something

addurn/-iadau *nm.* decoration

addurno *v.* to decorate

addurnol *adj.* decorative

addysgu *v.* to educate, to teach

adeg/-au *nf.* period, time
adeilad/-au *nm.* building
adeiladol *adj.* constructive
adeiladu *v.* to build
adeiladwr/adeiladwyr *nm.* builder
aderyn/adar *nm.* bird
adfail/adfeilion *nm.* ruin
adfer *v.* to restore
adio *v.* to add
adlais/adleisiau *nm.* echo
adlewyrchiad/-au *nm.* reflection
adlewyrchu *v.* to reflect
adloniant *nm.* entertainment
adnabod *v.* to know *(a person, a place)*
adnewyddu *v.* to renew
adnod/-au *nf.* verse *(Biblical)*
adnodd/-au *nm.* resource
adolygiad/-au *nm.* review
adolygu *v.* to revise, to review
adran/-au *nf.* department, section
adre, adref *adv.* homewards
adrodd *v.* to recite, to report
adroddiad/-au *nm.* report, recitation
adwaith/adweithiau *nm.* reaction
adweithio *v.* to react
aeddfed *adj.* mature, ripe
aeddfedu *v.* to mature, to ripen
ael/-iau *nf.* brow
aelod/-au *nm.* member; ~ **Cynulliad** *nm.* Assembly
     Member; ~ **Seneddol** *nm.* Member of Parliament
aer *nf.* air; /ion *nm.* heir
aeron *npl.* berries
afal/-au *nm.* apple
Affrica *nf.* Africa
Affricanaidd *adj.* African
Affricanes/-au *nf.* African
Affricanwr/Affricanwyr *nm.* African
aflonyddu *v.* to disturb, to molest
afon/-ydd *nf.* river
afresymol *adj.* unreasonable

agor *v.* to open

agos *adj.* near; ~ **i'r dref** near the town

agwedd/-au *nmf.* attitude, aspect

ai *inter.* used before nouns, verb-nouns, pronouns and adjectives

ail *adj.* second

ailadrodd *v.* to repeat

ail law *adj.* secondhand

alcohol *nm.* alcohol

alergedd/-au *nm.* allergy

allan *adv.* out

allanfa/allanfeydd *nf.* exit

allanol *adj.* exterior, external

allfudo *v.* to emigrate

allwedd/-i *nf.* key

allweddell/-au *nf.* keyboard (*piano*)

Almaeneg *nf.* German language

Almaenes/-au *nf.* German

Almaenig *adj.* German

Almaenwr/Almaenwyr *nm.* German

am *prep.* + *S.M.* for

amau *v.* to doubt, to suspect

ambell *adj.* occasional, few

ambwilans/-ys *nm.* ambulance

am byth *adv.* forever

amcangyfrif *v.* to estimate

amddiffyn *v.* to defend

amddiffynfa/amddiffynfeydd *nf.* defense (*physical*)

amddiffyniad/-au *nm.* defense

America *f.* America

Americanes/-au *nf.* American

Americanwr/Americanwyr *nm.* American

amgáu *v.* to enclose

amgueddfa/amgueddfeydd *nf.* museum; ~ **Genedlaethol Cymru** Welsh National Museum; ~ **Werin Cymru** National Museum of Welsh Life

amgylchedd/-au *nm.* environment

amgylchiad/-au *nm.* circumstance

amheuaeth/-au *nf.* doubt

amhosibl *adj.* impossible

aml *adv.* often

amlen/-ni *nf.* envelope

amlwg *adj.* obvious, clear, evident

amrwd *adj.* raw, rough

amryw *adj.* several, various

amrywiaeth/-au *nm.* variety

amrywiol *adj.* various

amser/-au *nm.* time; **~ llawn** *nm.* full time

amserlen/-ni *nf.* timetable

amsugno *v.* to absorb

amwys *adj.* ambiguous

anabl *adj.* disabled

anaddas *adj.* unsuitable

anadl/-au *nmf.* breath

anadlu *v.* to breathe

anaf/-iadau *nm.* injury

anafu *v.* to injure

analluog *adj.* unable

anarferol *adj.* unusual

anferth *adj.* huge

anfon *v.* to send; **~ ymlaen** *v.* to forward, to send on

anfwytadwy *adj.* inedible

angel/angylion *nm.* angel

angen/anghenion *nm.* need; **~ rhywbeth ar rywun**
    someone needs something

angenrheidiol *adj.* essential, necessary

anghenfil/angenfilod *nm.* monster

anghofio *v.* to forget

anghredadwy *adj.* unbelievable

anghwrtais *adj.* discourteous

anghyfarwydd *adj.* unfamiliar

anghyfreithlon *adj.* illegal

anghysurus *adj.* uncomfortable

anghywir *adj.* wrong, incorrect

angladd/-au *nmf.* funeral

angor/-au,-ion *nf.* anchor

anhapus *adj.* unhappy

anhysbys *adj.* unknown

anifail/anifeiliaid *nm.* animal; **~ anwes** *nm.* pet

annhebyg *adj.* unlikely

annhebygol *adj.* improbable
annibynnol *adj.* independent
Annibynwyr *npl.* Independents (*religious denomination*)
annioddefol *adj.* unbearable
anniogel *adj.* unsafe
annog *v.* to urge
annwyl *adj.* dear
anodd *adj.* difficult, hard
anrheg/-ion *nf.* present, gift
anrhydedd/-au *nm.* honor
ansawdd/-ansoddau *nmf.* quality, condition, texture
ansoddair/ansoddeiriau *nm.* adjective
antur/-iau *nm.* venture
anwastad *adj.* uneven
anwesu *v.* to caress
anwybyddu *v.* to disregard
anymwybodol *adj.* unconscious
apwyntiad/-au *nm.* appointment
ar *prep.+ S.M.* on
Arab/-iaid *nm.* Arab
araf *adj.* slow
ar agor open; **~ ben** finished, over; **~ draws** across;
    ~ frys in haste; **~ gael** available; **~ ganol** in the
    middle of; **~ gau** closed; **~ gof** in memory; **~ goll**
    lost; **~ hap** accidentally; **ar hyd** *prep.* along; **~ ôl**
    prep. after; *adv.* left over; **~ unwaith** at once;
    ~ wahân separate, apart; **~ werth** for sale
araith/areithiau *nf.* speech
arall *adj.* other
arbenigrwydd *nm.* specialty
arbennig *adj.* special
arch/eirch *nf.* coffin
archfarchnad/-oedd *nf.* supermarket
archwilio *v.* to inspect
archwiliwr/archwilwyr *nm.* inspector, auditor
ardal/-oedd *nf.* area, region
arddangos *v.* to display
arddangosfa/arddangosfeydd *nf.* exhibition
arddegwyr *npl.* teenagers
ardderchog *adj.* excellent

arddodiad/arddodiaid *nm.* preposition
arddwrn/arddyrnau *nm.* wrist
aren/-nau *nf.* kidney
arfer/-ion *nm.* practice, habit
arferol *adj.* usual
arfordir/-oedd *nm.* coast
argyhoeddi *v.* to convince
argymell *v.* to recommend
argymhelliad/argymhellion *nm.* recommendation
arholi *v.* to examine
arholiad/-au *nm.* examination
arian *nm.* money, silver; *adj.* silver; ~ **mân** *nm.* small
    change; ~ **parod** *nm.* cash
ariannol *adj.* financial
ariannwr/arianwyr *nm.* cashier
arlywydd/-ion *nm.* president
arnofio *v.* to float
arogl/-euon *nm.* smell, scent
arogli *v.* to smell
arolygu *v.* to survey, to supervise
arolygydd/arolygwyr *nm.* inspector, superintendent
aros *v.* to wait, to stay
artiffisial *adj.* artificial
artist/-iaid *nm.* artist
arwain *v.* to lead
arweiniad *nm.* lead
arweinydd/-ion *nm.* leader, conductor
arwydd/-ion *nmf.* sign
arwyddo *v.* to sign
as *nf.* ace
asen/-nau *nf.* rib
asgwrn/esgyrn *nm.* bone
asgwrn cefn *nm.* backbone
Asia *nf.* Asia
Asiad/Asiaid *nm.* Asian
asiantaeth/-au *nf.* agency
astudiaeth/-au *nf.* study
astudio *v.* to study
at *prep.* + *S.M.* at, towards, to, as far as
atalnod/-au *nm.* punctuation mark

ateb/-ion *nm.* answer; *v.* to answer
atgoffa *v.* to remind
athletau *npl.* athletics
athletig *adj.* athletic
athletwr/athletwyr *nm.* athlete
athrawes/-au *nf.* teacher
athro/athrawon *nm.* teacher
aur *nm.* gold; *adj.* gold
awdur/-on *nm.* author
awdurdod/-au *nm.* authority
awdurdodi *v.* to authorize
awel/-on *nf.* breeze
Awst *nm.* August
awtomatig *adj.* automatic
awyr *nf.* sky; ~ **agored** *nf.* open air; ~ **iach** *nf.* fresh air
awyren/-nau *nf.* airplane
awyrol *nf.* aerial
awyru *v.* to ventilate

B

baban/-od *nm.* baby
bach *adj.* small
bachgen/bechgyn *nm.* boy
bachu *v.* to hook
bachyn/bachau *nm.* hook
baco *nm.* tobacco
bacteria *nm.* bacteria
bad/-au *nm.* boat
bad achub *nm.* lifeboat
bae/-au *nm.* bay
bag/-iau *nm.* bag
bai/beiau *nm.* fault
balans/-au *nm.*balance
balch *adj.* proud, glad
bale *nm.* ballet
banc/-iau *nm.* bank
bancio *v.* to bank
banciwr/bancwyr *nm.* banker

band/-iau *nm.* band
band rwber *nm.* rubber band
baner/-i *nm.* flag
bannod *nf.* article (*grammar*)
bar/-iau *nm.* bar
bara *nm.* bread
barbwr/barbwyr *nm.* barber
barddoniaeth *nf.* poetry
bargen/bargeinion *nf.* bargain
bargyfreithiwr/bargyfreithwyr *nm.* barrister
barn/-au *nf.* opinion, judgement
barnu *v.* to judge
barnwr/barnwyr *nm.* judge
bas *adj.* shallow
basged/-i *nf.* basket
basn/-au *nm.* basin
bath/baddonau *nm.* bath
bathdy brenhinol *nm.* royal mint (for making money,
      situated at Llantrisant, south Wales)
batri/-s *nm.* battery
baw *nm.* dirt
bawd/bodiau *nmf. thumb*
bedd/-au *nm.* grave
bedydd *nm.* baptism
bedyddio *v.* to baptize
Bedyddiwr/Bedyddwyr *nm.* Baptist
Beibl/-au *nm.* Bible
beic/-iau *nm.* bicycle
beichiog *adj.* pregnant
beic modur *nm.* motor bike
beirniadaeth/-au *nf.* adjudication, criticism
beirniadu *v.* to criticize
beiro/-s *nm.* ballpoint pen
Belgiad/Belgiaid *nm.* Belgian
bendithio *v.* to bless
ben i waered *adv.* upside down
benthyca *v.* to borrow, to lend
benthyciad/-au *nm.* loan
benthyg *v.* to borrow, to lend
benyw/-od *nf.* woman

benywaidd *adj.* feminine
berf/-au *nf.* verb
berwi *v.* to boil
beth *interrog.* what
betio *v.* to bet
bil/-iau *nm.* bill
biliwn/biliynau *nf.* billion
bin sbwriel *nm.* trash can
blaen/-au *nm.* front
blaenorol *adj.* previous
blanced/-i *nm.* blanket
blas/-au *nm.* taste
blasu *v.* to taste
blasus *adj.* tasty
blawd *nm.* flour
blew'r llygad *npl.* eyelashes
blewyn/blew *nm.* body hair
blin *adj.* sorry, tiresome; **mae'n flin gen i** I'm sorry
blino *v.* to tire
bloc/-iau *nm.* block
blodyn/-au *nm.* flower
blodyn haul *nm.* sunflower
bloedd/-iadau *nm.* shout, cry
bloeddio *v.* to shout
blows/-ys *nf.* blouse
blwch/blychau *nm.* box; ~ **llwch** *nm.* ashtray; ~ **postio**
    nm. post box
blwyddyn/blynyddoedd *nf.* year; ~ **naid** *nf.* leap year;
    B~ Newydd Dda! Happy New Year!
blynyddol *adj.* annual
bob *adj. see* pob; ~ **amser** always; ~ **dydd** every day
boch/-au *nf.* cheek
bod *v.* to be; *pron.* that
bodlon *adj.* contended, satisfied
bodloni *v.* to satisfy
bodolaeth *nf.* existence
bodoli *v.* to exist
bol/-iau *nm.* stomach, belly
bola/boliau *nm.* belly
bollt/byllt *nf.* bolt

bom/-iau *nm.* bomb

bonedd *nm.* aristocracy

bore/-au *nm.* morning; ~ **da** good morning; ~ **'ma** this morning

bos/-ys *nm.* boss

botwm/botymau *nm.* button; ~ **bol** *nm.* belly button

braf *adj.* fine

braich/breichiau *nf.* arm

braster/-au *nm.* fat

bratiaith *nf.* patois

brawd/brodyr *nm.* brother

brawddeg/-au *nf.* sentence

brawd yng nghyfraith *nm.* brother-in-law

brecwast/-au *nm.* breakfast

bregus *adj.* frail

breichled/-au *nf.* bracelet

brenhines/breninesau *nf.* queen

brenhinol *adj.* royal

brenin/brenhinoedd *nm.* king

brest *nf.* breast, chest

brifo *v.* to hurt

brig/-au *nm.* top, summit

briwsion *npl.* crumbs

bro/-ydd *nf.* area, region

brodor/-ion *nm.* inhabitant, native

brodorol *adj.* native

broga/-od *nm.* frog

bron/-nau *nf.* breast; *adv.* almost

brown *adj.* brown

brwd *adj.* enthusiastic

brwdfrydedd *nm.* enthusiasm

brwsh/-ys *nm.* brush; ~ **dannedd** toothbrush

brwsio *v.* to brush

bryn/-iau *nm.* hill

bryniog *adj.* hilly

brys *nm.* haste

brysio *v.* to hurry

buan *adj.* soon

buarth/-au *nm.* yard

budd/-ion *nm.* benefit

bugail/bugeiliaid *nm.* shepherd
busnes/-au *nm.* business
busneslyd *adj.* nosy, meddlesome
buwch/buchod *nf.* cow
bwa/bwâu *nm.* bow
bwced/-i *nmf.* bucket
bwlch/bylchau *nm.* gap, pass (*mountain*)
bwled/-i *nf.* bullet
bwrdd/byrddau *nm.* table; ~ **smwddio** *nm.* ironing board;
    B~ yr Iaith Gymraeg *nm.* Welsh Language Board
bwrw *v.* to hit; ~ **cesair** *v.* to hail; ~ **eira** *v.* to snow;
    ~ **glaw** *v.* to rain
bws/bysus *nm.* bus
bwyd/-ydd *nm.* food
bwydlen/-ni *nf.* menu
bwydo *v.* to feed
bwyler/-i *nm.* boiler
bwytadwy *adj.* edible
bwyty/bwytai *nm.* restaurant
byd/-oedd *nm.* world
byddar *adj.* deaf
byddin/-oedd *nf.* army
byd-eang *adj.* worldwide
bydysawd *nm.* universe
bygwth *v.* to threaten
bygythiad/-au *nm.* threat
bylb/-iau *nm.* bulb
byr *adj.* short
byr-bryd/-au *nm.* snack
byrfyfyr *adj.* impromptu
byrhau *v.* to shorten
bys/-edd *nm.* finger
bys bawd *nm.* thumb
bysellfwrdd *nm.* keyboard (*computer*)
bys troed *nm.* toe
byth *adv.* ever, never
bythgofiadwy *adj.* unforgettable
byw *v.* to live; *adj.* alive
bywyd/-au *nm.* life

C

cabol *nm.* polish
caboli *v.* to polish
cacynen/cacwn *nf.* wasp
cadair/cadeiriau *nf.* chair
cadair freichiau *nf.* armchair
cadarn *adj.* strong, steady
cadarnhaol *adj.* positive
cadarnhau *v.* to confirm
cadw *v.* to keep; ~ **lle** *v.* to keep a place; **sŵn** *v.* to make a noise
cadwyn/-au *nf.* chain
cae/-au *nm.* field
cael *v.* to have, to obtain, to get; ~ **gafael ar** *v.* to get hold of
caffe/-s *nm.* café
cais/ceisiadau *nm.* application
cais/ceisiau *nmf.* try (*rugby*)
Calan *nm.* New Year's Day
Calan Gaeaf *nm.* Halloween
Calan Mai *nm.* May Day
caled *adj.* hard, difficult
calendr/-au *nm.* calendar
calon/-nau *nf.* heart
cam/-au *nm.* step, wrong
camddeall *v.* to misunderstand
camddealltwriaeth *nf.* misunderstanding
cam-drin *v.* to abuse, to misuse
camera/camerâu *nm.* camera
camera digidol *nm.* digital camera
camera fideo *nm.* video camera
camsyniad/-au *nm.* mistake
camu *v.* to step
cân/caneuon *nf.* song
Canada *nf.* Canada
Canades/-au *nf.* Canadian
Canadiad/Canadiaid *nm.* Canadian
canfod *v.* to find, to discover
caniatáu *v.* to allow

canlyniad/-au *nm.* result
cannwyll/canhwyllau *nf.* candle
canol/-au *nm.* middle
canol dydd *nm.* midday
canolfan groeso *nf.* tourist information center
canol nos *nm.* midnight
canolog *adj.* central
canol y dref *nm.* town center
canrif/-oedd *nf.* century
canser/-au *nm.* cancer
cant/cannoedd *nm.* hundred
canu *v.* to sing
canŵ/-au *nm.* canoe
canwr/cantorion *nm.* singer
cap/-iau *nm.* cap
capel/-i *nm.* chapel
capten/capteiniaid *nm.* captain
car/ceir *nm.* car
carchar/-au *nm.* prison
carco *v.* to baby-sit
cardfwrdd *nm.* cardboard
cardota *v.* to beg
cardotyn/cardotwyr *nm.* beggar
caredig *adj.* kind
caredigrwydd *nm.* kindness
cariad/-on *nm.* lover, love
cario *v.* to carry
carped/-i *nm.* carpet
carreg/cerrig *nf.* stone; ~ **fedd** *nf.* gravestone; ~ **filltir**
    nf. milestone
carthen/-ni *nf.* quilt
cartref/-i *nm.* home
caru *v.* to love
cas *adj.* nasty
casáu *v.* to hate
casgliad/-au *nm.* collection
casglu *v.* to collect
casineb *nm.* hate
castell/cestyll *nm.* castle
catalog/-au *nm.* catalogue

cath/-od *nf.* cat
Catholig *adj.* Catholic
Catholigwr/Catholigion *nm.* Catholic
Catholigwraig/Catholigwragedd *nf.* Catholic
cau *v.* to close
cawl/-iau *nm.* soup
cawod/-ydd *nf.* shower
caws *nm.* cheese
CD/au *nm.* CD
CD-ROM *nm.* CD-ROM
cebl/-au *nm.* cable
ceffyl/-au *nm.* horse
cefn/-au *nm.* back
cefnder/cefndyr *nm.* cousin
cefnfor/-oedd *nm.* ocean
cegin/-au *nf.* kitchen
ceisio *v.* to try, to attempt
celficyn/celfi *nm.* furniture
celfyddyd *nf.* art
cell/-oedd *nf.* cell
Celt/-iaid *nm.* Celt
celwydd/-au *nm.* lie, untruth
celwyddgi/celwyddgwn *nm.* liar
cemegol *adj.* chemical
cenedl/cenhedloedd *nf.* nation
cenedlaethol *adj.* national
cenhinen/cennin *nf.* leek
cenhinen Bedr *nf.* daffodil
centimetr/-au *nm.* centimeter
cerdd/-i *nf.* poem, song
cerddor/-ion *nm.* musician
cerddorfa/cerddorfeydd *nf.* orchestra
cerddoriaeth *nf.* music
cerddwr/cerddwyr *nm.* walker
cerdyn/cardiau *nm.* card
cerdyn credyd *nm.* credit card
cerdyn post *nm.* postcard
cerflun/-iau *nm.* statue
cês/cesys *nm.* case
cesail/ceseiliau *nf.* armpit

cesair *nm.* hail

cig/-oedd *nm.* meat

cigydd/-ion *nm.* butcher

cildwrn/cildyrnau *nm.* tip (*money*)

cilo/-s *nm.* kilo

cilometr/-au *nm.* kilometer

cinio/ciniawau *nmf.* dinner, lunch

cist/-iau *nf.* safe, box

cist car *nf.* car boot

claddu *v.* to bury

claear *adj.* lukewarm

clais/cleisiau *nf.* bruise

clasurol *adj.* classical

clefyd/-au *nm.* disease, illness; ~ **gwenerol** venereal disease

cleient/-iaid *nm.* client

clinig/-au *nm.* clinic

clir *adj.* clear

clo/-eon *nm.* lock

cloc/-iau *nm.* clock; ~ **larwm** alarm clock

cloch/clychau *nm.* bell

cloff *adj.* lame

cloffi *v.* to limp

clogwyn/-i *nm.* cliff

cloi *v.* to lock

clorian/-nau *nf.* scales (*for weighing*)

clun/-iau *nf.* hip

clustog/-au *nf.* cushion

clwb/clybiau *nm.* club; ~ **dawnsio** dancing club

clwyd/-i *nf.* gate

clyfar *adj.* clever, smart

clymu *v.* to tie

clyw *nm.* hearing

clywed *v.* to hear

cneuen/cnau *nf.* nut

cnoc/-iau *nm.* knock

cnocio *v.* to knock

cnoi *v.* to bite

coch *adj.* red

cod/-au *nm.* code; ~ **post** postal code

codi *v.* to pick up, to rise, to get up; ~ **arian** to raise money

codiad/-au *nm.* rise, erection; ~ **cyflog** pay raise; ~ **haul** sunrise

coeden/coed *nf.* tree

coes/-au *nf.* leg

cof/-ion *nm.* memory; **~ion gorau** best wishes

coffi *nm.* coffee

cofiadwy *adj.* memorable

cofio *v.* to remember; **cofiwch fi at Huw** give Huw my regards

cofnod/-ion *nm.* minute, record

cofnodi *v.* to record

cofrestr/-i/-au *nf.* register

cofrestru *v.* to register

cofrodd/-ion *nf.* souvenir

coginio *v.* to cook

cogydd/-ion *nm.* cook

cogyddes/-au *nf.* cook

coleg/-au *nm.* college; ~ **addysg bellach** technical school

colled/-ion *nf.* loss

colli *v.* to lose

colofn/-au *nf.* column

colur/-on *nm.* make-up

comisiwn/comisiynau *nm.* commission

concrit *nm.* concrete

condemnio *v.* to condemn

condom/-au *nm.* condom

conswl/consylau *nm.* consul

copa/-on *nf.* summit

copi/copïau *nm.* copy

copïo *v.* to copy

corcyn/cyrc *nm.* cork

corff/-cyrff *nm.* body

corfforol *adj.* physical

corn/cyrn *nm.* horn

cornel/-i *nmf.* corner

cors/-ydd *nf.* bog, fen

cortyn/-nau *nm.* string

cosb/-au *nf.* punishment

cosbi *v.* to punish

cosi *v.* to tickle, to itch

cot/-iau *nf.* coat; ~ **fawr** overcoat

cotwm *nm.* cotton
crac/-iau *nm.* crack; *adj.* angry
cracio *v.* to crack
crafu *v.* to scratch
cragen/cregyn *nf.* shell
crai *adj.* raw
craidd/creiddiau *nm.* core
craig/creigiau *nf.* rock
craith/creithiau *nf.* scar
crebachu *v.* to shrink
cred/-au *nf.* belief
credu *v.* to believe
crefft/-au *nf.* craft
crefftwr/crefftwyr *nm.* craftsman
crefydd/-au *nf.* religion
crefyddol *adj.* religious
creu *v.* to create
crib/-au *nf.* comb, ridge
cribo *v.* to comb
criced *nm.* cricket
crio *v.* to cry
Cristion/-ogion, Cristnogion *nm.* Christian
Cristnogol *adj.* Christian
criw/-iau *nm.* crew
crochenwaith *nm.* pottery
croen/crwyn *nm.* skin
croes/-au *nf.* cross; *adj.* cross
croesair/croeseiriau *nm.* crossword
croesi *v.* to cross
croeso *nm.* welcome
crogi *v.* to hang
cromlech/-i *nf.* cromlech, dolmen
cropian *v.* to crawl
crwn *adj.* round
crwt/cryts *nm.* boy, lad
cryf *adj.* strong
cryno *adj.* brief, concise
crynodeb/-au *nm.* summary
crys/-au *nm.* shirt
cuddio *v.* to hide
cul *adj.* narrow

cur calon *nm.* heart attack
curiad calon *nm.* heartbeat
curo *v.* to beat
cur pen *nm.* headache [*N.W.*]
cusan/-au *nf.* kiss
cusanu *v.* to kiss
cwch/cychod *nm.* boat; ~ **gwenyn** beehive; ~ **hwylio** sailboat
cweryla *v.* to quarrel
cwestiwn/cwestiynau *nm.* question
cwlwm/clymau *nm.* knot
cwm/cymoedd *nm.* valley
cwmni/cwmnïau *nm.* company; ~ **awyrennau** airline
cwmwl/cymylau *nm.* cloud
cwningen/cwningod *nf.* rabbit
cwpan/-au *nmf.* cup
cwpwrdd/cypyrddau *nm.* cupboard; ~ **llyfrau** bookcase
cwrdd/cyrddau *nm.* meeting; *v.* to meet; **rwy'n falch o gwrdd â chi** I'm glad to meet you
cwrs/cyrsiau *nm.* course
cwrtais *adj.* courteous
cwrw *nm.* beer
cwsg *nm.* sleep
cwsmer/-iaid *nm.* customer
cwt/cytau *nm.* queue
cwyn/-ion *nmf.* complaint
cwyno *v.* to complain
cybydd/-ion *nm.* miser
cybyddlyd *adj.* miserly
cychwyn *v.* to start
cychwynnol *adj.* initial
cydnabod *v.* to acknowledge
cydnabyddiaeth/-au *nf.* acknowledgement
cydraddoldeb *nm.* equality
cydymdeimlad *nm.* sympathy
cyfaddef *v.* to admit
cyfaddefiad/-au *nm.* admission
cyfaill/cyfeillion *nm.* friend
cyfan *adj.* whole
cyfandir/-oedd *nm.* continent
cyfansoddi *v.* to compose

cyfansoddwr/cyfansoddwyr *nm.* composer
cyfanswm/cyfansymiau *nm.* total
cyfarch *v.* to greet
cyfarfod/-ydd *nm.* meeting; *v.* to meet
cyfartal *adj.* equal
cyfartaledd/-au *nm.* average
cyfateb *v.* to correspond
cyfathrebu *v.* to communicate
cyfeillgar *adj.* friendly
cyfeiriad/-au *nm.* address, direction
cyfeirio *v.* to direct
cyfenw/-au *nm.* surname
cyffredin *adj.* common
cyffredinol *adj.* general
cyffro/-adau *nm.* excitement
cyffroi *v.* to excite
cyffrous *adj.* exciting
cyffur/-iau *nm.* drug
cyffwrdd *v.* to touch
cyfiawnder *nm.* justice
cyfieithu *v.* to translate
cyfieithydd/cyfieithwyr *nm.* translator
cyflawn *adj.* complete
cyflawni *v.* to accomplish
cyfleus *adj.* convenient
cyflog/-au *nmf.* pay, salary
cyflwr/cyflyrau *nm.* condition.
cyflwyniad/-au *nm.* presentation, introduction
cyflwyno *v.* to present, to introduce
cyflym *adj.* fast, quick
cyflymder/-au *nm.* speed
cyflymu *v.* to accelerate
cyfnewid *v.* to exchange
cyfnither/-od *nf.* cousin
cyfnod/-au *nm.* period, era
cyfoes *adj.* contemporary
cyfoeth *nm.* wealth
cyfoethog *adj.* rich
cyfog *nm.* vomit
cyfoglyd *adj.* sickening
cyfradd/-au *nf.* rate; ~ **gyfnewid** exchange rate

cyfraith/cyfreithiau *nf.* law
cyfredol *adj.* current
cyfreithiwr/cyfreithwyr *nm.* solicitor
cyfres/-i *nf.* series
cyfrif/-on *nm.* account; *v.* to count
cyfrifiadur/-on *nm.* computer; ~ **pen-lin** laptop
cyfrifiannell/-au *nf.* calculator
cyfrifo *v.* to count
cyfrifol *adj.* responsible
cyfrifoldeb/-au *nm.* responsibility
cyfrifydd/-ion *nm.* accountant
cyfrinach/-au *nf.* secret
cyfrinachol *adj.* secret
cyfun *adj.* comprehensive
cyfuniad/-au *nm.* combination
cyf-weld *v.* to interview
cyfweliad /-au *nm.* interview
cyfyng *adj.* narrow, constricted
cyfyngu *v.* to restrict
cyhoeddi *v.* to publish
cyhoeddiad/-au *nm.* publication
cyhoeddus *adj.* public
cyhoeddwr/cyhoeddwyr *nm.* publisher
cyhuddo *v.* to accuse
cyhyr/-au *nm.* muscle
cyhyrog *adj.* muscular
cylch/-oedd *nm.* circle; ~ **chwarae** playgroup
cylchfan/-nau *nf.* roundabout
cylchgrawn/cylchgronau *nm.* magazine
cyllell/cyllyll *nf.* knife; ~ **boced** pocketknife; ~ **fara** bread knife
cyllideb/-au *nf.* budget
cymdeithas/-au *nf.* society; **C~ yr Iaith** Welsh Language Society
cymdogol *adj.* neighborly
cymedrol *adj.* moderate
cymeradwyo *v.* to approve
cymeriad/-au *nm.* character
cymhariaeth/cymariaethau *nf.* comparison
cymharu *v.* to compare

cymhelliad/cymhellion *nm.* motive
cymorth/cymhorthion *nm.* aid, help
cymryd *v.* to take
cymydog/cymdogion *nm.* neighbor
cymysg *adj.* mixed
cymysgu *v.* to mix
cyn *prep.* before
cynefino *v.* to familiarize
cyngerdd/cyngherddau *nmf.* concert
cynghrair/cynghreiriau *nm.* league
cyngor/ion *nm.* advice
cyngor/cynghorion *nm.* council
cynhadledd/cynadleddau *nf.* conference; ~ **fideo** video
    conference
cynhaeaf/cynaeafau *nm.* harvest
cynhwysydd/cynwysyddion *nm.* container
cynhyrchu *v.* to produce
cynllun/-iau *nm.* plan
cynnes *adj.* warm
cynnig/cynigion *nm.* offer; *v.* to offer
cynnwys *nm.* contents; *v.* to contain
cynnydd *nm.* increase
cynnyrch/cynhyrchion *nm.* produce
cynorthwyo *v.* to aid, to help
cynorthwywr/cynorthwywyr *nm.* helper
cynorthwywraig/cynorthwywragedd *nm.* helper
cynorthwy-ydd/cynorthwy-yddion *nm.* helper
cynrychioli *v.* to represent
cynrychiolydd/cynrychiolwyr *nm.* delegate, representative
cyntaf *adj.* first
cyntedd/-au *nm.* hallway
cyntun *nm.* nap
cynulliad/-au *nm.* assembly, gathering; **C~ Cenedlaethol
    Cymru** National Assembly for Wales
cynyddu *v.* to increase
cyplysnod/-au *nm.* hyphen
cyrliog *adj.* curly
cyrraedd *v.* to arrive
cysgod/-ion *nm.* shadow, shelter
cysgodi *v.* to shelter

cysgu *v.* to sleep
cyson *adj.* regular
cystadleuaeth/cystadlaethau *nf.* competition
cystadlu *v.* to compete
cysuro *v.* to comfort
cysurus *adj.* comfortable
cyswllt/cysylltau *nm.* connection
cysylltiad/-au *nm.* connection
cysylltu *v.* to connect
cytsain/cytseiniaid *nf.* consonant
cytundeb/-au *nm.* agreement
cytuno *v.* to agree
cyw/-ion *nm.* chicken; ~ **iâr** chicken
cywilydd *nm.* shame
cywilyddus *adj.* shameful, disgraceful
cywir *adj.* correct
cywiro *v.* to correct

CH

chi *pron.* you
chwaer/chwiorydd *nf.* sister
chwaer yng nghyfraith *nf.* sister-in-law
chwaethus *adj.* tasteful
chwalu *v.* demolish, shatter
chwant bwyd appetite; **mae ~ arna i** I'm hungry
chwarae *v.* to play; ~ **teg** fair play
chwaraeon *npl.* games, sport
chwaraewr/chwaraewyr *nm.* player; ~ **CD** CD player
chwarter/-i *nm.* quarter
chwe *num.* six (*used in front of nouns*)
chwech *num.* six
chwedl/-au *nf.* tale, legend
Chwefror *nm.* February
chwerthin *v.* to laugh
chwerw *adj.* bitter
chwilio *v.* to search, to look for; ~ **am** to look for
chwistrell/-au *nf.* syringe, spray; ~ **gwallt** *nf.* hair spray
chwistrellu *v.* to spray, to inject

chwith *adj.* left
chwyddo *v.* to swell
chwyddwydr/-au *nm.* magnifying glass
chwydu *v.* to vomit
chwyrnu *v.* to snore

D

da *adj.* good
dad *nm.* dad
dadl/-euon *nf.* debate
dadlaith *v.* to thaw
dadlwytho *v.* to unload
dadwisgo *v.* to undress
daear/-au *nf.* earth
daearyddiaeth *nf.* geography
dal *v.* to catch, to continue; ~ **i weithio** to continue
    working
dalen/-nau *nf.* page
dall *adj.* blind
dallineb *nm.* blindness
damwain/damweiniau *nf.* accident; **ar ddamwain**
    accidentally
dan *prep.* + *S.M.* under; ~ **do** indoors
danfon *v.* to send
dangos *v.* to show
dannodd *nf.* toothache
dant/dannedd *nm.* tooth
darbodus *adj.* economical
darlith/-iau/-oedd *nf.* lecture
darlithio *v.* to lecture
darlithydd/darlithwyr *nm.* lecturer
darllen *v.* to read
darllenydd/darllenwyr *nm.* reader
darlun/iau *nm.* picture
darlunio *v.* to illustrate
darn/-au *nm.* piece; ~ **arian** coin; ~ **sbâr** spare part
darpariaeth/-au *nf.* provision
darparu *v.* to provide

datgan *v.* to declare
datganiad/-au *nm.* declaration
dathlu *v.* to celebrate
datod *v.* to untie
dau *num. m.* + *S.M.* two
dawnsio *v.* to dance
dde *adj.* right
ddoe *adv.* yesterday
de *nm.* south; *adj.* right
deall *v.* to understand
deallus *adj.* intelligent, smart
deallusrwydd *nm.* intelligence
dechrau *v.* to start
dechreuad/-au *nm.* start, beginning
dechreuwr/dechreuwyr *nm.* learner
deffro *v.* to waken, to awake
defnydd/-iau *nm.* use, material
defnyddio *v.* to use
defnyddiol *adj.* useful
deg *num.* ten
degawd/-au *nm.* decade
dehongli *v.* to interpret
deilen/dail *nf.* leaf
delfryd/-au *nf.* ideal
delfrydol *adj.* ideal
delio *v.* to deal
delwedd/-au *nf.* image
deniadol *adj.* attractive
denu *v.* to attract
derbyn *v.* to accept
derbyniad/-au *nm.* reception
derbynneb/derbynebau *nf.* receipt
derbynnydd/derbynyddion *nm.* receptionist
dethol *v.* to select; *adj.* select
detholiad/-au *nm.* selection
deunydd/-iau *nm.* material
dewin/-iaid *nm.* magician
dewis/-iadau *nm.* choice; *v.* to choose
dianc *v.* to escape
diangen *adj.* unnecessary

dibynadwy *adj.* dependable
dibynnu *v.* to depend
dicter *nm.* rage, anger
diddanu *v.* to entertain
diddiwedd *adj.* endless
diddordeb/-au *nm.* interest
diddorol *adj.* interesting
diderfyn *adj.* endless
difetha *v.* to destroy
diffodd *v.* to extinguish
diffoddwr/diffoddwyr *nm.* extinguisher
diffyg/-ion *nm.* lack, defect, fault; **~ cwsg** lack of sleep;
    ~ traul indigestion
difrifol *adj.* serious
dig *adj.* angry
digon *nm.* enough; **~ o fwyd** enough food
digwydd *v.* to happen
digwyddiad/-au *nm.* happening
dihareb/diarhebion *nf.* proverb
di-hid *adj.* indifferent
dileu *v.* to delete
dillad *npl.* clothes; **~ gwely** bedclothes, bed linens;
    ~ isaf underwear
dilledyn/dillad *nm.* garment
dilyn *v.* to follow
dilys *adj.* genuine
dilysu *v.* to verify
dim *nm.* nothing; **~ byd** nothing; **~ ond** only
dinas/-oedd *nf.* city
dinesydd/dinasyddion *nm.* citizen
diniwed *adj.* innocent
diod/-ydd *nf.* drink
dioddef *v.* to suffer
diog *adj.* lazy
diogel *adj.* safe
diogelwch *nm.* safety
diogyn *nm.* lazybones
diolch/-iadau *nm.* thanks; **~ yn fawr** thank you very much
diolchgar *adj.* thankful
diosg *v.* to undress, to take off

dirwy/-on *nf.* fine (*punishment*)
di-rym *adj.* powerless
disglair *adj.* bright
disgleirio *v.* to shine
disgownt/-iau *nm.* discount
disgwyl *v.* to expect
disgwyliad/-au *nm.* expectation
disodli *v.* to replace
distrywio *v.* to destroy
diwedd/-au *nm.* end
diweddar *adj.* recent
di-werth *adj.* valueless
diwethaf *adj.* last
diwrnod/-au *nm.* day
diwydiannol *adj.* industrial
diwydiant/diwydiannau *nm.* industry
diwylliannol *adj.* cultural
diwylliant/diwylliannau *nm.* culture
do *adv.* yes
dod *v.* to come; ~ **â** to bring; ~ **yn** to become
dodwy *v.* to lay (*egg*)
dolur/-iau *nm.* pain
doniol *adj.* funny
dosbarth/dosbarthiadau *nm.* class; ~ **meithrin** kindergarten
drama/dramâu *nf.* drama
drewi *v.* to stink
dringo *v.* to climb
dros *prep.* + *S.M.* over; ~ **dro** temporary
drud *adj.* expensive
drwg *adj.* bad, naughty
drwgdybio *v.* to suspect
drych/-au *nm.* mirror
dryll/-au *nmf.* gun
du *adj.* black
dull/-iau *nm.* method
dur *nm.* steel
duw/-iau *nm.* god
dweud *v.* to say; ~ **wrth** + *S.M.* to tell
dwfn *adj.* deep
dŵr *nm.* water; ~ **tap** tap water

dwrn/dyrnau *nm.* fist
dwy *num. f.*+ *S.M.* two
dwyieithog *adj.* bilingual
dwyn *v.* to steal
dwyrain *nm.* east
dy *pron.*+ *S.M.* your
dychmygu *v.* to imagine
dychwelyd *v.* to return
dychymyg/dychmygion *nm.* imagination
dydd/-iau *nm.* day; **D~ Calan** New Year's Day; **D~ Llun**
    Monday; **~ gwaith** weekday
dyddiad/-au *nm.* date
dyddiol *adj.* daily
dyfais/dyfeisiau *nf.* device
dyfalu *v.* to guess
dyfarniad/-au *nm.* adjudication
dyfarnwr/dyfarnwyr *nm.* referee
dyfeisio *v.* to devise
dyffryn/-noedd *nm.* vale
dyfnder/-au *nm.* depth
dyfodol *nm.* future
dyfyniad/-au *nm.* quotation
dyled/-ion *nf.* debt
dymuno *v.* to wish
dyn/-ion *nm.* man; **~ tân** fireman
dynesu *v.* to approach
dynol *adj.* human
dysgu *v.* to learn, to teach
dyweddïad/-au *nm.* engagement
dyweddïo *v.* to become engaged

E

eang *adj.* broad
eangfrydig *adj.* broadminded
ebol/-ion *nm.* foal
ebost *nm.* e-mail
Ebrill *nm.* April
echdoe *adv.* day before yesterday

edifarhau *v.* to regret

edmygu *v.* to admire

edrych *v.* to look; **~ ar ôl** to look after

ef *pron.* he

efallai *adv.* perhaps

efelychiad/-au *nm.* imitation

efelychu *v.* to imitate

effeithio *v.* to effect

eglwys/-i *nf.* church; **~ gadeiriol** cathedral; **yr E~ yng Nghymru** the Church in Wales

egni/egnïon *nm.* energy

egnïol *adj.* energetic

egwyddor/-ion *nf.* principle

ei *pron.* his + *S.M.*, her + *SP.M.*

eich *pron.* your

Eidaleg *nf.* Italian (*language*)

Eidales/-au *nf.* Italian

Eidalwr/Eidalwyr *nm.* Italian

eiddigedd *nm.* jealousy

eiddigeddus *adj.* jealous

eiddo *nm.* property

eillio *v.* to shave

eilliwr/eillwyr *nm.* razor

ein *pron.* our

eira *nm.* snow; **bwrw ~** to snow

eisiau *nm.* want; **mae ~ te arna i** I want tea

eisoes *adv.* already

eistedd *v.* to sit

eisteddfod/-au *nf.* Welsh cultural competitive festival; **E~ Genedlaethol Cymru** Welsh National Eisteddfod

eitem/-au *nf.* item

eithaf/-ion *nm.* extremity; *adv.* quite

eithafol *adj.* extreme

eithriad/-au *nm.* exception

elw *nm.* profit

enaid/eneidiau *nm.* soul

enfawr *adj.* huge

enfys/-au *nf.* rainbow

enghraifft/enghreifftiau *nf.* example

ennill *v.* to win

ennyd *nf.* moment
ensyclopedia *nm.* encyclopedia
enw/-au *nm.* name; **~ da** reputation; **~ blaen** first name;
    ~ morwynol maiden name
enwog *adj.* famous
enwogrwydd *nm.* fame
er *pron.* although
eraill *adj.* other; *npl.* others
erchyll *adj.* horrible
ergyd/-ion *nf.* shot
erioed *adv.* ever
ers *pron.* since
erthygl/-au *nf.* article (*magazine*)
erthyliad/-au *nm.* abortion
esboniad/-au *nm.* explanation
esbonio *v.* to explain
esgid/-iau *nf.* shoe; **esgidiau glaw** wellingtons; **esgidiau**
    sglefrio skates
esgus/-odion *nm.* excuse
esgusodi *v.* to excuse
esgyn *v.* to rise, to ascend
esiampl/-au *nf.* example
estron *adj.* foreign
estronwr/estroniaid *nm.* stranger
eto *adv.* yet, again
eu *pron.* their
euog *adj.* guilty
euogrwydd *nm.* guilt
ewro/-s *nm.* euro
Ewrop *nf.* Europe
Ewropead/Ewropeaid *nm.* European
Ewropeaidd *adj.* European
ewythr/-edd *nm.* uncle

F

fan/-iau *nf.* van
fanila *nm.* vanilla
fan yma *adv.* here

fe *pron.* he
fel *conj.* like; ~ **arfer** usually, as usual
felly *adv.* so
fi *pron.* me
fin nos *adv.* at nightfall
fisa/-s *nm.* visa
fitamin/-au *nm.* vitamin
fod *v.* to be; *pron.* that
foltedd/-au *nm.* voltage
fy *pron.* + *N.M.* my

FF

ffa *npl.* beans; ~ **dringo** runner beans
ffafr/-au *nf.* favor
ffefryn/-nau *nm.* favorite
ffeil/-iau *nf.* file
ffeindio *v.* to find
ffenest/-ri *nf.* window
ffenestr/-i *nf.* window
ffens/-ys *nf.* fence
fferi/s *nf.* ferry
fferyllydd/fferyllwyr *nm.* pharmacist
ffi/ffioedd *nm.* fee
ffibr/-au *nm.* fiber
ffilm/-iau *nf.* film
ffin/-iau *nf.* border, frontier
ffit *adj.* fit
ffitio *v.* to fit
ffiws/-ys *nm.* fuse
fflach/-iadau *nm.* flash
fflachlamp/-au *nf.* torch
fflam/-au *nf.* flame
fflat/-iau *nf.* flat; *adj.* flat
ffliw *nm.* flu
ffôl *adj.* foolish
ffon/ffyn *nf.* stick
ffôn/ffonau *nm.* telephone; ~ **bach** mobile phone; ~ **lôn**
    mobile phone

ffonio *v.* to telephone
fforc/ffyrc *nf.* fork
ffordd/ffyrdd *nf.* way
fforddio *v.* to afford
fforest/-ydd *nf.* forest
fformiwla/fformiwlâu *nf.* formula
ffotograff/-au *nm.* photograph
Ffrainc *nf.* France
ffrâm/fframiau *nf.* frame
Ffrances/-au *nf.* Frenchwoman
Ffrancwr/Ffrancwyr *nm.* Frenchman
Ffrangeg *f.* French
ffres *adj.* fresh
ffrind/-iau *nm.* friend
ffrio *v.* to fry
ffrwd/ffrydiau *nf.* stream
ffrwydrad/-au *nm.* explosion
ffrwydro *v.* to explode
ffrwyth/-au *nm.* fruit
ffurf/-iau *nf.* form
ffurfio *v.* to form
ffurfiol *adj.* formal
ffŵl/ffyliaid *nm.* fool
ffwng *nm.* fungus
ffwr *nm.* fur
ffwrn/ffyrnau *nf.* oven
ffynnon/ffynhonnau *nf.* fountain

G

gadael *v.* to leave
gaeaf/-au *nm.* winter
gafael *v.* to grasp; *nf.* grasp
gafr/geifr *nf.* goat
gair/geiriau *nm.* word
galar *nm.* mourning
gallu *nm.* ability; *v.* to be able; ~ **gweld** to be able to see
galluog *adj.* able
galw/-adau *nm.* call; *v.* to call

galwyn/-i *nm.* gallon

gamblo *v.* to gamble

gan *prep.* + *S.M.* by, with

gardd/gerddi *nf.* garden

garddwr/garddwyr *nm.* gardener

garej/-ys *nm.* garage

garlleg *nf.* garlic

gartref *adv.* at home

gât/gatiau *nm.* gate

gefell/gefeilliaid *nm.* twin

geirfa/geirfâu *nf.* vocabulary

geiriadur/-on *nm.* dictionary

gelyn/-ion *nm.* enemy

gem/-au *nm.* gem

gêm/gemau *nf.* game; ~ **ryngwladol** international game

gemwaith *nm.* jewelry

gemydd/-ion *nm.* jeweller

gen *prep.* have; **mae car** ~ **i** I have a car

gên/genau *nf.* chin

geneth/-od *nf.* girl

geni *v.* to be born; **ces i fy ngeni yn …** I was born in …

ger *prep.* near, by

gerllaw *adv.* nearby

germ/-au *nm.* germ

glan/-nau *nf.* bank (*of river*)

glân *adj.* clean

glas *adj.* blue

glaswellt *npl.* grass

glaw *nm.* rain; **bwrw** ~ to rain

glendid *nm.* cleanliness

gliniadur/-on *nm.* laptop computer

glud/-ion *nm.* glue

glynu *v.* to stick

gobaith/gobeithion *nm.* hope

gobeithio *v.* to hope

godineb *nm.* adultery

godre/-on *nm.* bottom; ~**'r mynydd** the foot of the mountain

gofal/-on *nm.* care; ~ **dydd** day care

gofalu *v.* to care; ~ **am** to look after

gofalus *adj.* careful
gofalwr/gofalwyr *nm.* caretaker
gofidio *v.* to worry
gofod/-au *nm.* space
gofyn *v.* to ask
gogledd *nm.* north
gohebiaeth *nf.* correspondence
gohebydd/-ion *nm.* correspondent
gôl/golau *nf.* goal
golau/goleuadau *nm.* light
golchi *v.* to wash
goleuo *v.* to light
gollwng *v.* to drop
golwg/golygon *nf.* appearance
golygfa/golygfeydd *nf.* scene
golygu *v.* to mean
golygus *adj.* handsome
gorau *adj.* best
gorchudd/-ion *nm.* cover
gorchuddio *v.* to cover
gorffen *v.* to finish
Gorffennaf *nm.* July
gorffennol *nm.* past
gorffwys *v.* to rest
gorfodol *adj.* compulsory
gorliwio *v.* to exaggerate
gorllewin *nm.* west
gormod *adv., nm.* too much; ~ **o fwyd** too much food
goroesi *v.* to survive
gorsaf/-oedd *nf.* station; ~ **heddlu** police station
gorwedd *v.* to lie down
gosod *v.* to put
gostwng *v.* to lower
gostyngiad/-au *nm.* reduction
gradd/-au *nf.* degree, grade
graddfa/graddfeydd *nf.* scale
graddio *v.* to graduate
gram/-au *nm.* gram
gramadeg/-au *nm.* grammar
grant/-iau *nm.* grant

grawnwin *npl.* grapes **Grawys** *nm.* Lent

gril/-iau *nm.* grill

grilio *v.* to grill

gris/-iau *nm.* step, stair

groser/-iaid *nm.* grocer

grŵp/grwpiau *nm.* group

grym/-oedd *nm.* force

gwacáu *v.* to empty

gwaed *nm.* blood

gwaedu *v.* to bleed

gwael *adj.* bad

gwaeth *adj.* worse

gwag *adj.* empty

gwahanu *v.* to separate

gwahardd *v.* to prohibit

gwahodd *v.* to invite

gwahoddiad/-au *nm.* invitation

gwair/gweiriau *nm.* grass, hay

gwaith *nm.* work; ~ **cartref** homework; ~ **tŷ** housework

gwaith/gweithfeydd *nm.* work (*plant*)

gwall/-au *nm.* error

gwallgo *adj.* mad

gwallt *npl.* hair; ~ **melyn** blond hair

gwan *adj.* weak

gwanwyn *nm.* spring

gwarant/-au *nm.* guarantee

gwarantu *v.* to guarantee

gwarchod *v.* to protect

gwaredu *v.* to rid

gwareiddiad/-au *nm.* civilization

gwario *v.* to spend

gwartheg *npl.* cattle

gwarthus *adj.* disgraceful

gwas/gweision *nm.* servant

gwasanaeth/-au *nm.* service

gwasg/gweisg *nf.* publisher, printing press

gwasgu *v.* to press

gwastad *adj.* flat

gwau *v.* to knit

gwawr *nf.* dawn

gwddf/gyddfau *nm.* neck
gweddïo *v.* to pray
gweddw *adj.* widowed
gwefan/-nau *nf.* website
gwefus/-au *nf.* lip
gweiddi *v.* to shout
gweinidog/-ion *nm.* minister
gweinydd/-ion *nm.* waiter
gweinyddes/-au *nf.* waitress
gweinyddiaeth/-au *nf.* administration
gweithgar *adj.* active
gweithgaredd/-au *nm.* activity
gweithred/-oedd *nf.* deed
gweld *v.* to see
gwell *adj.* better; **mae'n well gen i** I prefer
gwella *v.* to get better
gwellt *npl.* straw, hay
gwelltyn/gwellt *nm.* straw (*drinking*)
gwelw *adj.* pale
gwely/-au *nm.* bed
gwendid *nm.* weakness
Gwener *nm.* Friday
gwenith *npl.* wheat
gwennol/gwenoliaid *nf.* swallow
gwenu *v.* to smile
gwenwyn *nm.* poison
gwenwynig *adj.* poisonous
gwenynen/gwenyn *nf.* bee
gwerin/-oedd *nf.* folk
gweriniaeth/-au *nf.* republic
gwers/-i *nf.* lesson
gwersyll/-oedd *nm.* camp
gwersylla *v.* to camp
gwerth/-oedd *nm.* value
gwerthu *v.* to sell
gwerthuso *v.* to evaluate
gwerthwr/gwerthwyr *nm.* seller
gwestai/gwesteion *nm.* host, guest
gwibdaith/gwibdeithiau *nf.* trip
gwin/-oedd *nm.* wine; ~ **coch** red wine; ~ **gwyn** white wine

gwinllan/-nau *nf.* vineyard

gwir *adj.* true

gwirfoddolwr/gwirfoddolwyr *nm.* volunteer

gwirio *v.* to check

gwirionedd *nm.* truth

gwirioneddol *adj.* real

gwirod/-ydd *nm.* spirit (*alcoholic*)

gwisg/-oedd *nf.* dress; **~ nofio** swimming costume;
    ~ ysgol school uniform

gwisgo *v.* to wear

gwlad/gwledydd *nf.* country

gwladaidd *adj.* rustic

Gwlad Belg *nf.* Belgium

gwladwriaeth/-au *nf.* state

gwlân *nm.* wool

gwledd/-oedd *nf.* feast

gwleidydd/-ion *nm.* politician

gwleidyddol *adj.* political

gwlyb *adj.* wet

gwlychu *v.* to wet, to get wet

gwm *nm.* gum

gwn/gynnau *nm.* gun

gŵn/gynau *nm.* gown; **~ nos** nightgown

gwneud ~ cais to make an application; *v.* to do, to make;
    ~ cawl to make a mess

gwnïo *v.* to sew

gwobr/-au *nf.* prize

gŵr/gwŷr *nm.* husband, man

gwraig/gwragedd *nf.* wife

gwrando *v.* to listen

gwregys/-au *nm.* belt

gwres *nm.* heat

gwresogydd *nm.* heater

gwrthdaro *v.* to conflict

gwrthdrawiad/-au *nm.* collision

gwrthod *v.* to refuse

gwrthrych/-au *nm.* object

gwrthwynebiad/-au *nm.* opposition

gwrthwynebu *v.* to object

gwrthwynebydd/gwrthwynebwyr *nm.* opponent

gwryw *adj.* male
gwrywaidd *adj.* male
gwter/-i *nf.* gutter
gwthio *v.* to push
gwybedyn/gwybed *nm.* fly, gnat
gwybod *v.* to know
gwybodaeth *nf.* knowledge
gwych *adj.* great, excellent
gwyddbwyll *nm.* chess
gwyddoniaeth *nf.* science
gwyddonol *adj.* scientific
gwyddonydd/gwyddonwyr *nm.* scientist
gwyddor/-au *nf.* science, alphabet
gwydn *adj.* tough
gwydr/-au *nm.* glass
gwydraid *nm.* glassful
gŵyl/gwyliau *nf.* festival
gwyliau *npl.* holidays
gwylio *v.* to watch
gwyliwr/gwylwyr *nm.* spectator
gwyllt *adj.* wild
gwymon *npl.* seaweed
gwyn *adj.* white
gwynt/-oedd *nm.* wind
gwyrdd *adj.* green
gwythïen/gwythiennau *nf.* vein
gyda *prep.* +*SP.M.* with; ~ **'i gilydd** together

H

haearn *nm.* iron
haen/-au *nf.* strata, layer
haerllug *adj.* cheeky
haf/-au *nm.* summer
haint/heintiau *nf.* disease
halen *nm.* salt
hallt *adj.* salty
ham *nm.* ham
hambwrdd/hambyrddau *nm.* tray

hamdden *nm.* leisure

hanes *nm.* history

hanesydd/haneswyr *nm.* historian

hanesyddol *adj.* historic

hanfodol *adj.* essential

hanner/haneri *nm.* half

hapchwarae *v.* to gamble

hapus *adj.* happy

hapusrwydd *nm.* happiness

harbwr *nm.* harbor

hardd *adj.* beautiful, handsome

haul/heuliau *nm.* sun

heb *prep.*+ *S.M.* without; ~ **awdurdod** without authority

heblaw *prep.* apart from

Hebraeg *nf.* Hebrew

hebrwng *v.* to accompany

heddiw *adv.* today

heddlu/-oedd *nm.* police

heddwas/heddweision *nm.* policeman

heddwch *nm.* peace

hedfan *v.* to fly

hediad/-au *nm.* flight

hefyd *adv.* also

heini *adj.* sprightly, fit

heintio *v.* to infect

heintus *adj.* infectious

hela *v.* to hunt

helmed/-au *nf.* helmet

helo *inter.* hello

help *nm.* help

helpu *v.* to help

helpwr/helpwyr *nm.* helper

hen *adj.* old; ~ **dad-cu** *nm.* great-grandfather; ~ **fam-gu**
  nf. great-grandmother; ~ **ferch** *nf.* spinster; ~ **fyd**
  nm. antiquity; ~ **lanc** *nm.* bachelor; ~ **ffasiwn** *adj.*
  old-fashioned

heno *adv.* tonight

henoed *npl.* elderly people

heol/-ydd *nf.* road

het/-iau *nf.* hat

heulog *adj.* sunny
hi *pron.* she
hil/-iau *nf.* race (*people*)
hiliaeth *nf.* racism
hinsawdd/hinsoddau *nf.* climate
hiraeth *nm.* longing
hiwmor *nm.* humor
hoci *nm.* hockey; ~ **iâ** ice hockey
hoelen/hoelion *nf.* nail
hoelio *v.* to nail
hoff *adj.* favorite
hofrennydd/hofrenyddion *nm.* helicopter
holi *v.* to ask
holl *adj.* all; **yr** ~ **wlad** all the country
hon *pron./adj. f.* this, this one
hongian *v.* to hang
hosan/-au *nf.* sock
hostel/-i *nf.* hostel; ~ **ieuenctid** youth hostel
hoyw *adj.* gay
hud *nm.* magic
hufen *nm.* cream; ~ **eillio** shaving cream; ~ **haul** sun
     cream; ~ **iâ** ice cream
hunan *pron.* self
hunaniaeth *nf.* identity
hunanladdiad/-au *nm.* suicide
hunan-wasanaeth *nm.* self-service
hunllef/-au *nm.* nightmare
hurio *v.* to hire
hwn *pron./adj. m.* this, this one
hwy *pron.* they; *adj.* longer
hwyl/-iau *nf.* fun, mood, sail; **mewn hwyliau da** in a
     good mood; ~ **fawr** good-bye;
hwylio *v.* to sail
hwyr *adj.* late
hwyraf *adj.* latest
hyd/-oedd *nm.* length; *prep. + S.M.* along; ~ **yn oed** even
hyder *nm.* confidence
Hydref *nm.* October
hydref *nm.* autumn
hyfforddiant *nm.* training
hyfryd *adj.* lovely, pleasant

hylendid *nm.* cleanliness, hygiene

hylif/-au *nm.* fluid

hyn *prep./adj. pl.* this, these

hynafiaid *npl.* ancestors

hynafol *adj.* ancient

hysbyseb/-ion *nf.* advertisement

hysbysebu *v.* to advertise

hysbysrwydd *nm.* publicity

hysbysu *v.* to inform

I

i *prep.+ S.M.* to; ~ **ffwrdd** away; ~ **fyny** up; ~ **fyny'r grisiau** up the stairs; ~ **gyd** all; ~ **mewn i** into; ~ **'r chwith** to the left; ~ **'r dde** to the right

iâ *nm.* ice

iach *adj.* healthy

iaith/ieithoedd *nf.* language

Iau *nm.* Thursday

iawn *adj.* real; *adv.* very

iawndal/-iadau *nm.* compensation

Iddew/-on *nm.* Jew

Iddewes/-au *nf.* Jewess

Iddewig *adj.* Jewish

ie *adv.* yes

iechyd *nm.* health; **I~ da!** Good health! Cheers!

ieithyddol *adj.* linguistic

ieuenctid *nm.* youth

ifanc *adj.* young

ildio *v.* to yield

inc/-iau *nm.* ink

incwm/incymau *nm.* income

Ionawr *nm.* January

isaf *adj.* lowest, bottom

is-deitl/-au *nm.* subtitle

isel *adj.* low

isod *adv.* below

Israel *nf.* Israel

J

jam/-iau *nm.* jam
jar/-iau *nm.* jar
jîns *npl.* jeans
jôc/-s *nf.* joke

L

label/-i *nf.* label
labordy/labordai *nm.* laboratory
lafant *nm.* lavender
lager *nm.* lager
lamp/-iau *nf.* lamp
lan *adv.* up; ~ **llofft** upstairs
landlord/-iaid *nm.* landlord
lapio *v.* to wrap
larwm/larymau *nm.* alarm
lawnt/-iau *nf.* lawn
lawrlwytho *v.* download
lemwn/-au *nm.* lemon
lens/-ys *nf.* lens
lês *nf.* lease
licer *nm.* liquor
lifft/-iau *nm.* lift
liter/-au *nm.* liter
lolfa/lolfeydd *nf.* lounge
lôn/lonydd *nf.* lane
loncian *v.* to jog
londri *nm.* laundry
lorri/lorïau *nf.* lorry, bus
losin *npl.* sweets
lwc *nf.* luck; **pob** ~ good luck

LL

llac *adj.* slack
llacio *v.* to slacken

lladd *v.* to kill

lladrad/-au *nm.* theft

llaeth *nm.* milk [*S.W.*]

llaethdy *nm.* dairy

llafar *adj.* oral

llafariad/llafariaid *nf.* vowel

llafn/-fau *nf.* blade

llafur *nm.* labor

llai *adj.* less

llaid *nm.* mud

llais/lleisiau *nm.* voice

llaith *adj.* damp

llanast *nm.* mess

llanw *nm.* tide; *v.* to fill

llaw/dwylo *nf.* hand; **ail ~** secondhand

llawdriniaeth/-au *nf.* operation

llawen *adj.* happy; **Nadolig L~** Merry Christmas

llawenydd *nm.* joy

llawer *nm.* a lot, many

llawes/llewys *nf.* sleeve

llawfeddyg/-on *nm.* surgeon

llawlyfr/-au *nm.* handbook, brochure

llawn *adj.* full

llawr/lloriau *nm.* floor

lle/-oedd *nm.* place; **~ gwag** empty space; **~ tân** fireplace

lledr *nm.* leather

llefain *v.* to cry

llefaru *v.* to recite

llefrith *nm.* milk [*N.W.*]

lleiafrif/-oedd *nm.* minority

lleiafswm *nm.* minimum

lleidr/lladron *nm.* thief

lleihau *v.* to lessen, to diminish

lleithder *nm.* dampness

llen/-ni *nf.* curtain

llencyndod *nm.* adolescence

llenyddiaeth/-au *nf.* literature

lleol *adj.* local

lleoli *v.* to locate

lles *nm.* benefit, welfare

llethr/-au *nf.* slope
llety/-au *nm.* lodging
lleuad/-au *nf.* moon
llewygu *v.* to faint
lliain/llieniau *nm.* cloth; ~ **bwrdd** tablecloth
llid *nm.* anger
llifo *v.* to flow
llifogydd *npl.* flood
llinell/-au *nf.* line
llinyn/-nau *nm.* string
llithren/-nau *nf.* slide
llithro *v.* to slip
lliw/-iau *nm.* color; ~ **haul** suntan
lloches/-au *nf.* shelter
Lloegr *nf.* England
llofnod/-ion *nm.* autograph, signature
llofrudd/-ion *nm.* murderer
llofruddiaeth/-au *nf.* murder
llofruddio *v.* to murder
llogi *v.* to rent, to hire
llon *adj.* happy
llond *adv.* full; ~ **llaw** handful
llong/-au *nf.* ship
llongyfarch *v.* to congratulate
llongyfarchiadau *npl.* congratulations
llosgi *v.* to burn
lludw *nm.* ash, ashes
llun/-iau *nm.* picture
Llun *nm.* Monday
llungopïo *v.* to photocopy
lluniaeth *nmf.* refreshment, food
lluosi *v.* to multiply
lluosog *nm.* plural
llwch *nm.* dust
llwgu *v.* to starve
llwnc *nm.* throat
llwy/-au *nf.* spoon; ~ **de** teaspoon; ~ **fwrdd** tablespoon
llwybr/-au *nm.* path; ~ **cyhoeddus** public footpath
llwyd *adj.* gray
llwyddiant/llwyddiannau *nm.* success

llwyddo *v.* to succeed

llwyfan/-au *nmf.* stage

llwyth/-au *nm.* tribe; **/-i** *nm.* load

llydan *adj.* wide

llyffant/-od *nf.* frog, toad

llyfr/-au *nm.* book; **~ ffôn** phone book; **~ gosod** textbook; **~ nodiadau** notebook

llyfrgell/-oedd *nf.* library; **L~ Genedlaethol Cymru** Welsh National Library

llyfrgellydd/llyfrgellwyr *nm.* librarian

llygad/llygaid *nm.* eye

llygoden/llygod *nf.* mouse; **~ fawr** rat

llygru *v.* to corrupt

llymeitian *v.* to sip

llyn/-noedd *nm.* lake

llyncu *v.* to swallow

llynges/-au *nf.* navy

llys/-oedd *nm.* court

llysenw/-au *nm.* nickname

llysfam/llysfamau *nf.* stepmother

llysfwytawr/llysfwytawyr *nm.* vegetarian

llysgenhadaeth/llysgenadaethau *nf.* consulate

llysgennad/llysgenhadon *nm.* consul, ambassador

llysiau *npl.* vegetables

llystad/llystadau *nm.* stepfather

llythyr/-au *nm.* letter (*post*)

llythyren/llythrennau *nm.* letter (*of a word*)

llywio *v.* to guide, to steer

llywodraeth/-au *nf.* government; **~ leol** local government

llywydd/-ion *nm.* president

M

mab/meibion *nm.* son

mabwysiadu *v.* to adopt

mab yng nghyfraith *nm.* son-in-law

machlud/-oedd *nm.* sunset

madarchen/madarch *nf.* mushroom

maddau *v.* to forgive

maes/meysydd *nm.* field; **~ awyr** airport; **~ parcio** parking lot, parking garage

maestref/-i *nf.* suburb

maethlon *adj.* nutritious

Mai *nm.* May

mainc/meinciau *nf.* bench

maint/meintiau *nm.* size

malu *v.* to destroy, to grind; **~ awyr** to talk nonsense

mam/-au *nf.* mother

mam-gu/mamau cu *nf.* grandmother [*S.W.*]

mamol *adj.* motherly

mamwlad/mamwledydd *nf.* mother country

mam yng nghyfraith *nf.* mother-in-law

man/-nau *nmf.* place; **~ gwyliau** holiday resort

maneg/menig *nf.* glove

mantais/manteision *nf.* advantage

map/-iau *nm.* map

marc/-iau *nm.* mark

marchnad/-oedd *nf.* market

marcio *v.* to mark

marw *v.* to die; **buodd e farw** he died

marwol *adj.* deadly

marwolaeth/-au *nf.* death

masg/-iau *nm.* mask

masnach *nf.* trade

masnachu *v.* to trade

masnachwr/masnachwyr *nm.* trader

mat/-iau *nm.* mat

mater/-ion *nm.* matter

math/-au *nm.* type; **pa fath o?** what kind of?

matras/matresi *nm.* mattress

mawr *adj.* big

Mawrth *nm.* March

mecanig *nm.* mechanic

mecanyddol *adj.* mechanical

meddal *adj.* soft

meddiannu *v.* to possess, to occupy

meddiant/meddiannau *nm.* possession

meddw *adj.* drunk; **mae e'n feddw** he's drunk

meddwl *v.* to think

meddyg/-on *nm.* doctor
meddygol *adj.* medical
Medi *nm.* September
Mehefin *nm.* June
meirioli *v.* to thaw
meistr/-i *nm.* master
meistroli *v.* to master
meithrinfa/meithrinfeydd *nf.* playgroup, nursery
mêl *nm.* honey
melin/-au *nf.* mill
mellten/mellt *nf.* lightning
melyn *adj.* yellow
melys *adj.* sweet
mentro *v.* to venture
menyw/-od *nf.* woman
merch/-ed *nf.* girl, daughter
Mercher *nm.* Wednesday
merch yng nghyfraith *nf.* daughter-in-law
mesur *v.* to measure
metalig *adj.* metallic
metel/-au *nm.* metal
methiant/methiannau *nm.* failure
Methodistiaid *npl.* Methodists
methu *v.* to fail; **~ â gweld** to fail to see
metr/-au *nm.* meter
mewn *prep.* in
mewnforio *v.* to import
mewnfudo *v.* to immigrate
mewnfudwr/mewnfudwyr *nm.* immigrant
mewnol *adj.* inner, inside
migwrn/migyrnau *nm.* ankle
mil/-oedd *nf.* thousand
miliwn/miliynau *nf.* million
milltir/-oedd *nf.* mile
milwr/milwyr *nm.* soldier
milwrol *adj.* military
min *nm.* edge
miniog *adj.* sharp
minlliw *nm.* lipstick
mintys *npl.* mint

minws *prep.* minus

mis/-oedd *nm.* month

misol *adj.* monthly

modd/-ion *nm.* means

moddion *npl.* medicine

model/-au *nm.* model

modem *nm.* modem

modern *adj.* modern

modfedd/-i *nf.* inch

modrwy/-on *nf.* ring (*finger*); **~ briodas** wedding ring

modryb/-edd *nf.* aunt

modur/-on *nm.* motor, car

moel *adj.* bald

moeth/-au *nm.* luxury

moethus *adj.* luxurious

moment/-au *nf.* moment

môr/moroedd *nm.* sea

mordaith/mordeithiau *nf.* voyage

morddwyd/ydd *nf.* hip

morgais/morgeisi *nm.* mortgage

morwr/morwyr *nm.* sailor

morwyn/morynion *nf.* maid

mud *adj.* mute, dumb

mudiad/-au *nm.* movement; **M~ Ysgolion Meithrin** Welsh Playgroup Movement

munud/-au *nmf.* minute

mur/-iau *nm.* wall

mwclis/-au *nm.* necklace

mwd *nm.* mud

mwg *nm.* smoke

mwnci/mwncïod *nm.* monkey

mwstard *nm.* mustard

mwstás *nm.* moustache

mwy *adj./nm.* more; **~ na thebyg** probably

mwyaf *adj.* most, greatest

mwyafrif/-oedd *nm.* majority

mwyafswm *nm.* most, maximum

mwydyn/mwydod *nm.* worm

mwyhau *v.* to enlarge

mwynhau *v.* to enjoy

myfyriwr/myfyrwyr *nm.* student
mynach/-od *nm.* monk
mynachdy/mynachdai *nm.* monastery
mynachlog/-ydd *nf.* monastery
mynd *v.* to go; ~ **â** + *SP.M.* to take; ~ **am dro** to go for a
    walk; ~ **i mewn** to go in; ~ **yn** to become
mynedfa/mynedfeydd *nf.* entrance (*door*)
mynediad/-au *nm.* entrance
mynegai/mynegeion *nm.* index
mynegfys/-edd *nm.* index finger
mynegi *v.* to express
mynnu *v.* to insist
mynwent/-ydd *nf.* cemetery

N

na *adv.* no; *prep.+ SP.M.* than; *pron +S.M./+SP.M*
    before 'c', 'p', t'. that not
naddo *adv.* no
Nadolig *nm.* Christmas; ~ **Llawen** Merry Christmas
nai/neiaint *nm.* nephew
naill ai *conj.* either; ~ **...** **neu** either ... or
nain/neiniau *nf.* grandmother [*N.W.*]
nam/-au *nm.* fault
nant/nentydd *nf.* stream
natur *nf.* nature
naturiol *adj.* natural
naw *num.* nine
nawdd *nm.* sponsorship
nawr *adv.* now
neb *pron.* no one
nef *nf.* heaven
nefoedd *nf.* heaven
neges/-au/-euon *nf.* message
negesydd/negeswyr *nm.* messenger
negyddol *adj.* negative
neidio *v.* to jump
neidr/nadredd *nf.* snake

neis *adj.* nice
nen *nf.* heaven, sky
nenfwd/nenfydau *nm.* ceiling
nerf/-au *nm.* nerve
nerfus *adj.* nervous
nerth/-oedd *nm.* strength
nesaf *adj.* next
neu *conj.* or
neuadd/-au *nf.* hall; **~ breswyl** hostel
newid *v.* to change
newydd *adj.* new
newyddion *npl.* news
newyn *nm.* hunger
nhw *pron.* they, them
ni *pron.* we, us
nid *neg.* not
nifer/-oedd *nmf.* number
niferus *adj.* numerous
nith/-oedd *nf.* niece
niwed/niweidiau *nm.* damage
niweidio *v.* to damage
niwl/-oedd *nm.* mist, fog
niwtral *adj.* neutral
nodi *v.* note
nodweddiadol *adj.* typical
nodwydd/-au *nf.* needle
nodyn/nodiadau *nm.* note
noeth *adj.* naked
nofel/-au *nf.* novel
nofelydd/nofelwyr *nm.* novelist
nofio *v.* to swim
normal *adj.* normal
nos/-au *nf.* night; **N~ Galan** New Year's Eve; **~ yfory** tomorrow night
noswaith/nosweithiau *nf.* evening; **~ dda** good evening
nwy/-on *nm.* gas
nwyddau *npl.* goods
nyrs/-ys *nf.* nurse
nyth/-od *nmf.* nest

O

o *prep.* + *S.M.* of, from; ~ **o dan** + *S.M.* under; ~ **fewn** within; ~ **flaen** in front of; ~ **gwmpas** around; ~ **hyd** still, always; ~ **leiaf** at least

ochr/-au *nf.* side

ocsigen *nm.* oxygen

ocsiwn/ocsiynau *nm.* auction

od *adj.* odd, strange

oed *nm.* age

oedi *v.* to delay

oedolyn/oedolion *nm.* adult

oedran/-nau *nm.* age

oedrannus *adj.* elderly

oer *adj.* cold

oergell/-oedd *nf.* refrigerator

offeiriad/-on *nm.* priest

offer *npl.* equipment

offeryn/offer *nm.* instrument; ~ **cerdd** musical instrument

ofn/-au *nm.* fear

ofnadwy *adj.* awful

ofnus *adj.* afraid, fearful

ogof/-âu *nf.* cave

oherwydd *prep.* because

ôl/olion *nm.* remain, trace

olaf *adj.* last

olew/-on *nm.* oil

olewllyd *adj.* oily

oll *adj.* all

olwyn/-ion *nf.* wheel; ~ **sbâr** spare tire

ond *conj.* but

ongl/-au *nf.* angle

oni bai *conj.* but for, except that

optegydd/optegwyr *nm.* optician

oren/-nau *nmf.* orange

organ/-au *nf.* organ

oriawr/oriorau *nm.* watch

oriel/-au *nf.* gallery

os *conj.* if; ~ **gwelwch yn dda** please

osgoi *v.* to avoid

owns/-ys *nm.* ounce

P

pa *interrog.* + *S.M.* which, what; ~ **fath o** what kind of

pab/au *nm.* pope

pabell/pebyll *nf.* tent

Pabydd/Pabyddion *nm.* Catholic, papist

Pabyddes/Pabyddesau *nf.* Catholic, papist

pabyddol *adj.* Catholic

pacio *v.* to pack

padell/-i *nf.* pan; ~ **ffrio** frying pan

paent *nm.* paint

paffio *v.* to box

pafin *nm.* sidewalk

pam *interrog.* why

pans *nm.* briefs

papur/-au *nm.* paper; ~ **meddyg** prescription; ~ **newydd**
    newspaper; ~ **tŷ bach** toilet paper

pâr/parau *nm.* pair

paratoi *v.* to prepare

parc/-iau *nm.* park

parhad *nm.* continuation

parhau *v.* to continue

parlysu *v.* to paralyze

parod *adj.* ready

parti/partïon *nm.* party

partner/-iaid *nm.* partner

pasbort/-au *nm.* passport

pasio *v.* to pass

past dannedd *nm.* toothpaste

pawen/-nau *nf.* paw

pe *conj.* if

pedair *num. f.* four

pedal/-au *nm.* pedal

pedwar *num. m.* four

peg pabell/pegiau pabell *nm.* tent peg

pegwn/pegynau *nm.* pole

pei/-s *nm.* pie

peilot/-iaid *nm.* pilot

peintio *v.* to paint

peintiwr/peintwyr *nm.* painter

peiriannwr/peirianwyr *nm.* engineer

peiriant/peiriannau *nm.* engine; **~ golchi** washing machine

pêl/peli *nf.* ball; **~ bluen** badminton; **~ -droed** football, soccer; **~ -droed Americanaidd** American football; **~ -fas** baseball; **~ fasged** basketball

pelydr/-au *nm.* ray; **~ X** X ray

pen/-nau *nm.* head; **~ blwydd** birthday; **P~ blwydd hapus!** Happy birthday!; **~ mawr** hangover; **~ tost** headache

pencadlys/-oedd *nm.* headquarters

pencampwriaeth/-au *nf.* championship

penderfyniad/-au *nm.* decision

penderfynu *v.* to decide

pendics *nm.* appendix (*body*)

pendro *nm.* dizziness

pen-lin/-iau *nm.* knee

pennaeth/penaethiaid *nm.* head, chief, school principal

pennawd/penawdau *nm.* heading

pennod/penodau *nf.* chapter

pensaer/penseiri *nm.* architect

pensaernïaeth *nf.* architecture

pensil/-iau *nm.* pencil

pensiynwr/pensiynwyr *nm.* pensioner, retiree

pentref /-i *nm.* village

pentwr/pentyrrau *nm.* heap, pile

penwisg/-oedd *nf.* wig

penwythnos/-au *nm.* weekend

perchen *v.* to own

perchennog/perchenogion *nm.* owner

perffaith *adj.* perfect

peri *v.* to cause

perl/-au *nm.* pearl

perlysieuyn/perlysiau *nm.* herb

persawr/-au *nm.* scent

person/-au *nm.* person; /-iaid *nm.* parson

perthyn *v.* to belong

perthynas/perthnasau *nf.* relation

perygl/-on *nm.* danger

peryglus *adj.* dangerous

peswch/pesychiadau *nm.* cough; **mae ~ arna i** I have a cough

pesychu *v.* to cough

peth/-au *nm.* thing

petruso *v.* to hesitate

pib/-au *nf.* pipe

piben/pibau *nf.* pipe; **~ ddŵr** water pipe; **~ wacáu** exhaust pipe

picnic/-au *nm.* picnic

pigiad/-au *nm.* sting

pigo *v.* to sting

pilsen/pils *nf.* pill

pin/-nau *nm.* pin; **~ cau** safety pin

pinsio *v.* to pinch

pinswrn/pinsyrnau *nm.* pincers

piws *adj.* purple

plaen *adj.* plain

plaid/pleidiau *nf.* party (*political*) **P~ Cymru** The Party of Wales; **y Blaid Geidwadol** the Conservative Party; **y Blaid Lafur** the Labour Party

planed/-au *nf.* planet

planhigyn/planhigion *nm.* plant

plastig/-au *nm.* plastic

plât/platiau *nm.* plate

pleidlais/pleidleisiau *nf.* vote;

pleidleisio *v.* to vote; **~ dros** to vote for

plentyn/plant *nm.* child

plentyndod *nm.* childhood

pleser/-au *nm.* pleasure

plesio *v.* to please

plismon/plismyn *nm.* policeman

plismones/-au *nf.* policewoman

pluen/plu *nf.* feather; **~ eira** snowflake

plwg/plygiau *nm.* plug

plws *prep.* plus

plygu *v.* to bend, to fold

plymer/plymeriaid *nm.* plumber

pob *adj.* every; all; baked; **~ hwyl** good-bye

pobl/-oedd *nf.* people

poblogaeth/-au *nf.* population

pobydd/-ion *nm.* baker
poced/-i *nm.* pocket
poen/-au *nmf.* pain
poeni *v.* to hurt, to worry
poenus *adj.* painful
poer *nm.* spit
polisi/polisïau *nm.* policy
polyn/polion *nm.* pole; ~ **pabell** tent pole
pont/-ydd *nf.* bridge
porc *nm.* pork
porcyn *adj.* nude
porfa/porfeydd *nf.* grass
porffor *adj.* purple
portread/-au *nm.* portrait
porthladd/-oedd *nm.* harbor
posibl *adj.* possible
post *nm.* post; ~ **awyr** air mail
postio *v.* to post
pot/-iau *nm.* pot
potel/-i *nf.* bottle
pothell/-au *nf.* blister
powdr/-au *nm.* powder
powlen/-ni *nf.* bowl
prawf/profion *nm.* test
preifat *adj.* private
preifatrwydd *nm.* privacy
prentis/-iaid *nm.* apprentice
prentisiaeth *nf.* apprenticeship
presennol *adj.* present; *nm.* present
preswyl *adj.* residential
preswylio *v.* to live, to reside
pridd/-oedd *nm.* soil, earth
prif *adj.* main; ~ **weinidog** prime minister
prifathro/prifathrawon *nm.* headteacher
prifddinas/-oedd *nf.* capital city
priffordd/priffyrdd *nf.* main road
prifysgol/-ion *nf.* university
prin *adj.* rare
priodas/-au *nf.* marriage
priodfab *nm.* groom

priodferch *nf.* bride
priodi *v.* to marry, to get married
priodol *adj.* appropriate
pris/-iau *nm.* price
prisio *v.* to price
problem/-au *nf.* problem
proffesiwn/proffesiynau *nm.* profession
proffil/-iau *nm.* profile
profi *v.* to prove, to test
profiad/-au *nm.* experience
promenâd/promenadau *nm.* promenade
prosiect/-au *nm.* project
Protestant/Protestaniaid *nm.* Protestant
protestio *v.* to protest
pryd/-au *nm.* meal; *interrog.* when
Prydain *nf.* Britain
pryder/-on *nm.* worry
prydferth *adj.* beautiful
pryf/-ed *nm.* insect; ~ **copyn** spider
pryfyn/pryfed *nm.* insect
prynhawn/-au *nm.* afternoon; ~ **'ma** this afternoon;
     ~ **heddiw** this afternoon
prynu *v.* to buy
prysur *adj.* busy
pump *num.* five
punt/punnoedd *nf.* pound (£)
pupur *nm.* pepper
pur *adj.* pure
pwdin/-au *nm.* pudding
pwdr *adj.* rotten
pwll/pyllau *nm.* pond; ~ **glo** coal mine; ~ **nofio** swimming
     pool
pwmp/pympiau *nm.* pump
pwmpio *v.* to pump
pwnc/pynciau *nm.* subject
pwrpas/-au *nm.* purpose
pwrs/pyrsiau *nm.* purse
pwy *interrog.* who
pwyllgor/-au *nm.* committee
pwynt/-iau *nm.* point
pwyntio *v.* to point

pwys/-au *nm.* weight; /-i *nm.* pound (*lb*)
pwysig *adj.* important
pwysigrwydd *nm.* importance
pwyso *v.* to weigh
pwyth/-au *nm.* stitch
pwytho *v.* to stitch
pyjamas *nm.* pajamas
pyls *nm.* pulse
pysgodyn/pysgod *nm.* fish; **pysgod cragen** shellfish
pysgota *v.* to fish
pysgotwr/pysgotwyr *nm.* fisherman

R

'r *art.* the
raced/-i *nf.* racket
radio *nm.* radio
RAM *nm.* RAM (Random Access Memory)
ramp/-iau *nm.* ramp
ras/-ys *nf.* race
real *adj.* real
record/-iau *nmf.* record
reid/-iau *nf.* ride
reis *nm.* rice
restio *v.* to arrest
risg/-iau *nm.* risk
rôl/rolau *nf.* role
rygbi *nm.* rugby
rysáit/ryseitiau *nm.* recipe

RH

rhad *adj.* cheap
rhaff/-au *nf.* rope
rhag *prep.* from, lest; **RHAG** Parents for Welsh Education
rhagenw/-au *nm.* pronoun
Rhagfyr *nm.* December
rhaglen/-ni *adj.* program

rhagolwg/rhagolygon *nm.* forecast; **rhagolygon y tywydd**
weather forecast

rhagor *nm.* more

rhagori *v.* to excel

rhai *pron.* some

rhaid *nm.* necessity; **mae ~ i fi** I must

rhain *pron.* these

rhamant/-au *nf.* romance

rhan/-nau *nf.* part

rhan-amser *adj.* part-time

rhanbarth/-au *nm.* district

rhedeg *v.* to run

rhegi *v.* to swear

rheilffordd/rheilffyrdd *nf.* railway

rheiny *pron.* those

rhent/-i *nm.* rent

rheol/-au *nf.* rule

rheolaeth/-au *nf.* control

rheolaidd *adj.* regular

rheoli *v.* to rule, to control

rheolwr/rheolwyr *nm.* ruler

rhes/-i *nf.* row

rhestr/-i *nf.* list

rhestru *v.* to list

rheswm/rhesymau *nm.* reason

rhesymu *v.* to reason

rhewgell/-oedd *nf.* freezer

rhewllyd *adj.* icy

rhiant/rhieni *nm.* parent; **rhieni cu** grand-parents

rhif/-au *nm.* number

rhiw/-iau *nmf.* hill

rhodd/-ion *nf.* gift

rhoddi *v.* to give

rhoi *v.* to give; **~ gwybod** to inform

rholio *v.* to roll

rholyn/rholiau *nm.* roll

rhuban/-au *nm.* ribbon

rhugl *adj.* fluent

rhuthro *v.* to rush

rhwd *nm.* rust

rhwng *prep.* between
rhwyd/-i *nm.* net
rhwydwaith/rhwydweithiau *nm.* network
rhwym *adj.* bound, constipated
rhwymyn/rhwymau *nm.* bandage
rhwystr/-au *nm.* impediment, hindrance
rhybudd/-ion *nm.* warning
rhybuddio *v.* to warn
rhyddhad *nm.* relief
rhyddid *nm.* freedom
rhydu *v.* to rust
rhyfedd *adj.* strange
rhyfeddu *v.* to wonder
rhyfel/-oedd *nm.* war
rhyngrwyd *nm.* Internet
rhyngwladol *adj.* international
rhythm/-au *nm.* rhythm
rhyw/-iau *nf.* sex, gender; *nmf.* sort; *adj.* some
rhywbeth *nm.* something
rhywiol *adj.* sexy
rhywle *adv.* somewhere
rhywrai *pron.* some people
rhywun *nm.* someone

S

Sabath *nm.* Sabbath
sach/-au *nf.* sack; ~ **gefn** backpack; ~ **gysgu** sleeping bag
Sadwrn *nm.* Saturday
saer/seiri *nm.* carpenter
Saesneg *nf.* English
Saesnes/-au *nf.* Englishwoman
saeth/-au *nf.* arrow
saethu *v.* to shoot
safle/-oedd *nm.* position
safon/-au *nf.* standard
sail/seiliau *nm.* foundation
sain/seiniau *nm.* sound
Sais/Saeson *nm.* Englishman

saith *num.* seven
sâl *adj.* ill
salad/-au *nm.* salad
salw *adj.* ugly
salwch *nm.* illness; **~ môr** seasickness
sampl/-au *nm.* sample
sanctaidd *adj.* holy
sandal/-au *nm.* sandal
sarhad *nm.* insult
sarhau *v.* to insult
sawdl/sodlau *nmf.* heel
sawl *adj.* several; *interrog.* how many
Sbaen *nf.* Spain
Sbaeneg *nf.* Spanish language
Sbaenes/-au *nf.* Spanish woman
Sbaenwr/Sbaenwyr *nm.* Spaniard
sbardun/-au *nm.* accelerator
sbectol/-au *nf.* spectacles; **~ haul** sunglasses
sbwng *nm.* sponge
sbwriel *nm.* trash
sbwylio *v.* to spoil
sebon/-au *nm.* soap
sedd/-au/-i *nf.* seat
sefydliad/-au *nm.* institution
sefydlu *v.* to establish
Seisnig *adj.* English
sêl/-s *nf.* sale
seler/-ydd *nf.* cellar
seremoni/seremonïau *nf.* ceremony
seren/sêr *nf.* star
set/-iau *nf.* set; **~ deledu** television set
setlo *v.* to settle
sgarff/-iau *nf.* scarf
sgert/-iau *nf.* skirt
sgi/-s *nm.* ski
sgio *v.* to ski; **~ dŵr** to water-ski
sglefrio *v.* to skate; **~ iâ** to ice-skate
sgrifennu *v.* to write
sgrin/-au *nf.* screen; **~ haul** sunscreen
sgwâr/sgwarau *nm.* square

sgwrs/sgyrsiau *nf.* conversation, chat
sgwrsio *v.* to chat, to converse
shwmae *inter.* hello, how are you
siaced/-i *nf.* jacket; ~ **achub** life jacket
siampŵ/-s *nm.* shampoo
siarad *v.* to talk; ~ **â** to talk to
siarc/-od *nm.* shark
siawns/-au *nf.* chance
sicrwydd *nm.* certainty
sidan/-au *nm.* silk
sidanaidd *adj.* silky
siec/-iau *nf.* check; ~ **deithio** traveler's check
sigâr/sigarau *nf.* cigar
sigarét/-s/-au *nf.* cigarette
silff/-oedd *nf.* shelf; ~ **lyfrau** bookshelf
sillafu *v.* to spell
sinc *nm.* sink
sinema/sinemâu *nf.* cinema
sioc/-iau *nm.* shock
sioe/-au *nf.* show
siom/-au *nmf.* disappointment
siomi *v.* to disappoint
Siôn Corn *nm.* Santa Claus
siop/-au *nf.* shop; ~ **bapur** newsagent; ~ **ddillad**
    clothing store; ~ **goffi** coffee shop; ~ **lyfrau**
    bookstore
siopa *v.* to shop
siswrn/sisyrnau *nm.* scissors
siwgr/-au *nm.* sugar
siwmper/-i *nf.* jumper, pullover
siŵr *adj.* sure
siwrnai/siwrneiau *nf.* journey
siwt/-iau *nf.* suit; ~ **nofio** swimsuit
smalio *v.* to joke
smwddio *v.* to iron
soffa *nf.* sofa
solid *adj.* solid
sôn *v.* to mention
stadiwm/stadiymau *nm.* stadium
staen/-au *nm.* stain

staer *npl.* stairs

stafell/-oedd *nf.* room; ~ **wely** bedroom; ~ **ymolchi** bathroom

stamp/-iau *nm.* stamp

stecen/stêcs *nf.* steak

stôl/stolion *nf.* stool

stordy/stordai *nm.* warehouse, storeroom

stori/storïau *nf.* story

storio *v.* to store

storm/-ydd *nf.* storm

straen *nm.* strain

stryd/-oedd *nf.* street

stumog/-au *nf.* stomach

sudd/-oedd *nm.* juice; ~ **lemwn** lemon juice; ~ **oren** orange juice

suddo *v.* to sink

sugno *v.* to suck

sugnydd llwch *nm.* vacuum cleaner

Sulgwyn *nm.* Whitsun

sur *adj.* sour

sut *interrog.* how

sw/sŵau *nm.* zoo

swigen/swigod *nf.* bubble

Swisiad/Swisiaid *nm.* Swiss person

swits/-ys *nm.* switch

swm/symiau *nm.* sum

sŵn/synau *nm.* sound, noise

swnllyd *adj.* noisy

swper/-au *nmf.* supper

swydd/-i *nf.* job, post; ~ **wag** vacancy

swyddfa/swyddfeydd *nf.* office; ~ **dwristaidd** tourist office; ~ **post** post office

swyddog/-ion *nm.* officer

swyn/-ion *nm.* charm

sych *adj.* dry

syched *nm.* thirst; **mae ~ arna i** I'm thirsty

sychedig *adj.* thirsty

sychu *v.* to dry

sylw/-adau *nm.* observation

sylweddol *adj.* substantial

sylweddoli *v.* to realize
sylwi *v.* to notice
syml *adj.* simple
symptom/-au *nm.* symptom
symud *v.* to move
symudiad/-au *nm.* movement
synagog/-au *nm.* synagogue
syniad/-au *nm.* idea
synnu *v.* to surprise
syr *nm.* sir
syrcas/-au *nm.* circus
syth *adj.* straight
sythu *v.* to shiver

T

tabl/-au *nm.* table
Tachwedd *nm.* November
tacsi/-s *nm.* taxi
tad/-au *nm.* father
tad bedydd *nm.* godfather
tad-cu/tadau cu *nm.* grandfather [*S.W.*]
tad yng nghyfraith *nm.* father-in-law
tafarn/-au *nmf.* public house
tafell/-au *nf.* slice
taflen/-ni *nf.* leaflet
taflu *v.* to throw
tafodiaith/tafodieithoedd *nf.* dialect
tagu *v.* to choke, to strangle
taid/teidiau *n.m.* grandfather [*N.W.*]
tair *num.f.* three
taith/teithiau *nf.* journey; ~ **gerdded** hike
tâl/taliadau *nm.* pay
talcen/-ni *nm.* forehead
taldra *nm.* height
tan *prep.*+ *S.M.* until
tân/tanau *nm.* fire; ~ **gwyllt** fireworks
tanddaear *adj.* underground
tanio *v.* to fire, to start (*engine*)

taniwr/tanwyr *nm.* lighter, starter
tanwydd/-au *nf.* fuel
tap/-iau *nm.* tap
taran/-au *nf.* thunder
tarfu *v.* to disturb
targed/-au *nm.* target
taro *v.* to hit, to strike
tarten/-au *nf.* tart
tatŵ/s *nm.* tattoo
tawel *adj.* quiet, silent
tawelwch *nm.* silence
te *nm.* tea
tebot/-au *nm.* teapot
tebyg *adj.* alike
teg *adj.* fair
tegan/-au *nm.* toy
tegell/-au *nm.* kettle
tei/-s *nm.* tie
teiar/-s *nm.* tire
teiliwr/teilwriaid *nm.* tailor
teimlad/-au *nm.* feeling
teimlo *v.* to feel
teisen/-nau *nf.* cake
teithio *v.* to travel
teithiwr/teithwyr *nm.* traveler
teleffôn/teleffonau *nm.* telephone
teitl/-au *nm.* title
teledu *nm.* television; **set deledu** *nf.* television set
telyn/-au *nf.* harp
teml/-au *nf.* temple
tenau *adj.* thin
tennis *nm.* tennis
teras/-au *nm.* terrace
terfyn/-au *nm.* limit, boundary
terfynol *adj.* final
terfysg/-oedd *nm.* riot
testun/-au *nm.* text, subject
teulu/-oedd *nm.* family
tew *adj.* fat
teyrnged/-au *nf.* tribute

theatr/-au *nf.* theater
thermomedr/-au *nm.* thermometer
ti *pron.* you
tîm/timau *nm.* team
tir/-oedd *nm.* land
tirfeddiannwr/tirfeddianwyr *nm.* landlord
tirlun/-iau *nm.* landscape
tisian *v.* to sneeze
tlawd *adj.* poor
to/toeon *nm.* roof
tocyn/nau *nm.* ticket
toes *nm.* dough
toiled/-au *nm.* toilet
toll/-au *nf.* toll, tax
torf/-eydd *nf.* crowd
toriad/-au *nm.* break; ~ **gwallt** haircut
torri *v.* to break, to cut; ~ **lawr** to break down
torrwr/torwyr *nm.* cutter; ~ **gwallt** barber
torth/-au *nf.* loaf
tra *adv.* + *SP.M.* quite, very; *conj.* while
traddodiad/-au *nm.* tradition
traddodiadol *adj.* traditional
traeth/-au *nm.* beach
trafferth/-ion *nf.* difficulty
traffig *nm.* traffic
trafnidiaeth *nf.* traffic; ~ **gyhoeddus** public transport
tragwyddol *adj.* everlasting, eternal
trais *nm.* violence, rape
tramor *adj.* foreign
tramorwr/tramorwyr *nm.* foreigner
traul/-treuliau *nf.* expense
tref/-i *nf.* town
trefn/-au *nf.* order
trefnu *v.* to order, to sort, to arrange
trefol *adj.* urban
treisgar *adj.* violent
treisio *v.* to violate, to rape
trên/trenau *nm.* train
treth/-i *nf.* tax
trethu *v.* to tax

treulio *v.* to spend
tri *num.m.* three
triniaeth/-au *nf.* treatment
trinydd gwallt *nm.* hairdresser
trist *adj.* sad
tro/troeon *nm.* turn, walk; **mynd am dro** to go for a walk
troed/traed *nf.* foot
troednoeth *adj.* barefoot
troi *v.* to turn
trosedd/-au *nmf.* crime
trosglwyddo *v.* to transfer
trosi *v.* to transfer, to translate, to convert
trowsus *nm.* pants
truan *nm.* wretch
trwm *adj.* heavy
trwsio *v.* to mend, to repair
trwy *prep.+ S.M.* through
trwydded/-au *nf.* license
trwyddedu *v.* to license
trwyn/-au *nm.* nose
trymaidd *adj.* heavy, close (*weather*)
trysor/-au *nm.* treasure
tsieni *nm.* china
tua *prep.+ SP.M.* around, about
tuag at *prep. + S.M.* towards
tudalen/-nau *nf.* page
tuedd/-au *nf.* tendency
tueddu *v.* to tend
tun/-iau *nm.* tin
tusw/-au *nm.* posy
twf *nm.* growth; **T~** organization for promoting use of Welsh in the home
twll/tyllau *nm.* hole; **~ y clo** keyhole
twnnel/twnelau *nm.* tunnel
twpsyn/twpsod *nm.* fool
tw^r/tyrau *nm.* tower
twrist/twristiaid *nm.* tourist
twristiaeth *nf.* tourism
twyllo *v.* to cheat
twym *adj.* warm

twymyn *nm.* fever; ~ **y gwair** hay fever

tŷ/tai *nm.* house; ~ **bach** toilet; ~ **tafarn** public house

tyfu *v.* to grow

tymer *nf.* temper

tymheredd *nm.* temperature

tymor/tymhorau *nm.* term, season

tyn *adj.* tight

tynnu *v.* to pull; ~ **i ffwrdd** to take away, to take off

tyrfa/-oedd *nf.* crowd

tyrnsgriw/-iau *nm.* screwdriver

tyst/-ion *nm.* witness

tystiolaeth/-au *nf.* evidence

tywel/-ion *nm.* towel; ~ **mislif** sanitary towel

tywod *nm.* sand

tywydd *nm.* weather

tywyll *adj.* dark

tywyllwch *nm.* darkness

tywys *v.* to guide, to lead

tywysydd/tywyswyr *nm.* guide

U

uchaf *adj.* highest

uchder *nm.* height

uchel *adj.* high

uchelgais *nmf.* ambition

uchelseinydd/-ion *nm.* loudspeaker

uffern *nf.* hell

un *num.* one

undeb/-au *nm.* union; **U~ Ewropeaidd** European Union

Undodiaid *npl.* Unitarians

uned/-au *nf.* unit

unieithog *adj.* monolingual

unig *adj.* only, lonely

unigrwydd *nm.* loneliness

unigryw *adj.* unique

union *adj.* straight; **yn ~** immediately

uno *v.* to join, to unite

Unol Daleithiau America *npl.* United States of America
unrhyw *adj.* any; ~ **un** anyone; ~ **beth** anything
unwaith *adv.* once
Urdd Gobaith Cymru *nf.* Welsh League of Youth
uwchben *prep.* above

W

wal/-iau *nf.* wall
waled/-i *nf.* wallet
wats/-ys *nm.* watch
wedi *prep.* after; *verbal* have; ~ **blino** tired; **wedi ei eni**
    born; ~ **'i ferwi** boiled; ~ **'i ffrio** fried
wedyn *adv.* then, afterwards
weithiau *adv.* sometimes
wincio *v.* to wink
wlser/-au *nm.* ulcer
wrth *prep.* + *S.M.* by, near; ~ **gwrs** of course; ~ **ochr** by
    the side of
wyneb/-au *nm.* face
wynwynen/wynwyn *nf.* onion
ŵyr/-ion *nm.* grandson
wyres/-au *nf.* granddaughter
wythnos/-au *nf.* week; ~ **nesaf** next week

Y

y *art.* the; ~ **ddau** *m.* both; ~ **ddwy** *f.* both; ~ **cant**
    percent; ~ **llynedd** last year; ~ **Môr Canoldir** the
    Mediterranean Sea; ~ **Pasg** Easter; **y Swistir**
    Switzerland; ~ **tu allan** outside; ~ **tu hwnt i**
    beyond; ~ **tu mewn** inside
ychwanegol *adj.* extra, additional
ychwanegu *v.* to add
ychydig *nm.* a little, a few
yfory *adv.* tomorrow
yma *adv.* here

ymadrodd/-ion *nm.* phrase
ymarfer *v.* to practice
ymarferol *adj.* practical
ymatal *v.* to refrain, to abstain
ymateb/-ion *nm.* response; *v.* to respond
ymbarél/ymbarelau *nm.* umbrella
ymchwil *nf.* research
ymchwilio *v.* to research
ymddangos *v.* to appear
ymddeol *v.* to retire
ymddiheuro *v.* to apologize
ymddiriedaeth *nf.* trust
Ymddiriedolaeth Genedlaethol *nf.* National Trust
ymddwyn *v.* to behave
ymddygiad *nm.* behavior
ymdrochi *v.* to bathe
ymgais/ymgeisiadau *nm.* attempt
ymgynnull *v.* to assemble
ymhlith *prep.* among
ymlacio *v.* to relax
ymladd *v.* to fight; ~ **â** + *SP.M.* to fight with
ymlâdd *adj.* **wedi** ~ exhausted
ymlaen *adv.* forward
ymolchi *v.* to wash
ymosodol *adj.* offensive
ymsefydlu *v.* to establish
ymuno *v.* to join
ymweld *v.* to visit; ~ **â** + *SP.M.* to visit
ymweliad/-au *nm.* visit
ymwelydd/ymwelwyr *nm.* visitor
ymwybodol *adj.* conscious
ymyl/-on *nf.* edge; **yn** ~ near
yn *prep.* + *N.M.* in; ~ **agos at** near; ~ **erbyn** against;
    ~ **lle** instead of; ~ **ôl** back
yn *introduces verb or noun; changes adjective to*
    adverb; ~ **aml** often; ~ **barod** ready; ~ **enwedig**
    especially; ~ **gywir** yours sincerely; according to;
    ~ **syth** straight, immediately; ~ **unig** only, lonely
yna *adv.* then

ynghanol *adv.* in the middle of
ynghwsg *adv.* asleep
ynghyd *adv.* together
yng nghanol *adv.* in the middle of
yno *adv.* there
ynys/-oedd *nf.* island
ynysu *v.* to isolate
yr *art.* the; ~ **Almaen** Germany; ~ **Eidal** Italy; ~ **un**
    each; ~ **unig** the only; ~ **Urdd** the Welsh League
    of Youth
ysbryd/-ion *nm.* spirit
ysbyty/ysbytai *nm.* hospital
ysgol/-ion *nf.* school, ladder; ~ **feithrin** nursery school;
    ~ **fonedd** private school; ~ **gyfun** comprehensive
    school; ~ **gynradd** primary school; ~ **uwchradd**
    secondary school
ysgoloriaeth/-au *nf.* scholarship
ysgrifbin/-nau *nf.* pen
ysgrifennu *v.* to write
ysgrifennwr/ysgrifenwyr *nm.* writer
ysgrifennydd/ysgrifenyddion *nm.* secretary
ysgrifenyddes/-au *nf.* secretary
ysgubo *v.* to sweep
ysgubor/-iau *nf.* barn
ysgwyd *v.* to shake; ~ **llaw** to shake hands
ysgwydd/-au *nf.* shoulder
ysgyfaint *npl.* lungs
ystad/-au *nf.* estate
ystafell/-oedd *nf.* room; ~ **aros** waiting room; ~ **fyw**
    living room
ystum/-iau *nm.* gesture
ystyr/-on *nmf.* meaning
ystyried *v.* to consider
yswiriant *nm.* insurance
yswirio *v.* to insure

ENGLISH–WELSH
DICTIONARY

A

a *art.* [no Welsh equivalent]
abbey *n.* abaty *m.*, mynachlog *f.*
ability *n.* gallu *m.*
able *adj.* galluog
  to be able to *v.* gallu
abolish *v.* dileu (*delete*); gwahardd (*ban*)
about *prep.* am + *S.M.* (*about, at+ time*); tua + *SP.M.*
  (*about+ time*); o gwmpas (*around*)
above *prep. + adv.* uwchben
abroad *adv.* dramor; *adj.* tramor
absent *adj.* absennol
absurd *adj.* ffôl (*foolish*); afresymol (*unreasonable*)
abuse *v.* camddefnyddio; *n.* camddefnydd *m.*
academy *n.* academi *f.*
accelerate *v.* cyflymu
accelerator *n.* sbardun *m.*
accent *n.* acen *f.*
accept *v.* derbyn
accident *n.* damwain *f.*
accommodation *n.* llety *m.*
accompany *v.* hebrwng (*across road*); cyfeilio (*on piano*)
accomplish *v.* cyflawni
according to *prep.* yn ôl
account *n.* cyfrif *m.*
accountant *n.* cyfrifydd *m.*
accurate *adj.* cywir
accusation *n.* cyhuddiad *m.*
accuse *v.* cyhuddo
accustomed *adj.* cyfarwydd
ace *n.* as *m.*
ache *n.* poen *mf.*; *v.* poeni, brifo

achieve *v.* cyflawni

achievement *n.* cyflawniad *m.*

acknowledge *v.* cydnabod

acknowledgement *n.* cydnabyddiaeth *f.*

acquaintance *n.* cyfaill *m.* (*friend*); cydnabod *m.*

acquire *v.* cael (*receive*); ennill (*gain*)

across *prep.* ar draws

act *n.* act/-au *f.*; *v.* actio

action *n.* gweithred *f.* (*deed*); hwyl *f* (*fun*)

active *adj.* bywiog (*lively*); gweithgar (*working*)

activity *n.* gweithgaredd *m.*

actor *n.* actor *m.*

actress *n.* actores *f.*

adapt *v.* addasu

add *v.* adio, ychwanegu

address *n.* cyfeiriad (*house*); araith (*speech*)

adjective *n.* ansoddair *m.*

administration *n.* gweinyddiaeth *f.*

admire *v.* edmygu

adolescence *n.* glasoed *m.*

adopt *v.* mabwysiadu

adult *n.* oedolyn *m.*

adultery *n.* godineb *m.*

advance *v.* mynd ymlaen

advantage *n.* mantais *f.*

adventure *n.* antur *m.*

advertise *v.* hysbysebu

advertisement *n.* hysbyseb *f.*

advice *n.* cyngor *m.*

affect *v.* effeithio

afford *v.* fforddio

afraid *adj.* ofnus; **I'm afraid** Mae ofn arna i

Africa *n.* Affrica *f.*

African *n.* Affricanwr *m.*, Affricanes *f.*; *adj.* Affricanaidd

after *prep.* ar ôl, wedi

afternoon *n.* prynhawn *m.*

again *adv.* eto

against *prep.* yn erbyn

age *n.* oed *m.*

agency *n.* asiantaeth *f.*

agent *n.* asiant *m.*

aggressive *adj.* ymosodol

ago *adv.* yn ôl

agree *v.* cytuno

agreement *n.* cytundeb *m.*

ahead *adv.* ymlaen, ar y blaen

air *n.* awyr *f.*; **fresh ~** awyr iach

airline *n.* cwmni awyrennau *m.*

airmail *n.* post awyr *m.*

airplane *n.* awyren *f.*

airport *n.* maes awyr *m.*

alarm *n.* larwm *m.*

alarm clock *n.* cloc larwm *m.*

alcohol *n.* alcohol *m.*

alien *adj.* dieithr

alike *adj.* tebyg

alive *adj.* byw

all *pron.* pawb

allergic *adj.* alergaidd

allergy *n.* alergedd *m.*

allow *v.* caniatáu

almost *adv.* bron

alone *adv.* ar ei ben ei hun *m.*, ar ei phen ei hun *f.*

aloud *adv.* yn uchel

alphabet *n.* gwyddor *f.*

already *adv.* yn barod, eisoes

also *adv.* hefyd

always *adv.* bob amser

amaze *v.* rhyfeddu

ambassador *n.* llysgennad

ambiguous *adj.* amwys

ambition *n.* uchelgais *m.*

ambulance *n.* ambiwlans *m.*

America *n.* America *f.*

American *n.* Americanwr *m.*, Americanes *f.*;
  adj. Americanaidd

among *prep.* ymhlith

amount *n.* swm *m.*

ancestor *n.* hynafiad *m.*

anchor *n.* angor *f.*

ancient *adj.* hynafol
and *conj.* a + *SP.M.*, ac
angel *n.* angel *m.*
anger *n.* dicter *m.*
angle *n.* ongl *f.*
angry *adj.* dig
animal *n.* anifail *m.*
ankle *n.* migwrn *m.*
anniversary *n.* blwyddiant *m.*
announcement *n.* cyhoeddiad *m.*
annual *adj.* blynyddol
another *adj.* arall
answer *n.* ateb *m.*
anxiety *n.* pryder *m.*
anxious *adj.* pryderus
any *adj.* unrhyw
anybody *n.* unrhyw un *mf.*
apart *prep.* ar wahân
apartment *n.* fflat *f.*
apologize *v.* ymddiheuro
appearance *n.* golwg *mf.*
appendicitis *n.* pendics *m.*
appetite *n.* archwaeth *m.*
applaud *v.* cymeradwyo
applause *n.* cymeradwyaeth *f.*
apple *n.* afal *m.*
appliance *n.* teclyn *m.*
application *n.* cais *m.*
apply *v.* ymgeisio, gwneud cais
appointment *n.* apwyntiad *m.*
apprentice *n.* prentis *m.*
apprenticeship *n.* prentisiaeth *f.*
approach *v.* nesáu
appropriate *adj.* addas, priodol
approve *v.* cymeradwyo
April *n.* Ebrill *m.*
Arab *n.* Arab *m.*; *adj.* Arabaidd
arch *n.* bwa *m.*
architecture *n.* pensaernïaeth *f.*
archive *n.* archif *m.*

area *n.* arwynebedd *m.*, ardal *f.* (*region*)
argument *n.* dadl *f.*
arm *n.* braich *f.*
armchair *n.* cadair freichiau *f.*
armpit *n.* cesail *f.*
army *n.* byddin *f.*
around *prep.* o gwmpas
arrest *v.* restio
arrival *n.* dyfodiad *m.*
arrive *v.* cyrraedd
arrow *n.* saeth *f.*
art *n.* celfyddyd *f.*; celf *f.*
article *n.* erthygl *f.*
artificial *adj.* artiffisial
artist *n.* artist *m.*
as *conj.* fel
ash *n.* lludw *m.*, llwch *m.*
ashtray *n.* blwch llwch *m.*
Asia *n.* Asia *f.*
Asian *n.* Asiad *m.*; *adj.* Asiaidd
ask *v.* gofyn
asleep *adv.* ynghwsg
assist *v.* cynorthwyo
assistant *n.* cynorthwywr *m.*, cynorthwywraig *f.*
association *v.* cymdeithas *f.*
assure *v.* sicrhau
at *prep.* ger, wrth + *S.M.*, yn (*in*) + *N.M.*
athlete *n.* athletwr *m.*
ATM *n.* peiriant arian *m.*
attempt *v.* ceisio; *n.* ymdrech *f.*
attention *n.* sylw *m.*
attitude *n.* agwedd *f.*
attorney *n.* cyfreithiwr *m.*
attract *v.* denu
attractive *adj.* deniadol
auction *n.* ocsiwn *f.*
August *n.* Awst *m.*
aunt *n.* modryb *f.*
Australia *n.* Awstralia *f.*
Austria *n.* Awstria *f.*

authentic *adj.* dilys
author *n.* awdur *m.*, awdures *f.*
authority *n.* awdurdod *m.*
authorize *v.* awdurdodi
automatic *adj.* awtomatig
available *adj.* ar gael
avenue *n.* rhodfa *f.*
average *n.* cyfartaledd *m.*
avoid *v.* osgoi
aware *adj.* ymwybodol
away *adv.* i ffwrdd
awful *adj.* ofnadwy

B

baby *n.* baban *m.*
baby-sit *v.* gwarchod
baby-sitter *n.* gofalwr *m.*, gofalwraig *f.*
bachelor *n.* hen lanc *m.*
back *adv.* yn ôl; *n.* cefn *m.*
backbone *n.* asgwrn cefn *m.*
backpack *n.* sach gefn *f.*
backwards *adv.* tuag yn ôl
bacteria *n.* bacteria *mpl.*
bad *adj.* gwael, drwg
bag *n.* bag *m.*
baggage *n.* bagiau *mpl.* **bake** *v.* pobi
baker *n.* pobydd *m.*
balance *v.* cydbwyso; *n.* balans *m.* (*bank*)
balcony *n.* balconi *m.*, balcon *m.*
bald *adj.* moel
ball *n.* pêl *f.*
ballet *n.* bale *m.*
ballpoint pen *n.* beiro *m.*
ban *v.* gwahardd; *n.* gwaharddiad *m.*
band *n.* band *m.*
bandage *n.* rhwymyn *m.*
bank *n.* banc *m.*
banker *n.* banciwr *m.*

banquet *n.* gwledd *f.*

baptism *n.* bedydd *m.*

baptize *v.* bedyddio

bar *n.* bar *m.*

barber *n.* barbwr *m.*, torrwr gwallt *m.*

bard *n.* bardd *m.*

bare *adj.* noeth

barefoot *adj.* troednoeth

bargain *n.* bargen *f.*

barn *n.* ysgubor *m.*

basement *n.* llawr gwaelod *m.*

basin *n.* basn *m.*

basis *n.* sail *f.*

basket *n.* basged *f.*

bath *n.* bath *m.*

bathe *v.* ymdrochi

bathroom *n.* stafell ymolchi *f.*

bathtub *n.* bath *m.*

battery *n.* batri *m.*

bay *n.* bae *m.*

be *v.* bod

beach *n.* traeth *m.*

beard *n.* barf *f.*

beat *v.* curo; *n.* curiad *m.*

beautiful *adj.* prydferth

beauty *n.* prydferthwch *m.*

because *conj.* achos, oherwydd

become *v.* dod yn

bed *n.* gwely *m.*

bedding *n.* dillad gwely *mpl.*

bedroom *n.* stafell wely *f.*

bee *n.* gwenynen *f.*

beer *n.* cwrw *m.*

before *prep.* cyn

beg *v.* cardota

begin *v.* dechrau

beginner *n.* dechreuwr *m.*

beginning *n.* dechreuad *m.*

behave *v.* ymddwyn

behind *prep.* y tu ôl i

Belgian *n.* Belgiad *mf.*; *adj.* Belgaidd
Belgium *n.* Gwlad Belg *f.*
belief *n.* cred *f.*
believe *v.* credu
bell *n.* cloch *f.*
belly *n.* bola *m.*
belong *v.* perthyn
belongings *n.* eiddo *m.*
below *prep.* dan + *S.M.*; *adv.* isod
belt *n.* gwregys *m.*
bench *n.* mainc *f.*
benefit *n.* lles *m.*
beside *prep.* ger, wrth
best *adj.* gorau
bet *v.* betio
better *adj.* gwell
between *prep.* rhwng
beverage *n.* diod *f.*
beware *inter.* gofal
beyond *prep.* y tu hwnt i
bib *n.* bib *m.*
Bible *n.* Beibl *m.*
bicycle *n.* beic *m.*
big *adj.* mawr
bikini *n.* bicini *m.*
bilingual *adj.* dwyieithog
bill *n.* bil *m.*
billion *num.* biliwn *f.*
bird *n.* aderyn *m.*
birth *n.* genedigaeth *f.*
birth control pill *n.* pilsen gwrthgenhedlu *f.*
birthday *n.* pen blwydd *m.*
bit *n.* darn *m.*; **a bit** *adv.* ychydig
bitter *adj.* chwerw
black *adj.* du
blade *n.* llafn *f.*
blanket *n.* blanced *f.*
bleed *v.* gwaedu
blend *v.* cymysgu
bless *v.* bendithio

blind *adj.* dall
blindness *n.* dallineb *m.*
blister *n.* pothell *f.*
block *n.* bloc *m.*
blond *adj.* golau
blood *n.* gwaed *m.*
blouse *n.* blows *f.*
blow *v.* chwythu
blue *adj.* glas
board *n.* bwrdd *m.*
boarding school *n.* ysgol breswyl *f.*
boat *n.* cwch *m.*, bad *m.*
body *n.* corff *m.*
boil *v.* berwi
bolt *n.* bollt *f.*
bomb *n.* bom *m.*
bone *n.* asgwrn *m.*
book *n.* llyfr *m.*; *v.* archebu, cadw lle (*keep a room/seat*)
bookcase *n.* cwpwrdd llyfrau *m.*
bookstore *n.* siop lyfrau *f.*
boot *n.* cist *f.*
border *n.* ffin *f.*
born *v.* geni
boss *n.* bos *m.*
both *adv., pron.* y ddau
bother *v.* poeni
bottle *n.* potel *f.*
bow *n.* bwa *m.*
bowl *n.* powlen *f.*
box *n.* blwch *m.*
bracelet *n.* breichled *f.*
bread *n.* bara *m.*
break *v.* torri
break down *v.* torri lawr
breakfast *n.* brecwast *m.*; **for ~** i frecwast
breast *n.* bron *f.*
breath *n.* anadl *f.*
breathe *v.* anadlu
breeze *n.* awel *f.*
bride *n.* priodferch *f.*

bridge *n.* pont *f.*
brief *adj.* byr, cryno
briefs *n.* pans *m.*
bright *adj.* disglair
bring *v.* dod â + *SP.M.*
brother *n.* brawd *m.*
brother-in-law *n.* brawd yng nghyfraith *m.*
brown *adj.* brown
bruise *n.* clais *m.*
brush *n.* brwsh *m.*
bubble *n.* swigen *f.*
bucket *n.* bwced *m.*
budget *n.* cyllideb *f.*
build *v.* adeiladu
building *n.* adeilad *m.*
bulb *n.* bwlb *m.*
bullet *n.* bwled *f.*
bunch *n.* tusw *m.*
burglar *n.* lleidr *m.*
burn *v.* llosgi
burst *v.* torri
bury *v.* claddu
bus *n.* bws *m.*
business *n.* busnes *m.*
busy *adj.* prysur
but *conj.* ond
butcher *n.* cigydd *m.*
button *n.* botwm *m.*
buy *v.* prynu
by *prep.* wrth +*S.M.*
bye-bye *inter.* hwyl fawr, pob hwyl

C

cab *n.* tacsi *m.*
cable *n.* cebl *m.*
café *n.* caffe *m.*
cage *n.* cawell *m.*
cake *n.* teisen *f.*, cacen *f.*

calculate *v.* cyfrifo

calculator *n.* cyfrifiannell

calendar *n.* calendr *m.*

call *v.* galw; *n.* galwad *f.*

calling card *n.* cerdyn galw *m.*

camera *n.* camera *m.*

camp *n.* gwersyll *m.*

can *v.* gallu; *n.* tun *m.*

Canada *n.* Canada *f.*

Canadian *n.* Canadiad *m.*; *adj.* Canadaidd

cancel *v.* dileu, canslo

cancer *n.* canser *m.*

candle *n.* cannwyll *f.*

candy *n.* losin *pl.*

canoe *n.* canŵ *m.*

cap *n.* cap *m.*

capable *adj.* galluog

capital *n.* prifddinas *f.*

captain *n.* capten *m.*

car *n.* car *m.*

card *n.* cerdyn *m.*

cardboard *n.* cardfwrdd *m.*

care *n.* gofal *m.*; *v.* gofalu

careful *adj.* gofalus

carpet *m.* carped

carry *v.* cario

carton *n.* carton *m.*

case *n.* cês *m.* (*bag*); achos *m.* (*law*)

cash *n.* arian *m.*

cashier *n.* ariannwr *m.*

casino *n.* casino *m.*

castle *n.* castell *m.*

casual *adj.* hamddenol (*leisurely*), achlysurol (*now and again*)

cat *n.* cath *f.*

catalogue *n.* catalog *m.*

catch *v.* dal

cathedral *n.* eglwys gadeiriol *f.*

Catholic *adj.* Catholig

Catholicism *n.* Catholigaeth *f.*

caution *n.* gofal *m.*
cautious *adj.* gofalus
cave *n.* ogof *f.*
CD *n.* CD *m.*
CD player *n.* chwaraewr CD *m.*
CD-ROM *n.* CD-ROM *m.*
ceiling *n.* nenfwd *m.*
celebrate *v.* dathlu
cell *n.* cell *f.*
cellar *n.* seler *f.*
cemetery *n.* mynwent *f.*
center *n.* canol *m.*
centimeter *n.* centimetr *m.*
central *adj.* canolog
century *n.* canrif *f.*
ceremony *n.* seremoni *f.*
chain *n.* cadwyn *f.*
chair *n.* cadair *f.*
chance *n.* siawns *f.*
change *v.* newid; *n.* newid *m.*
chapter *n.* pennod *f.*
character *n.* cymeriad *m.*
charge *v.* codi tâl
charges *n.* taliadau *mpl.*
chat *v.* sgwrsio; *n.* sgwrs *f.*
cheap *adj.* rhad
cheat *v.* twyllo
check *v.* gwirio, edrych (*look*)
cheek *n.* boch *f.*
Cheers! *inter.* Iechyd da!
cheese *n.* caws *m.*
chemical *adj.* cemegol
chess *n.* gwyddbwyll *m.*
chest *n.* brest *f.*
chew *v.* cnoi
child *n.* plentyn *m.*
childhood *n.* plentyndod *m.*
chin *n.* gên *f.*
china *n.* tsieni *m.*
choice *n.* dewis *m.*

choke *v.* tagu

choose *v.* dewis

Christian *n.* Cristion *m.*; *adj.* Cristnogol

Christianity *n.* Cristnogaeth *f.*

Christmas *n.* Nadolig *m.*; **Merry ~** Nadolig Llawen

church *n.* eglwys *f.*

cigar *n.* sigâr *f.*

cigarette *n.* sigarét *f.*

circle *n.* cylch *m.*

circumstance *n.* amgylchiad *m.*

circus *n.* syrcas *m.*

citizen *n.* dinesydd *m.*

city *n.* dinas *f.*

civil *adj.* sifil

civilian *n.* dinesydd *m.*

civilization *n.* gwareiddiad *m.*

classic *adj.* clasurol

clean *adj.* glân

clear *adj.* clir

clever *adj.* clyfar

client *n.* cleient *m.*

cliff *n.* clogwyn *m.*

climate *n.* hinsawdd *f.*

climb *v.* dringo

clinic *n.* clinig *m.*

clock *n.* cloc *m.*

close *v.* cau

closed *adv.* ar gau

cloth *n.* lliain *m.*

clothe *v.* dilladu, gwisgo

clothes *n.* dillad *pl.*

cloud *n.* cwmwl *m.*

coast *n.* arfordir *m.*

coat *n.* cot *f.*

cobbler *n.* crydd *m.*

code *n.* cod *m.*

coffee *n.* coffi *m.*

coffee shop *n.* siop goffi *f.*

coffin *n.* arch *f.*

coin *n.* darn arian *m.*

cold *adj.* oer
collect *v.* casglu
collection *n.* casgliad *m.*
college *n.* coleg *m.*
collide *v.* gwrthdaro
collision *n.* gwrthdrawiad *m.*
color *n.* lliw *m.*
column *n.* colofn *f.*
comb *n.* crib *f.*
combination *n.* cyfuniad *m.*
come *v.* dod
comfort *n.* cysur *m.*
comfortable *adj.* cysurus
comma *n.* atalnod *m.*, coma *m.*
comment *n.* sylw *m.*
commission *n.* comisiwn *m.*
committee *n.* pwyllgor *m.*
common. *adj.* cyffredin
communicate *v.* cyfathrebu
company *n.* cwmni *m.*
compare *v.* cymharu
comparison *n.* cymhariaeth *f.*
compartment *n.* adran *f.*
compass *n.* cwmpawd *m.*
compensate *v.* gwneud iawn
competition *n.* cystadleuaeth *f.*
complain *v.* cwyno
complaint *n.* cwyn *mf.*
complete *v.* cwblhau; *adj.* cyflawn
compliment *n.* canmoliaeth *f.*
compose *v.* cyfansoddi
composer *n.* cyfansoddwr *m.*
composition *n.* cyfansoddiad *m.*
comprehensive *adj.* cyfun, cyflawn
computer *n.* cyfrifiadur *m.*
concern *n.* pryder *m.,* gofal *m.*
concert *n.* cyngerdd *mf.*
concrete *n.* concrit *m.*; *adj.* pendant
condemn *v.* condemnio
condition *n.* cyflwr *m.*, amod *mf.* (*term*)

condolences *n.* cydymdeimlad *m.*

condom *n.* condom *m.*

conductor *n.* arweinydd *m.*, tocynnwr *m.* (*bus*)

confess *v.* cyfaddef

confession *n.* cyffes *f.*

confidence *n.* hyder *m.*

confirm *v.* cadarnhau

conflict *v.* gwrthdaro

confuse *v.* cymysgu

congratulate *v.* llongyfarch

congratulations *inter.* llongyfarchiadau

connect *v.* cysylltu

connection *n.* cysylltiad *m.*

conscious *adj.* ymwybodol

consequence *n.* canlyniad *m.*

conserve *v.* gwarchod, cadw

consider *v.* ystyried

consonant *n.* cytsain *f.*

constipation *n.* rhwymedd *m.*

consul *n.* conswl *m.*

consulate *n.* llysgenhadaeth *f.*

contact *v.* cysylltu

contact lenses *n.* lensys cyswllt *fpl.*

contagious *adj.* heintus

contain *v.* cynnwys

container *n.* cynhwysydd *m.*

contaminate *v.* llygru

contempt *n.* dirmyg *m.*

content *adj.* bodlon

continent *n.* cyfandir *m.*

continue *v.* parhau

contraceptive *n.* gwrthgenhedlu *m.*

contract *n.* cytundeb *m.*, contract *m.*

control *v.* rheoli

convent *n.* cwfaint *m.*

conversation *n.* sgwrs *f.*

convert *v.* trosi

convince *v.* argyhoeddi

cook *v.* coginio; *n.* cogydd *m.*, cogyddes *f.*

cool *adj.* oer, oerllyd

copy *v.* copïo; *n.* copi *m.*

Cordially,... *inter.* Yn gywir,...

core *n.* craidd *m.*

cork *n.* corc *m.*

corner *n.* cornel *mf.*

corpse *n.* corff *m.*

correct *adj.* cywir; *v.* cywiro

correction *n.* cywiriad *m.*

correspondence *n.* gohebiaeth *f.* (*letters*), cyfatebiaeth *f.* (*similarity*)

cost *n.* cost *f.*; *v.* costio

cot *n.* cot *f.*

cotton *n.* cotwm *m.*

couch *n.* soffa *m.*

cough *v.* pesychu; *n.* peswch *m.*

count *v.* cyfrif

counter *n.* cownter *m.*

country *n.* gwlad *f.*

couple *n.* pâr *m.*

course *n.* cwrs *m.*

court *n.* llys *m.*

courtyard *n.* buarth *m.*

cousin *n.* cefnder *m.,* cyfnither *f.*

cover *n.* clawr *m.*; *v.* gorchuddio

cow *n.* buwch *f.*

cradle *n.* crud *m.*

craft *n.* crefft *f.*

craftsman *n.* crefftwr *m.*

crash *n.* gwrthdrawiad *m.*; *v.* crasio

crawl *v.* cropian

crazy *adj.* gwallgof, gwallgo

cream *n.* hufen *m.*

create *v.* creu

credit *n.* credyd *m.*; **~ card** *n.* cerdyn credyd *m.*

crew *n.* criw *m.*

crime *n.* trosedd *mf.*

criticism *n.* beirniadaeth *f.*

criticize *v.* beirniadu

cross *n.* croes *f.*; *v.* croesi; *adj.* dig

cruise *v.* mordeithio; *n.* mordaith *f.*

crumb *n.* briwsionyn *m.*
crumble *v.* chwalu
cry *v.* crio, llefain, wylo
culture *n.* diwylliant *m.*
cup *n.* cwpan *mf.*
cupboard *n.* cwpwrdd *m.*
cure *n.* gwellhad *m.*
curious *v.* chwilfrydig
curl *n.* cyrl *m.*
currency *n.* arian *m.*
current *adj.* cyfredol, presennol
curtain *n.* llen *f.*
curve *n.* tro *m.*
cushion *n.* clustog *f.*
custom *n.* arfer *mf.*
customer *n.* cwsmer *m.*
customs *n.* tollau *fpl.*; arferion *mpl.* (*habits*)
cut *v.* torri; *n.* cwt *m.*, toriad *m.*

D

dad *n.* dad *m.*
daily *adj.* dyddiol
dairy *n.* llaethdy *m.*
damage *n.* niwed *m.*
damp *adj.* llaith
dance *n.* dawns *f.*; *v.* dawnsio; ~ **club** clwb dawnsio
danger *n.* perygl *m.*
dangerous *adj.* peryglus
dare *v.* mentro
dark *adj.* tywyll
darkness *n.* tywyllwch *m.*
date *n.* dyddiad *m.*, oed *m.* (*appointment*)
daughter *n.* merch *f.*
daughter-in-law *n.* merch yng nghyfraith *f.*
dawn *n.* gwawr *f.*
day *n.* dydd *m.*, diwrnod *m.*
day care *n.* gofal dydd *m.*
dead *adj.* marw

deadly *adj.* marwol, angheuol
deaf *adj.* byddar
deafness *n.* byddardod *m.*
deal *v.* delio; *n.* bargen *f.*
dealer *n.* deliwr *m.*
dear *adj.* annwyl
death *n.* marwolaeth *f.*
debt *n.* dyled *f.*
decade *n.* degawd *mf.*
decaffeinated *adj.* digaffîn
deceive *v.* twyllo
December *n.* Rhagfyr *m.*
decide *v.* penderfynu
decision *n.* penderfyniad *m.*
declare *v.* cyhoeddi
decorate *v.* addurno
decoration *n.* addurn *m.*
decrease *v.* lleihau
deep *adj.* dwfn
defect *n.* nam *m.*
defend *v.* amddiffyn
defense *n.* amddiffyniad *f.*
define *v.* diffinio
definition *n.* diffiniad *m.*
degree *n.* gradd *f.*
delay *v.* oedi
delete *v.* dileu
delicious *adj.* blasus
deliver *v.* dosbarthu
demand *v.* hawlio
democracy *n.* democratiaeth *f.*
demonstration *n.* gwrthdystiad *m.*
dentist *n.* deintydd *m.*
departure *n.* ymadawiad *m.*
depend *v.* dibynnu
deposit *n.* ernes *m.*
depression *n.* iselder *m.*
depth *n.* dyfnder *m.*
descend *v.* disgyn
describe *v.* disgrifio

desert *n.* anialwch *m.*
deserve *v.* haeddu
desire *n.* dymuniad *m.*; *v.* dymuno
desk *n.* desg *f.*
dessert *n.* pwdin *m.*
destroy *v.* distrywio, dinistrio
detach *v.* datod
detail *n.* manylyn *m.*
detective *n.* ditectif *m.*
develop *v.* datblygu
devil *n.* diawl *m.*, diafol *m.*
dew *n.* gwlith *m.*
diabetes *n.* clefyd siwgr *m.*
dial *v.* deialu; *n.* deial *m.*
dialect *n.* tafodiaith *f.*
dialogue *n.* sgwrs *f.*, deialog *f.*
diamond *n.* diemwnt *mf.*
diaper *n.* cewyn *m.*
diary *n.* dyddiadur *m.*
dictionary *n.* geiriadur *m.*
die *v.* marw
diet *n.* deiet, diet *m.*
difference *n.* gwahaniaeth *m.*
different *adj.* gwahanol
difficult *adj.* anodd, caled
difficulty *n.* anhawster *m.*
digest *v.* treulio
digestion *n.* treuliad *m.*
digital *adj.* digidol; *n* ~ **camera** camera digidol *m.*
dimension *n.* dimensiwn *m.*
dine *v.* bwyta, ciniawa
dining room *n.* stafell fwyta *f.*
dinner *n.* cinio *mf.*
diplomacy *n.* diplomyddiaeth *f.*
direct *adj.* uniongyrchol, syth
direction *n.* cyfeiriad *m.*
director *n.* cyfarwyddwr *m.*
dirt *n.* baw *m.*
dirty *adj.* brwnt, budr
disagree *v.* anghytuno

disagreement *n.* anghytundeb *m.*
disappear *v.* diflannu
disappointment *n.* siom *m.*
disaster *n.* trychineb *f.*
discipline *n.* disgyblaeth *f.*; *v.* disgyblu
discount *n.* disgownt *m.*
discover *v.* darganfod
discuss *v.* trafod
discussion *n.* trafodaeth *f.*
disease *n.* haint *m.*, clefyd *m.*
disgusting *adj.* ffiaidd
dish *n.* dysgl *f.*
disk *n.* disg *m.*
dislike *v.* ddim yn hoffi
disobey *v.* anufuddhau
disposable *adj.* tafladwy
distance *n.* pellter *m.*
distinct *adj.* pendant, arbennig
distinguish *v.* gwahaniaethu
distribute *v.* dosbarthu
distribution *n.* dosbarthiad *m.*
disturb *v.* torri ar draws, aflonyddu
ditch *n.* ffos *f.*
dive *v.* plymio
diver *n.* plymiwr *m.*
divide *v.* rhannu
divorce *n.* ysgariad *m.*; *v.* ysgaru
do *v.* gwneud
doctor *n.* doctor *m.*, meddyg *m.*
dog *n.* ci *m.*
doll *n.* dol *f.*
dollar *n.* doler *m.*
donkey *n.* asyn *m.*
door *n.* drws *m.*
dose *n.* dos *f.*
dot *n.* dot *m.*
double *v.* dyblu
doubt *n.* amheuaeth *f.*
dough *n.* toes *m.*
down *adv.* lawr

dozen *n.* dwsin *m.*
draft *n.* drafft *m.*; awel *f.*
drama *n.* drama *f.*
draw *v.* tynnu
drawing *n.* darlun *m.*
dream *n.* breuddwyd *m.*
dress *n.* gwisg *f.*; *v.* gwisgo
drink *n.* diod *f.*; *v.* yfed
drive *v.* gyrru
driver *n.* gyrrwr *m.*
driver's license *n.* trwydded yrru *f.*
drop *v.* gollwng
drown *v.* boddi
drug *n.* cyffur *m.*
drunk *adj.* meddw, wedi meddwi
dry *v.* sychu
dryer *n.* sychwr *m.*
due *adj.* dyledus
dumb *adj.* mud (*unable to speak*), twp (*stupid*)
during *prep.* yn ystod
dusk *n.* cyfnos *m.*
dust *n.* llwch *m.*
duty *n.* dyletswydd *m.*
dye *v.* lliwio

E

each *adj.* pob
ear *n.* clust *f.*
early *adj.* cynnar
earn *v.* ennill
earnings *n.* enillion *pl.*
earring *n.* clustdlws *m.*
earth *n.* daear *f.*
easily *adv.* yn hawdd
east *n.* dwyrain *m.*
Easter *n.* Y Pasg *m.*
easy *adj.* hawdd
eat *v.* bwyta

economy *n.* economi *m.*

edge *n.* ymyl *f.*

education *n.* addysg *f.*

effect *n.* effaith *f.*

effort *n.* ymdrech *f.*

egg *n.* wy *m.*; **boiled ~** wy wedi'i ferwi; **fried ~** wy wedi'i ffrio

eight *num.* wyth

elastic *n.* elastig *m.*

elbow *n.* penelin *mf.*

electric *adj.* trydanol

electrician *n.* trydanwr *m.*

electricity *n.* trydan *m.*

elegant *adj.* gosgeiddig

elevator *n.* lifft *m.*

eleven *num.* un deg un, un ar ddeg

else *adj.* arall

e-mail *n.* ebost *m.*

embarrass *v.* codi gwrid

embassy *n.* llysgenhadaeth *f.*

emergency *n.* argyfwng *m.*

emigrate *v.* allfudo

employee *n.* gweithiwr *m.*

employer *n.* cyflogwr *m.*

employment *n.* cyflogaeth *f.*, gwaith *m.*

empty *adj.* gwag

enclose *v.* amgáu

encounter *v.* cyfarfod

encyclopedia *n.* ensyclopedia *m.*

end *v.* gorffen; *n.* diwedd *m.*

endless *adj.* diddiwedd

enemy *n.* gelyn *m.*

energetic *adj.* egnïol

energy *n.* egni *m.*, ynni *m.*

engage *v.* dyweddïo

engagement *n.* dyweddïad *m.*

engine *n.* peiriant *m.*

engineer *n.* peiriannydd *m.*

England *n.* Lloegr *f.*

English *n.* Saesneg *f.* (*language*); *adj.* Seisnig

Englishman *n.* Sais *m.*
Englishwoman *n.* Saesnes *f.*
enjoy *v.* mwynhau
enjoyment *n.* mwynhad *m.*
enlarge *v.* mwyhau, helaethu
enormous *adj.* enfawr
enough *adj.* digon; ~ **food** digon o fwyd
enter *v.* mynd i mewn
entertain *v.* diddanu
enthusiasm *n.* brwdfrydedd *m.*
entire *adj.* cyfan
entrance *n.* mynedfa *f.* (*door*); mynediad *m.*
envelope *n.* amlen *f.*
environment *n.* amgylchedd *m.*
epidemic *n.* haint *m.*, pla *m.*
equal *adj.* cyfartal
equality *n.* cydraddoldeb *m.*
equipment *n.* offer *mpl.*
era *n.* cyfnod *m.*
erase *v.* dileu
eraser *n.* rhwber *m.*
error *n.* camsyniad *m.*
escalator *n.* lifft *m.*
escape *v.* ffoi, dianc
especially *adv.* yn enwedig
essential *adj.* angenrheidiol
establish *v.* sefydlu
estate *n.* ystâd *f.*
estimate *v.* amcangyfrif
eternal *adj.* tragwyddol
euro *n.* ewro *m.*
Europe *n.* Ewrop *f.*
European *adj.* Ewropeaidd; *n.* Ewropead *m.*
European Union *n.* Yr Undeb Ewropeaidd *m.*
evacuate *v.* gwacáu
evaluate *v.* gwerthuso
even *adj.* gwastad; *adv.* hyd yn oed
evening *n.* noswaith *f.*
event *n.* digwyddiad *m.*
ever *adv.* erioed

every *adj.* pob

everybody *n./pron.* pawb

everyday *adj.* cyffredin, pob dydd

evidence *n.* tystiolaeth *f.*

exact *adj.* union

exaggerate *v.* gorliwio

examination *n.* arholiad *m.*

examine *v.* arholi

example *n.* enghraifft *f.*

excellent *adj.* ardderchog

except *prep.* ac eithrio, heblaw

exception *n.* eithriad *m.*

exchange *v.* cyfnewid

exchange rate *n.* cyfradd gyfnewid *f.*

excite *v.* cyffroi

excitement *n.* cyffro *m.*

exclude *v.* cau allan

excursion *n.* gwibdaith *f.*

excuse *n.* esgus *m.*; *v.* esgusodi

execute *v.* gwneud (*do*); dienyddio (*kill*)

exercise *n.* ymarfer *m.*; *v.* ymarfer

exhaust *n.* piben wacáu *f.*

exhibit *v.* arddangos

exhibition *n.* arddangosfa *f.*

exist *v.* bodoli

existence *n.* bodolaeth *f.*

exit *n.* allanfa *f.*

expect *v.* disgwyl

expectation *n.* disgwyliad *m.*

expel *v.* taflu allan

expense *n.* traul *f.*

expensive *adj.* drud

experience *n.* profiad *m.*

expert *n.* arbenigwr *m.*

expire *v.* dod i ben

explain *v.* esbonio

explanation *n.* esboniad *m.*

explosion *n.* ffrwydrad *m.*

express *v.* mynegi

external *adj.* allanol

extinguish *v.* diffodd
extinguisher *n.* diffoddwr *m.*
extra *adj.* ychwanegol
extract *v.* tynnu allan; *n.* darn *m.*
extraordinary *adj.* arbennig
extreme *adj.* eithafol
eye *n.* llygad *m.*
eyebrow *n.* ael *f.*

F

fabric *n.* defnydd *m.*
face *n.* wyneb *m.*
fail *v.* methu
failure *n.* methiant *m.*
faint *v.* llewygu
fair *adj.* teg; ~ **play** chwarae teg
faith *n.* ffydd *m.*
faithful *adj.* ffyddlon
fall *v.* syrthio, cwympo
false *adj.* ffug
family *n.* teulu *m.*
famous *adj.* enwog
fan *n.* cefnogwr *m.* (*supporter*), gwyntyll *m.* (*air*)
far *adj.* pell
farm *n.* fferm *f.*
farmer *n.* ffermwr *m.*
fashion *n.* ffasiwn *m.*
fast *adj.* cyflym
fasten *v.* clymu (*tie*), cyflymu (*speed*)
fat *adj.* tew
father *n.* tad *m.*
father-in-law *n.* tad yng nghyfraith *m.*
fault *n.* bai *m.*
favor *n.* ffafr *f.*
favorite *adj.* hoff
fear *n.* ofn *m.*
feather *n.* pluen *f.*
February *n.* Chwefror *m.*

fee *n.* ffi *m.*
feed *v.* bwydo
feel *v.* teimlo
feeling *n.* teimlad *m.*
female *adj.* benywaidd; *n.* benyw *f.*
feminine *adj.* benywaidd
fence *n.* ffens *f.*
ferry *n.* fferi *m.*
festival *n.* gŵyl *f.*
fever *n.* twymyn *m.*
few *pron.* ychydig
field *n.* cae *m.*
fight *v.* ymladd
fill *v.* llenwi, llanw
film *n.* ffilm *f.*; *v.* ffilmio
filter *n.* hidlydd *m.*
filthy *adj.* brwnt
final *adj.* terfynol
financial *adj.* ariannol
find *v.* canfod, ffeindio
fine *adj.* braf
finger *n.* bys *m.*
fingerprint *n.* ôl bys *m.*
finish *v.* gorffen
fire *n.* tân *m.*
fireman *n.* dyn tân *m.*
fireplace *n.* lle tân *m.*
fireworks *n.* tân gwyllt *m.*
firm *adj.* cadarn
first *adj.* cyntaf
fish *n.* pysgodyn *m.*
fisherman *n.* pysgotwr *m.*
fist *n.* dwrn *m.*
fit *v.* ffitio
five *num.* pump
fix *v.* glynu
flag *n.* baner *f.*
flame *n.* fflam *f.*
flash *v.* fflachio
flashlight *n.* fflachlamp *f.*

flat *adj.* gwastad
flavor *n.* blas *m.*
flea *n.* lleuen *f.*
flight *n.* hediad *m.*
float *v.* arnofio
flood *n.* llifogydd *pl.*
floor *n.* llawr *m.*
florist *n.* gwerthwr blodau *m.*
flour *n.* blawd *m.*
flow *v.* llifo
flower *n.* blodyn *m.*
flu *n.* ffliw *m.*
fluently *adv.* yn rhugl
fly *v.* hedfan
fog *n.* niwl *m.*
fold *v.* plygu
folk *n.* gwerin *f.*
follow *v.* dilyn
food *n.* bwyd *m.*
fool *n.* ffŵl *m.*
foot *n.* troed *f.*
football *n.* pêl-droed *f.*
for *prep.* am, i
forbid *v.* gwahardd
force *n.* grym *m.*
forefinger *n.* mynegfys *m.*
forehead *n.* talcen *m.*
foreign *adj.* estron, tramor
foreigner *n.* estronwr *m.*, tramorwr *m.*
forest *n.* fforest *f.*, coedwig *f.*
forever *adv.* am byth
forget *v.* anghofio
forgive *v.* maddau
fork *n.* fforc *f.*
form *n.* ffurf *f.*; *v.* ffurfio
formal *adj.* ffurfiol
former *adj.* cyn
forward *n.* blaenwr *m.*; *adv.* ymlaen
foundation *n.* sail *f.*
four *num.* pedwar *m.*, pedair *f.*

fragile *adj.* bregus
frame *n.* ffrâm *f.*
France *n.* Ffrainc *f.*
free *adj.* rhydd
freedom *n.* rhyddid *m.*
freeze *v.* rhewi
freezer *n.* rhewgell *f.*
French *adj.* Ffrengig; *n.* Ffrangeg *f.*
Frenchman *n.* Ffrancwr *m.*
frequent *adv.* aml
fresh *adj.* ffres
Friday *n.* Gwener *m.*
friend *n.* ffrind *m.*, cyfaill *m.*, cyfeilles *f.*
friendly *adj.* cyfeillgar
friendship *n.* cyfeillgarwch *m.*
frog *n.* broga *m.*
from *prep.* o +*S.M.*, oddi wrth +*S.M.* (*letter*)
front *n.* blaen *m.*
fruit *n.* ffrwyth *m.*
fry *v.* ffrio
frying pan *n.* padell ffrio *f.*
fuel *n.* tanwydd *m.*
full *adj.* llawn; ~ **time** amser llawn
fun *n.* hwyl *f.*
funeral *n.* angladd *f.*
funny *adj.* doniol
fur *n.* ffwr *m.*
furniture *n.* celfi *mpl.*
fuse *n.* ffiws *mf.*
future *n.* dyfodol *m.*

G

gallery *n.* oriel *f.*
gallon *n.* galwyn *m.*
gamble *v.* gamblo, hapchwarae
game *n.* gêm *f.*
gap *n.* bwlch *m.*

garage *n.* garej *m.*, modurdy *m.*

garbage *n.* sbwriel *m.*

garden *n.* gardd *f.*

gardener *n.* garddwr *m.*

garlic *n.* garlleg *fpl.*

gas *n.* nwy *m.*

gate *n.* gât *m.*, clwyd *f.*

gather *v.* casglu

gay *adj.* hapus, hoyw

geography *n.* daearyddiaeth *f.*

germ *n.* germ *m.*

German *n.* Almaeneg *f.*; *adj.* Almaenig

Germany *n.* Yr Almaen *f.*

get *v.* cael

gift *n.* anrheg *f.*, rhodd *f.*

girl *n.* merch *f.*

give *v.* rhoi, rhoddi

glad *adj.* balch

glass *n.* gwydryn *m.*

glasses *n.* sbectol *f.*

glove *n.* maneg *f.*

glue *n.* glud *m.*

go *v.* mynd

goal *n.* gôl *f.*

goat *n.* gafr *f.*

God *n.* Duw *m.*

godfather *n.* tad bedydd *m.*

godmother *n.* mam fedydd *f.*

gold *n.* aur *m.*

good *adj.* da

good-bye *inter.* hwyl fawr

goods *n.* nwyddau *pl.*

government *n.* llywodraeth *f.*

gown *n.* gŵn *f.*

grab *v.* gafael

graduate *v.* graddio

gram *n.* gram *m.*

grammar *n.* gramadeg *m.*

grandchild *n.* ŵyr *m.*

granddaughter *n.* wyres *f.*

grandfather *n.* tad-cu *m.*[*S.W.*], taid *m.* [*N.W.*]

grandmother *n.* mam-gu *f.* [*S.W.*], nain *f.* [*N.W.*]

grandson *n.* ŵyr *m.*

grant *n.* grant *m.*; *v.* rhoi

grapes *n.* grawnwin *pl.*

grass *n.* glaswellt *pl.* porfa *f.*

grave *n.* bedd *m.*

gravestone *n.* carreg fedd *f.*

graveyard *n.* mynwent *f.*

gray *adj.* llwyd

great *adj.* mawr

Great Britain *n.* Prydain *f.*

great-grandfather *n.* hen dad-cu *m.* [*S.W.*], hen daid *m.* [*N.W.*]

great-grandmother *n.* hen fam-gu *f.* [*S.W.*], hen nain *f.* [*N.W.*]

green *adj.* gwyrdd

greet *v.* cyfarch

grief *n.* galar *m.*

grill *v.* grilio

grind *v.* malu

grocer *n.* groser *m.*

grocery store *n.* siop groser *f.*

ground *n.* tir *m.*

group *n.* grŵp *m.*

grow *v.* tyfu

grown-up *n.* oedolyn *m.*

growth *n.* twf *m.*

guarantee *n.* gwarant *m.*; *v.* gwarantu

guard *v.* gwarchod

guess *v.* dyfalu

guide *v.* tywys; *n.* tywysydd *m.*

guilt *n.* euogrwydd *m.*

guilty *adj.* euog

gum *n.* gwm *m.*

gun *n.* dryll *m.*

gutter *n.* gwter *m.*

gynecologist *n.* gynecolegydd *m.*

H

hail *n.* cesair *m.*; *v.* bwrw cesair
hair *n.* gwallt *pl.*
haircut *n.* toriad gwallt *m.*
hairdresser *n.* trinydd gwallt *m.*
hairspray *n.* chwistrell gwallt *f.*
half *n.* hanner *m.*
hall *n.* neuadd *f.*
Halloween *n.* Calan Gaeaf *m.*
ham *n.* ham *m.*
hammer *n.* morthwyl *m.*
hand *n.* llaw *f.*
handful *n.* llond llaw *f.*
handicap *n.* anfantais *f.*
handle *v.* trin; *n.* dolen *f.*
handy *adj.* hwylus
hang *v.* hongian
hangover *n.* pen mawr *m.*
happen *v.* digwydd
happiness *n.* hapusrwydd *m.*
happy *adj.* hapus
harass *v.* poeni
harbor *n.* harbwr *m.*, porthladd *m.*
hard *adj.* caled, anodd *(difficult)*
harm *v.* niweidio; *n.* niwed *m.*
harp *n.* telyn *f.*
harvest *n.* cynhaeaf *m.*
hat *n.* het *f.*
hate *n.* casineb *m.*
have *v.* cael *(obtain)*, mae … gan *(possess)*
hay *n.* gwellt *pl.*
hay fever *n.* twymyn y gwair *m.*
hazard *n.* perygl *m.*
he *pron.* fe, ef
head *n.* pen *m.*
headache *n.* pen tost *m.* [*S.W.*], cur pen *m.* [*N.W.*]
headlight *n.* prif olau *m.*
headline *n.* pennawd *m.*
headquarters *n.* pencadlys *m.*

heal *v.* gwella
health *n.* iechyd *m.*
healthy *adj.* iach
hear *v.* clywed
hearing *n.* clyw *m.*
heart *n.* calon *f.*
heat *n.* gwres *m.*
heater *n.* gwresogydd *m.*
heaven *n.* nefoedd *f.*, nef *f.*
heavy *adj.* trwm
heel *n.* sawdl *mf.*
height *n.* uchder *m.*; taldra *m.* (*of person*)
helicopter *n.* hofrennydd *m.*
hell *n.* uffern *f.*
hello *inter.* helo, shwmae
help *n.* help *m.*, cymorth *m.*; *v.* helpu
her *pron.* hi; *poss.pron* ei + *SP.M.*
herb *n.* perlysieuyn *m.*
here *adv.* yma
hesitate *v.* petruso
hi *inter.* shwmae
hide *v.* cuddio
high *adj.* uchel; *n.* ~ **school** ysgol uwchradd *f.*
highway *n.* priffordd *f.*
hike *v.* heicio
hill *n.* bryn *m.*
him *pron.* fe, ef
hip *n.* clun *m.*
hire *v.* llogi, hurio
historic *adj.* hanesyddol
history *n.* hanes *m.*
hit *v.* taro
hold *v.* dal
hole *n.* twll *m.*
holiday *n.* gwyliau *pl.*
holy *adj.* sanctaidd
home *n.* cartref *m.*; *adv.* adref; **at ~** gartref
homeland *n.* mamwlad *f.*
homesickness *n.* hiraeth *m.*
homework *n.* gwaith cartref *m.*

honey *n.* mêl *m.*

hook *n.* bachyn *m.*; *v.* bachu

hope *n.* gobaith *m.*; *v.* gobeithio

horn *n.* corn *m.*

hornet *n.* cacynen *f.*

horse *n.* ceffyl *m.*

hose *n.* pibell *f.*

hospital *n.* ysbyty *m.*

host *n.* gwestai *m.*; gwestywr *m.*

hostess *n.* gwestywraig *f.*

hot *adj.* poeth

hotel *n.* gwesty *m.*

hour *n.* awr *f.*

house *n.* tŷ *m.*

how *interrog.* sut

hug *v.* cofleidio

human *adj.* dynol

humid *adj.* trymaidd

hundred *num.* cant

hunger *n.* newyn *m.*

hungry *adj.* chwant bwyd *m.*; **I'm ~** mae chwant bwyd arna i

hunt *v.* hela; *n.* helfa *f.*

hunter *n.* helwr *m.*

hurricane *n.* corwynt *m.*

hurry *v.* brysio

hurt *v.* brifo

husband *n.* gŵr *m.*

hygiene *n.* glendid *m.*, hylendid *m.*

hygienic *adj.* hylan

hyphen *n.* cyplysnod *m.*

I

I *pron.* fi, i, mi

ice *n.* iâ *m.*; **~ cream** hufen iâ *m.*; **~ cube** iâ *m.*; **~ hockey** hoci iâ *m.*

icy *adj.* rhewllyd

idea *n.* syniad *m.*

ideal *adj.* delfrydol
identical *adj.* tebyg
identify *v.* adnabod
identity *n.* hunaniaeth *f.*; ~ **card** cerdyn adnabod
idiot *n.* ffŵl *m.*
if *conj.* os
ignition *n.* peiriant tanio *m.* (*car*)
ignore *v.* anwybyddu
ill *adj.* sâl
illegal *adj.* anghyfreithlon
illness *n.* salwch *m.*
illustration *n.* darlun *m.*
image *n.* delwedd *f.*
imagination *n.* dychymyg *m.*
imagine *v.* dychmygu
imitate *v.* efelychu
immediately *adv.* ar unwaith
import *v.* mewnforio
importance *n.* pwysigrwydd *m.*
important *adj.* pwysig
impossible *adj.* amhosibl
in *prep.* yn + *N.M.* (+ *definite noun*), mewn (+ *indefinite noun*)
inappropriate *adj.* anaddas
inch *n.* modfedd *f.*
incline *v.* tueddu; *n.* rhiw *f.*
include *v.* cynnwys
income *n.* incwm *m.*
increase *v.* cynyddu; *n.* cynnydd *m.*
index *n.* mynegai *m.*
indicate *v.* nodi
indifferent *adj.* di-hid
indigestion *n.* diffyg traul *m.*
industry *n.* diwydiant *m.*
inedible *adj.* anfwytadwy
infect *v.* heintio
infection *n.* haint *m.*
inform *v.* rhoi gwybod
information *n.* gwybodaeth *f.*
inhabitant *n.* trigolyn *m.*

initial *adj.* cychwynnol
inject *v.* chwistrellu
injection *n.* chwistrelliad *m.*
injure *v.* niweidio
injury *n.* niwed *m.*, anaf *m.*
ink *n.* inc *m.*
inn *n.* tafarn *mf.*
innocent *adj.* diniwed
inquire *v.* holi
insect *n.* trychfilyn *m.*
inside *prep.* y tu mewn i +*S.M.*; *adv.* y tu mewn
insist *v.* mynnu
inspect *v.* archwilio
inspector *n.* arolygydd *m.*
install *v.* gosod i mewn
instead of *prep.* yn lle
instrument *n.* offeryn *m.*
insulate *v.* ynysu
insulation *n.* ynysiad *f.*
insult *v.* sarhau; *n.* sarhad *m.*
insurance *n.* yswiriant *m.*
insure *v.* yswirio
intelligence *n.* deallusrwydd *m.*
interest *n.* diddordeb *m.*; llog *m.* (*finance*)
interesting *adj.* diddorol
interior *n.* y tu mewn *m.*; *adj.* mewnol
international *adj.* rhyngwladol
Internet *n.* rhyngrwyd *m.*
interpret *v.* dehongli
intervene *v.* ymyrryd
interview *v.* cyf-weld; *n.* cyfweliad *m.*
intestine *n.* coluddyn *m.*
into *prep.* mewn i + *S.M.*
intoxicated *adj.* meddw
introduce *v.* cyflwyno
introduction *n.* cyflwyniad *m.*
invent *v.* dyfeisio
invention *n.* dyfais *f.*
investigate *v.* ymchwilio, archwilio
invitation *n.* gwahoddiad *m.*

invite *v.* gwahodd
iron *n.* haearn *m.*
ironing board *n.* bwrdd smwddio *m.*
Islam *n.* Islam *m.*
island *n.* ynys *f.*
isolate *v.* ynysu
issue *v.* rhoi, cyhoeddi (*publish*)
it *pron.* ef *m.*, hi *f.*
Italy *n.* Yr Eidal *f.*
Italian *adj.* Eidalaidd; *n.* Eidalwr *m.*, Eidales *f.*, Eidaleg *f.*
　　(*language*)
itch *v.* cosi
item *n.* eitem *f.*

J

jacket *n.* siaced *f.*
jail *n.* carchar *m.*
jam *n.* jam *m.*
January *n.* Ionawr *m.*
jar *n.* jar *m.*
jealous *adj.* eiddigeddus
jealousy *n.* eiddigedd *m.*
jeans *n.* jins *pl.*
jelly *n.* jeli *m.*; ~ **fish** slefren fôr
jet *n.* jet *m.*
Jew *n.* Iddew *m.*, Iddewes *f.*
jewel *n.* gem *f.*
jeweler *n.* gemydd *m.*
jewelery *n.* gemwaith *m.*
Jewish *adj.* Iddewig
job *n.* swydd *f.* (*employment*), tasg *f.* (*task*)
jog *v.* loncian
join *v.* ymuno
joint *n.* cymal *m.*; *adj.* cyd
joke *n.* jôc *f.*; *v.* smalio
journal *n.* cylchgrawn *m.*
journalist *n.* gohebydd *m.*

journey *n.* taith *f.*

joy *n.* llawenydd *m.*

judge *n.* barnwr *m.*; *v.* barnu

judgment *n.* barn *f.*

juice *n.* sudd *m.*

July *n.* Gorffennaf *m.*

jump *n.* neidio

June *n.* Mehefin *m.*

just *adv.* dim ond

justice *n.* cyfiawnder *m.*

juvenile *n.* glaslanc *m.*

K

keep *v.* cadw

kettle *n.* tegell *m.*

key *n.* allwedd *f.* [*S.W.*], (a)goriad *m.* [*N.W.*]

keyboard *n.* allweddell *f.* (*piano*), bysellfwrdd *m.* (*computer*)

keyhole *n.* twll clo *m.*

kid *n.* plentyn *m.*

kidney *n.* aren *f.*

kill *v.* lladd

killer *n.* llofrudd *m.*

kilo *n.* cilo *m.*

kilometer *n.* cilometr *m.*

kind *adj.* caredig; *n.* math *m.*

kindergarten *n.* cylch chwarae *m.*

kindness *n.* caredigrwydd *m.*

king *n.* brenin *m.*

kingdom *n.* teyrnas *f.*

kiss *v.* cusanu; *n.* cusan *f.*

kitchen *n.* cegin *f.*

knee *n.* pen-lin *m.*

knife *n.* cyllell *f.*

knit *v.* gwau

knock *v.* curo

knot *n.* cwlwm *m.*; *v.* clymu

know *v.* gwybod (*fact*), adnabod (*person, place*)
knowledge *n.* gwybodaeth *f.*
kosher *adj.* cosher

L

label *n.* label *f.*
labor *n.* llafur *m.*
laboratory *n.* labordy *m.*
lack *n.* diffyg *m.*
ladder *n.* ysgol *f.*
lady *n.* boneddiges *f.*
lake *n.* llyn *m.*
lamp *n.* lamp *f.*
land *n.* tir *m.*
landlord *n.* landlord *m.*
landscape *n.* tirlun *m.*
lane *n.* lôn *f.*
language *n.* iaith *f.*
laptop computer *n.* gliniadur *m.*
large *adj.* mawr
last *adj.* olaf; *v.* parhau
late *adj.* hwyr, diweddar
later *adj.* hwyrach
laugh *v.* chwerthin; *n.* chwarddiad *m.*
laundry *n.* londri *m.*
lavender *n.* lafant *m.*
law *n.* cyfraith *f.*
lawful *adj.* cyfreithlon
lawn *n.* lawnt *f.*
lawsuit *n.* achos llys *m.*
lawyer *n.* cyfreithiwr *m.*
lay *v.* gosod, dodwy (*egg*)
lazy *adj.* diog
lead *v.* arwain
leader *n.* arweinydd *m.*
leaf *n.* deilen *f.*
league *n.* cynghrair *m.*
leak *v.* gollwng

lean *v.* pwyso; *adj.* tenau
leap *v.* neidio; ~ **year** blwyddyn naid
learn *v.* dysgu
lease *v.* llogi; *n.* les *m.*
least *adj.* lleiaf; **at** ~ o leiaf
leather *n.* lledr *m.*
leave *v.* gadael
lecture *n.* darlith *f.*
leek *n.* cenhinen *f.*
left *adj.* chwith
leg *n.* coes *f.*
legal *adj.* cyfreithiol
legend *n.* chwedl *f.*
legitimate *adj.* cyfreithlon
leisure *n.* hamdden *mf.*
lemon *n.* lemwn *m.*
lend *v.* benthyg
length *n.* hyd *m.*
lens *n.* lens *m.*
Lent *n.* Y Grawys *m.*
less *adj.* llai
lesson *n.* gwers *f.*
let *v.* gadael, llogi (*hire*); rhentu (*rent*)
letter *n.* llythyr *m.*, llythyren *f.* (*alphabet*)
liar *n.* celwyddgi *m.*
liberty *n.* rhyddid *m.*
librarian *n.* llyfrgellydd *m.*
library *n.* llyfrgell *f.*
license *n.* trwydded *f.*
lie *n.* celwydd *m.*; *v.* celwydda (*untruth*), gorwedd (*rest*)
life *n.* bywyd *m.*; ~ **jacket** siaced achub
lift *v.* codi; *n.* lifft *m.*
light *n.* golau *m.*
lighter *n.* taniwr *m.*
lightning *n.* mellten *f.*
like *v.* hoffi
limit *n.* ffin *f.*; *v.* cyfyngu
limp *v.* cloffi; *adj.* llipa
line *n.* llinell *f.*

linen *n.* lliain *m.*

link *n.* cyswllt *m.*; *v.* cysylltu

lip *n.* gwefus *f.*

lipstick *n.* minlliw *m.*

liquid *n.* hylif *m.*

liquor *n.* licer *m.*

list *n.* rhestr *f.*

listen *v.* gwrando

liter *n.* litr *m.*

literature *n.* llenyddiaeth *f.*

litter *n.* sbwriel *m.*

little *adj.* bach

live *v.* byw

liver *n.* afu *m.*

living room *n.* stafell fyw *f.*

loaf *n.* torth *f.*

loan *n.* benthyciad *m.*; *v.* benthyca, benthyg

lobby *n.* cyntedd *m.*

local *adj.* lleol

lock *v.* cloi; *n.* clo *m.*

log *n.* boncyff *m.* (*tree*), log *m.* (*record*); *v.* logio (*computer*)

loneliness *n.* unigrwydd *m.*

lonely *adj.* unig

long *adj.* hir

look *v.* edrych

lose *v.* colli

loss *n.* colled *f.*

lost *adj.* ar goll

loud *adj.* uchel

loudspeaker *n.* uchelseinydd *m.*

lounge *n.* lolfa *f.*

love *v.* caru; *n.* cariad *m.*

low *adj.* isel

luck *n.* lwc *f.*; **good ~** pob lwc

luggage *n.* bagiau *pl.*

lunch *n.* cinio *mf.*

lung *n.* ysgyfaint *m.*

luxurious *adj.* moethus

luxury *n.* moeth *m.*

M

machine *n.* peiriant *m.*
mad *adj.* gwallgo
madam *n.* madam *f.*
magic *n.* hud *m.*
magician *n.* dewin *m.*
magnet *n.* magned *m.*
magnifying glass *n.* chwyddwydr *m.*
maid *n.* morwyn *f.*
maiden name *n.* enw morwynol *m.*
mail *n.* post *m.*; *v.* postio
mailbox *n.* blwch post *m.*
main *adj.* prif
majority *n.* mwyafrif *m.*
make *n.* gwneud
makeup *n.* colur *m.*
male *adj.* gwrywaidd; *n.* gwryw *m.*
mall *n.* canolfan siopa *f.*
man *n.* dyn *m.*
manager *n.* rheolwr *m.*
manner *n.* dull *m.*
many *n.* llawer *m.*
map *n.* map *m.*
March *n.* Mawrth *m.*
margin *n.* ymyl *f.*
marine *adj.* morol
mark *v.* marcio
market *n.* marchnad *f.*; *v.* marchnata
marriage *n.* priodas *f.*
marry *v.* priodi
masculine *adj.* gwrywaidd
mask *n.* masg *m.*
mason *n.* saer maen *m.*
mass *n.* torf *f.* (*crowd*)
master *adj.* prif; *n.* meistr *m.*
match *v.* cyfateb; *n.* gêm *f.*
material *n.* deunydd *m.*
maternity *n.* mamolaeth *f.*

matter *n.* mater *m.*
mattress *n.* matras *m.*
mature *adj.* aeddfed
maturity *n.* aeddfedrwydd *m.*
maximum *n.* mwyafswm *m.*
May *n.* Mai *m.*
maybe *adv.* efallai
meal *n.* pryd *m.*
mean *v.* golygu; *adj.* cas
meaning *n.* ystyr *mf.*
means *n.* modd *m.*
measure *v.* mesur; *n.* mesuriad *m.*
meat *n.* cig *m.*
mechanic *n.* mecanig *m.*
mechanical *adj.* mecanyddol
medal *n.* medal *mf.*
medical *adj.* meddygol
medication *n.* moddion *pl.*
Mediterranean Sea *n.* Y Môr Canoldir *m.*
meet *v.* cyfarfod, cwrdd
meeting *n.* cyfarfod *m.*
melt *v.* toddi, dadlaith, dadmer
member *n.* aelod *m.*
memorize *v.* cofio
memory *n.* cof *m.*
mention *v.* sôn, crybwyll
menu *n.* bwydlen *f.* (*food*), dewislen *f.* (*computer*)
merchandise *n.* nwyddau *pl.*
Merry Christmas *inter.* Nadolig Llawen
mess *n.* llanast *m.*
message *n.* neges *f.*
messenger *n.* negesydd *m.*
metal *n.* metel *m.*
meter *n.* metr *m.*
middle *n.* canol *m.*
midnight *n.* canol nos *m.*
mild *adj.* tyner (*gentle*), gwan (*weak*)
mile *n.* milltir *f.*
milestone *n.* carreg filltir *f.*
military *adj.* milwrol

milk *n.* llaeth *m.* [*S.W.*], llefrith *m.* [*N.W.*]

mill *n.* melin *f.*

million *n.* miliwn *f.*

mind *n.* meddwl *m.*

minimum *n.* minimwm *m.*, lleiafswm *m.*

minister *n.* gweinidog *m.*

minor *adj.* lleiaf

minority *n.* lleiafrif *m.*

mint *n.* mintys *m.*

minus *n.* minws *m.*

minute *n.* munud *mf.*

mirror *n.* drych *m.*

miscellaneous *adj.* amrywiol

miss *v.* colli

mistake *n.* camsyniad *m.*

mister *n.* meistr *m.*

misunderstanding *n.* camddealltwriaeth *f.*

mix *v.* cymysgu

model *n.* model *m.*

modem *n.* modem *m.*

moderate *adj.* cymedrol

modern *adj.* modern

modify *v.* addasu

moist *adj.* llaith

moisture *n.* lleithder *m.*

mold *n.* ffwng *m.*

moment *n.* moment *f.*, eiliad *f.*

monastery *n.* mynachlog *f.*

Monday *n.* Llun *m.*

money *n.* arian *m.*

monk *n.* mynach *m.*

monkey *n.* mwnci *m.*

monster *n.* anghenfil *m.*

month *n.* mis *m.*

monument *n.* cofadail *m.*

mood *n.* tymer *f.*

moon *n.* lleuad *f.*

more *adj.* mwy

morning *n.* bore *m.*

mortgage *n.* morgais *m.*

mosque *n.* mosg *m.*
mosquito *n.* mosgito *m.*
most *adj.* mwyaf
mother *n.* mam *f.*
mother-in-law *n.* mam yng nghyfraith *f.*
motion *n.* symudiad *m.* (*movement*), cynnig *m.* (*conference*)
motivation *n.* ysgogiad *m.*
motive *n.* cymhelliad *m.*
motorbike *n.* beic modur *m.*
mountain *n.* mynydd *m.*
mouse *n.* llygoden *f.*
mouth *n.* ceg *f.*
move *v.* symud
movie *n.* ffilm *f.*
movie theater *n.* sinema *f.*
much *n.* llawer *m.*
mud *n.* llaid *m.*, mwd *m.*
multiply *v.* lluosi
murder *v.* llofruddio
murderer *n.* llofrudd *m.*
muscle *n.* cyhyr *m.*
museum *n.* amgueddfa *f.*
mushroom *n.* madarchen *f.*
music *n.* cerddoriaeth *f.*
musician *n.* cerddor *m.*
must *n.* rhaid *m.*; **I ~** mae rhaid i fi
mustache *n.* mwstás *m.*
mustard *n.* mwstard *m.*
mute *adj.* mud

N

nail *n.* hoelen *f.* (*metal*), ewin *m.* (*finger*)
naked *adj.* noeth
name *n.* enw *m.*
nap *n.* cyntun *m.*
napkin *n.* clwt *m.*
narrow *adj.* cul
nation *n.* cenedl. *f.*

nationality *n.* cenedligrwydd *m.*

native *adj.* brodorol

natural *adj.* naturiol

nature *n.* natur *f.*

nausea *n.* cyfog *m.*

navel *n.* botwm bol *m.*

navigate *v.* mordeithio

navy *n.* llynges *f.*

near *prep.* yn ymyl, ger

nearly *adv.* bron

neat *adj.* taclus

necessary *adj.* angenrheidiol

necessity *n.* anghenraid *m.*

neck *n.* gwddf *m.*

necklace *n.* mwclis *m.*

need *n.* angen *m.*; **I ~** mae angen arna i

needle *n.* nodwydd *f.*

negative *adj.* negyddol

neighbor *n.* cymydog *m.*

neighborhood *n.* cymdogaeth *f.*

neither *adv.* na chwaith

nephew *n.* nai *m.*

nerve *n.* nerf *m.*

nervous *adj.* nerfus

nest *n.* nyth *f.*

net *n.* rhwyd *f.*

network *n.* rhwydwaith *m.*

neutral *adj.* niwtral

never *adv.* byth

new *adj.* newydd; **Happy N~ Year** Blwyddyn Newydd Dda

news *n.* newyddion *pl.*

newspaper *n.* papur newydd *m.*

next *adj.* nesaf

nice *adj.* neis

nickname *n.* llysenw *m.*

niece *n.* nith *f.*

night *n.* nos *f.*

nightmare *n.* hunllef *f.*

nine *num.* naw

no *adv.* na

nobility *n.* bonedd *m.*
nobody *pron.* neb
noise *n.* sŵn *m.*
none *n.* dim *m.*
noon *n.* canol dydd *m.*
normal *adj.* normal
north *n.* gogledd *m.*
nose *n.* trwyn *m.*
nosy *adj.* busneslyd
not *adv.* ddim
note *n.* nodyn *m.*
notebook *n.* llyfr nodiadau *m.*
nothing *n.* dim *m.*
notice *n.* hysbysiad *m.*; *v.* sylwi
notify *v.* rhoi gwybod, hysbysu
noun *n.* enw *m.*
nourishing *adj.* maethlon
novel *n.* nofel *f.*
November *n.* Tachwedd *m.*
now *adv.* yn awr, nawr
nowadays *adv.* heddiw
nowhere *adv.* ddim yn unman
nude *adj.* noeth
number *n.* rhif *m.*
numerous *adj.* niferus
nun *n.* lleian *f.*
nurse *n.* nyrs *f.*
nut *n.* cneuen *f.*

O

obese *adj.* gordew
object *n.* gwrthrych *m.*
objection *n.* gwrthwynebiad *m.*
obscene *adj.* anllad
obscure *adj.* aneglur
observation *n.* sylw *m.*
observe *v.* sylwi
obstacle *n.* rhwystr *m.*

obtain *v.* cael
obvious *adj.* amlwg
occasion *n.* achlysur *m.*
occasional *adj.* achlysurol
occasionally *adv.* weithiau
occupation *n.* galwedigaeth *f.*
occupy *v.* meddiannu
occur *v.* digwydd
ocean *n.* cefnfor *m.*
October *n.* Hydref *m.*
odd *adj.* rhyfedd
odor *n.* arogl *m.*
of *prep.* o + *S.M.*
of course wrth gwrs
offend *v.* tramgwyddo
offer *v.* cynnig; *n.* cynnig *m.*
office *n.* swyddfa *f.*
official *adj.* swyddogol; *n.* swyddog *m.*
often *adv.* yn aml
oil *n.* olew *m.*
oily *adj.* olewllyd, seimllyd
old *adj.* hen
old-fashioned *adj.* henffasiwn
on *prep.* ar +*S.M.*
once *adv.* unwaith
one *num.* un
onion *n.* wynwynen *f.*
only *adv.* yn unig
open *adj.* agored; *adv.* ar agor
open-minded *adj.* meddwl agored
operate *v.* gweithredu
operation *n.* llawdriniaeth *f.* (*hospital*)
operator *n.* gweithredwr *m.*
opinion *n.* barn *f.*
opponent *n.* gwrthwynebydd *m.*
oppose *v.* gwrthwynebu
opposite *prep.* gyferbyn â +*SP.M.*
optician *n.* optegydd *m.*
option *n.* dewis *m.*
or *conj.* neu +*S.M.*

oral *adj.* llafar

orange *n.* oren *m.*

orchestra *n.* cerddorfa *f.*

order *n.* archeb *f.*, gorchymyn *m.* (*command*); *v.* archebu, gorchymyn (*command*)

ordinary *adj.* cyffredin

organ *n.* organ *mf.*

organization *n.* corff *m.*

organize *v.* trefnu

other *adj.* arall

ounce *n.* owns *m.*

our *pron.* ein

out *adv.* allan

outdoor *adv.* awyr agored

outside *adv.* y tu allan

oven *n.* ffwrn *f.*

over *prep.* dros +*S.M.*

overcoat *n.* cot *f.*, cot fawr *f.*

overtime *n.* goramser *m.*

owe *v.* ar +*S.M.*; **I ~ you ten pounds** mae arna i ddeg punt i chi

own *v.* perchenogi; gan +*S.M.* **I ~ a car** mae car gen i

owner *n.*, perchennog *m.*

oxygen *n.* ocsigen *m.*

P

pace *n.* cyflymder *m.*

pack *v.* pacio

page *n.* tudalen *mf.*

pain *n.* poen *mf.*

painful *adj.* poenus

paint *n.* paent *m.*

painting *n.* peintiad *m.*, darlun *m.*

pair *n.* pâr *m.*

pajamas *n.* pyjamas *m.*

pale *adj.* gwelw

pan *n.* padell *f.*

pants *n.* trowsus *m.*

paper *n.* papur *m.*

paralyze *v.* parlysu

parents *n.* rhieni *mpl.*

park *n.* parc *m.*; *v.* parcio.

parking lot *n.* lle parcio *m.*

part *n.* rhan *f.*

partner *n.* partner *m.*

part-time *adj.* rhan-amser

party *n.* parti *m.*

pass *v.* pasio; *n.* bwlch *m.* (*mountain*), pas *m.* (*ticket*)

passenger *n.* teithiwr *m.*

passport *n.* pasbort *m.*

past *n.* gorffennol *m.*

pastry *n.* toes *m.*

path *n.* llwybr *m.*

patient *n.* claf *m.*; *adj.* amyneddgar

paw *n.* pawen *f.*

pay *v.* talu; *n.* tâl *m.*

payment *n.* tâl *m.*

peace *n.* heddwch *m.*

peak *n.* copa *m.*

pearl *n.* perl *m.*

pebble *n.* carreg *f.*

pedal *n.* pedal *m.*

pedestrian *n.* cerddwr *m.*

pen *n.* ysgrifbin *m.*

pencil *n.* pensil *m.*

people *n.* pobl *f.*

pepper *n.* pupur *m.*

percent *adv.* y cant

perfect *adj.* perffaith

perfume *n.* persawr *m.*

perhaps *adv.* efallai

period *n.* cyfnod *m.*

permit *v.* caniatáu

person *n.* person *m.*

personal *adj.* personol

pet *n.* anifail anwes *m.*

petite *adj.* bychan

pharmacy *n.* fferyllfa *f.*
phone *n.* ffôn *m.*
phonebook *n.* llyfr ffôn *m.*
photo *n.* ffotograff *m.*
photocopy *n.* llungopi *m.*
photograph *n.* ffotograff *m.*
phrase *n.* ymadrodd *m.*
physical *adj.* corfforol
physician *n.* meddyg *m.*
picnic *n.* picnic *m.*
picture *n.* darlun *m.*
pie *n.* pei *m.*
piece *n.* darn *m.*
pile *n.* pentwr *m.*
pill *n.* pilsen *f.*
pillow *n.* clustog *f.*
pillowcase *n.* gorchudd clustog *m.*
pilot *n.* peilot *m.*
pin *n.* pin *m.*
pinch *v.* pinsio
pine *n.* pîn *m.*
pink *adj.* pinc
pint *n.* peint *m.*
pipe *n.* piben *f.*
place *n.* lle *m.*
plain *adj.* plaen
plan *n.* cynllun *m.*
plane *n.* awyren *f.*
planet *n.* planed *f.*
plant *n.* planhigyn *m.*
plastic *adj.* plastig
plate *n.* plât *m.*
play *v.* chwarae
please *adv.* os gwelwch yn dda
pleasure *n.* pleser *m.*
plug *n.* plwg *m.*
plumber *n.* plymer *m.*
plural *adj.* lluosog
plus *prep.* plws

pocket *n.* poced *f.*
pocketknife *n.* cyllell boced *f.*
poetry *n.* barddoniaeth *f.*
point *n.* pwynt *m.*
poison *n.* gwenwyn *m.*
poisonous *adj.* gwenwynig
pole *n.* polyn *m.*
police *n.* heddlu *m.*
police officer *n.* heddwas *m.*
police station *n.* gorsaf heddlu *f.*
policy *n.* polisi *m.*
polite *adj.* cwrtais
political *adj.* gwleidyddol
politics *n.* gwleidyddiaeth *f.*
pond *n.* pwll *m.*
pony *n.* merlyn *m.*
pool *n.* pwll *m.*; **swimming** ~ pwll nofio
poor *adj.* tlawd
pope *n.* pab *m.*
population *n.* poblogaeth *f.*
pork *n.* porc *m.*
portrait *n.* portread *m.*
position *n.* safle *m.*
positive *adj.* cadarnhaol
possible *adj.* posibl
post *n.* post *m.*; ~ **office** post office
postcard *n.* cerdyn post *m.*
pot *n.* pot *m.*
pottery *n.* crochenwaith *m.*
poultry *n.* ieir *pl.*
pound *n.* punt *f.* (£), pwys *m.* (*lb*)
powder *n.* powdr *m.*
power *n.* pŵer *m.*
practical *adj.* ymarferol
pray *v.* gweddïo
prayer *n.* gweddi *f.*
prefer *v.* gwell; **I** ~ mae'n well gen i
pregnant *adj.* beichiog
prepaid *adj.* wedi'i dalu o flaen llaw

prepare *v.* paratoi
prescription *n.* papur meddyg *m.*
present *adj.* presennol; *v.* cyflwyno
president *n.* llywydd *m.*
press *n.* gwasg *f.*; *v.* gwasgu
pressure *n.* gwasgedd *m.*
pretty *adj.* pert
prevent *v.* rhwystro, atal
previous *adj.* blaenorol
price *n.* pris *m.*
pride *n.* balchder *m.*
priest *n.* offeiriad *m.*
prime minister *n.* prif weinidog *m.*
principal *adj.* prif; *n.* pennaeth *m.*, prifathro *m.*
principle *n.* egwyddor *f.*
prison *n.* carchar *m.*
prisoner *n.* carcharor *m.*
privacy *n.* preifatrwydd *m.*
private *adj.* preifat
privilege *n.* braint *f.*
probably *adv.* yn ôl pob tebyg
problem *n.* problem *f.*
produce *v.* cynhyrchu
product *n.* cynnyrch *m.*
profession *n.* proffesiwn *m.*
professor *n.* athro *m.*
profile *n.* proffil *m.*
profit *n.* elw *m.*
program *n.* rhaglen *f.*
progress *n.* cynnydd *m.*
prohibit *v.* gwahardd
project *n.* prosiect *m.*
promenade *n.* promenâd *m.*
promise *v.* addo
proof *n.* prawf *m.*
property *n.* eiddo *m.*
proposal *n.* cynnig *m.*
propose *v.* cynnig
protect *v.* amddiffyn

protection *n.* amddiffyniad *m.*

protest *n.* protest *f.*; *v.* protestio

Protestant *n.* Protestant *m.*

proud *adj.* balch

prove *v.* profi

proverb *n.* dihareb *f.*

provide *v.* darparu

province *n.* talaith *f.*

prudent *adj.* call

pub *n.* tafarn *mf.*

public *n.* cyhoedd *m.*; *adj.* cyhoeddus; ~ **transport** cludiant cyhoeddus

publicity *n.* cyhoeddusrwydd *m.*

publish *v.* cyhoeddi

publisher *n.* cyhoeddwr *m.*

pull *v.* tynnu

pulse *n.* pyls *m.*, curiad calon *m.*

pump *n.* pwmp *m.*

purchase *v.* prynu

pure *adj.* pur

purple *adj.* porffor

purpose *n.* pwrpas *m.*

purse *n.* pwrs *m.*

push *v.* gwthio

put *v.* rhoi

Q

quality *n.* ansawdd *mf.*

quantity *n.* swm. *m.*

quarter *n.* chwarter *m.*

queen *n.* brenhines *f.*

question *n.* cwestiwn *m.*

quick *adj.* cyflym

quiet *adj.* tawel

quilt *n.* carthen *f.*

quite *adv.* eitha

quote *v.* dyfynnu; *n.* dyfyniad *m.*

R

rabbi *n.* rabi *m.*
rabbit *n.* cwningen *f.*
race *n.* ras *f.*
racism *n.* hiliaeth *f.*
racquet *n.* raced *f.*
radio *n.* radio *m.*
rage *n.* dicter *m.*
railroad *n.* rheilffordd *f.*
rain *n.* glaw *m.*; *v.* bwrw glaw
rainbow *n.* enfys *f.*
raincoat *n.* cot law *f.*
rainy *adj.* glawiog
raise *v.* codi
RAM (Random Access Memory) *n.* RAM *m.*
random *adj.* ar hap
range *n.* amrediad *m.*
rape *n.* trais *m.*; *v.* treisio
rare *adj.* prin
rash *n.* brech *f.*; *adj.* byrbwyll
rat *n.* llygoden fawr *f.*
rate *n.* cyfradd *f.*
raw *adj.* amrwd
razor *n.* eilliwr *m.*
razor blade *n.* llafn eillio *f.*
react *v.* adweithio
reaction *n.* adwaith *m.*
read *v.* darllen
reader *n.* darllenydd *m.*
ready *adj.* parod
real *adj.* gwirioneddol, real
reality *n.* gwirionedd *m.*
realize *v.* sylweddoli
rear *n.* cefn *m.*
reason *n.* rheswm *m.*
recall *v.* cofio
receipt *n.* derbynneb *f.*
receive *v.* derbyn
receiver *n.* derbynnydd *m.*

recent *adj.* diweddar
reception *n.* derbynfa *f.*
recipe *n.* rysáit *m.*
recommend *v.* argymell
record *n.* record *f.*, cofnod *m.* (*note*)
recover *v.* adfer
red *adj.* coch
reduce *v.* lleihau
reduction *n.* lleihad *m.*
refer *v.* cyfeirio
referee *n.* dyfarnwr *m.*
refreshment *n.* lluniaeth *f.*
refrigerator *n.* oergell *f.*
refund *v.* ad-dalu
regard *v.* ystyried
regarding *prep.* ynglŷn â +*SP.M.*
Regards *inter.* Cofion
region *n.* ardal *f.*
register *n.* cofrestr *f.*; *v.* cofrestru
regret *v.* edifarhau
regular *adj.* cyson
regulation *n.* rheoliad *m.*
relationship *n.* perthynas *f.*
relative *n.* perthynas *f.*; *adj.* perthnasol
relax *v.* ymlacio
reliable *adj.* dibynadwy
relief *n.* rhyddhad *m.*
relieve *v.* rhyddhau
religion *n.* crefydd *f.*
religious *adj.* crefyddol
rely *v.* dibynnu
remain *v.* aros
remark *n.* sylw *m.*
remember *v.* cofio
remind *v.* atgoffa
remote control *n.* cliciwr *m.*
remove *v.* symud
renew *v.* adnewyddu
renovate *v.* adnewyddu
renown *n.* enwogrwydd *m.*

rent *n.* rhent *m.*; *v.* rhentu
reorganize *v.* aildrefnu
repair *v.* trwsio
repeat *v.* ailadrodd
replace *v.* disodli
reply *v.* ateb; *n.* ateb *m.*
report *v.* adrodd; *n.* adroddiad *m.*
represent *v.* cynrychioli
representative *n.* cynrychiolydd *m.*
republic *n.* gweriniaeth *f.*
reputation *n.* enw da *m.*
request *v.* gwneud cais; *n.* cais *m.*
require *v.* angen; **I ~** mae angen arna i
rescue *v.* achub
research *n.* ymchwil *f.*
reservation *n.* cadw lle *m.*
reserve *v.* cadw lle
residence *n.* cartref *m.* (*home*)
resist *v.* ymwrthod
resort *n.* man gwyliau *mf.*
respect *n.* parch *m.*; *v.* parchu
respond *v.* ymateb
response *n.* ymateb *m.*
responsibility *n.* cyfrifoldeb *m.*
responsible *adj.* cyfrifol
rest *v.* gorffwys; *n.* **~ room** ystafell orffwys *f.*
restaurant *n.* bwyty *m.*
restore *v.* adfer
restrict *v.* cyfyngu
result *n.* canlyniad *m.*
retire *v.* ymddeol
return *v.* dychwelyd
reverse *v.* cefnu
review *v.* adolygu; *n.* adolygiad *m.*
reward *v.* gwobrwyo
rhythm *n.* rhythm *m.*
rib *n.* asen *f.*
ribbon *n.* rhuban *m.*
rice *n.* reis *m.*
rich *adj.* cyfoethog

ride *v.* marchogaeth
right *adj.* iawn (*correct*), de (*side*)
ring *n.* cylch *m.* (*circle*), modrwy *f.* (*finger*)
rinse *v.* golchi
riot *n.* terfysg *m.*
ripe *adj.* aeddfed
rise *v.* codi
risk *n.* risg *m.*
river *n.* afon *f.*
road *n.* heol *f.*
rob *v.* lladrata
robbery *n.* lladrad *m.*
robe *n.* gŵn *m.*
rock *n.* craig *f.*
rod *n.* rhoden *f.*
role *n.* rôl *f.*
roll *v.* rholio
romance *n.* rhamant *f.*
roof *n.* to *m.*
room *n.* stafell *f.*, ystafell *f.*
rope *n.* rhaff *f.*
rotten *adj.* pwdr
round *adj.* crwn
route *n.* ffordd *f.*
row *n.* rhes *f.*
royal *adj.* brenhinol
rubber band *n.* band rwber *m.*
rude *adj.* anfoesgar
ruin *n.* adfail *m.*; *v.* difetha
rule *n.* rheol *f.*; *v.* rheoli
run *v.* rhedeg
rush *v.* rhuthro
rust *n.* rhwd *m.*

S

Sabbath *n.* Sabath *m.*
sad *adj.* trist
saddle *n.* cyfrwy *m.*

safe *adj.* diogel, saff; *n.* sêff *f.*
safety *n.* diogelwch *m.*
safety pin *n.* pin cau *m.*
sail *v.* hwylio
sailboat *n.* cwch hwylio *m.*
sailor *n.* morwr *m.*
salad *n.* salad *m.*
salary *n.* cyflog *mf.*
sale *n.* gwerthiant *m.*, sêl *f.*
saliva *n.* poer *m.*
salt *n.* halen *m.*
same *adj.* tebyg, yr un
sample *n.* sampl *m.*
sand *n.* tywod *m.*
sandal *n.* sandal *m.*
sanitary pad *n.* tywel mislif *m.*
Santa Claus *n.* Siôn Corn *m.*
satisfy *v.* bodloni
Saturday *n.* Sadwrn *m.*
savory *adj.* sawrus
say *v.* dweud
scale *n.* graddfa *f.*
scar *n.* craith *f.*
scarf *n.* sgarff *f.*
scenery *n.* golygfa *f.*
scent *n.* persawr *m.*
schedule *n.* amserlen *f.* (*timetable*); *n.* trefnlen *f.* (*order*)
scholarship *n.* ysgoloriaeth *f.*
school *n.* ysgol *f.*
science *n.* gwyddoniaeth *f.*
scientific *adj.* gwyddonol
scissors *n.* siswrn *m.*
scratch *v.* crafu
scream *v.* gweiddi, sgrechian; *n.* sgrech *f.*
screen *n.* sgrin *f.*
screw *n.* sgriw *f.*
screwdriver *n.* tyrnsgriw *m.*
sculpture *n.* cerflun *m.*
sea *n.* môr *m.*
search *v.* chwilio

seasickness *n.* salwch môr *m.*

season *n.* tymor *m.*

seat *n.* sedd *f.*

seat belt *n.* gwregys diogelwch *m.*

seaweed *n.* gwymon *m.*

second *n.* eiliad *f.*; *adj.* ail

secret *n.* cyfrinach *f.*

secretary *n.* ysgrifennydd *m.*, ysgrifenyddes *f.*

security *n.* diogelwch *m.*

see *v.* gweld

seed *n.* hedyn *m.*

seem *v.* ymddangos

seize *v.* gafael

select *v.* dethol

selection *n.* detholiad *m.*

self *pron.* hunan

self-service *n.* hunanwasanaeth *m.*

sell *v.* gwerthu

send *v.* anfon

sender *n.* anfonwr *m.*

senior citizen *n.* pensiynwr *m.*

sentence *n.* brawddeg *f.*; dedfryd *f.* (*law*)

separate *v.* gwahanu; *adj.* ar wahân

separation *n.* gwahaniad *m.*

September *n.* Medi *m.*

series *n.* cyfres *f.*

serious *adj.* difrifol

service *n.* gwasanaeth *m.*

set *n.* set *f.*; *v.* gosod

settle *v.* ymsefydlu, setlo

seven *num.* saith

several *pron.* sawl

sew *v.* gwnïo

shade *n.* cysgod *m.*; *v.* cysgodi

shake *v.* ysgwyd; **~ hands** ysgwyd llaw

shallow *adj.* bas

shame *n.* cywilydd *m.*

shampoo *n.* siampŵ *m.*

shape *n.* siâp *m.*

share *v.* rhannu

shark *n.* siarc *m.*
sharp *adj.* miniog
shave *v.* eillio
shaving cream *n.* hufen eillio *m.*
she *pron.* hi
sheet *n.* dalen *f.*; cynfas *m.* (*bed*)
shelf *n.* silff *f.*
shell *n.* cragen *f.*
shellfish *n.* pysgod cragen *mpl.*
shelter *n.* cysgod *m.*; *v.* cysgodi
shine *v.* disgleirio
ship *n.* llong *f.*
shirt *n.* crys *m.*
shock *n.* sioc *m.*
shoe *n.* esgid *f.*
shoelace *n.* carrai esgid *f.*
shoe polish *n.* cabol esgidiau *m.*
shoot *v.* saethu
shop *n.* siop *f.*
shore *n.* glan *f.*
short *adj.* byr
shorten *v.* byrhau
shot *n.* ergyd *f.*
shoulder *n.* ysgwydd *f.*
shout *v.* gweiddi
show *v.* dangos; *n.* sioe *f.*
shower *n.* cawod *f.*
shrink *v.* cwtogi
shut *v.* cau
shutter *n.* caead *m.*
shuttle *n.* gwennol *f.*
sick *adj.* sâl; *n.* cyfog *m.*
side *n.* ochr *f.*
sidewalk *n.* pafin *m.*
sight *n.* golwg *mf.*
sign *n.* arwydd *mf.*; *v.* llofnodi
signal *n.* arwydd *mf.*, signal *m.*
signature *n.* llofnod *m.*
silence *n.* tawelwch *m.*
silent *adj.* tawel

silk *n.* sidan *m.*
silly *adj.* ffôl, twp
silver *n.* arian *m.*
similar *adj.* tebyg
simple *adj.* syml
since *prep.* er, ers
sincerely *adv.* yn gywir
sing *v.* canu
singer *n.* canwr *m.*, cantor *m.*, cantores *f.*
single *adj.* sengl
sink *n.* sinc *m.*
sip *v.* llymeitian
sir *n.* syr *m.*
sister *n.* chwaer *f.*
sister-in-law *n.* chwaer yng nghyfraith *f.*
sit *v.* eistedd
site *n.* safle *m.*
six *num.* chwech, chwe
size *n.* maint *m.*
skate *v.* sglefrio
ski *v.* sgio
skin *n.* croen *m.*
skirt *n.* sgert *f.*
sky *n.* awyr *f.*
slang *n.* slang *m.*
sleep *v.* cysgu
sleeping bag *n.* sach gysgu *f.*
sleeping pill *n.* pilsen gysgu *f.*
sleeve *n.* llawes *f.*
slice *n.* tafell *f.*
slide *v.* llithro
slipper *n.* llopan *m.*
slope *n.* llethr *mf.*
slow *adj.* araf
small *adj.* bach
smart *adj.* golygus (*handsome*), clyfar, deallus (*intelligent*)
smell *v.* arogli; *n.* arogl *m.*
smile *v.* gwenu
smoke *n.* mwg *m.*
snack *n.* byrbryd *m.*

snake *n.* neidr *f.*
sneeze *v.* tisian
snore *v.* chwyrnu
snow *n.* eira *m.*; *v.* bwrw eira
snowboard *v.* eirfyrddio
snowflake *n.* pluen eira *f.*
so *adv.* felly
soak *v.* gwlychu
soap *n.* sebon *m.*
soccer *n.* pêl-droed *f.*
sock *n.* hosan *f.*
sofa *n.* soffa *m.*
sofabed *n.* gwely soffa *m.*
soft *adj.* meddal
soil *n.* pridd *m.*; *v.* trochi
solid *adj.* solet
some *pron.* rhai
somebody *pron.* rhywun
something *pron.* rhywbeth
sometimes *adv.* weithiau
son *n.* mab *m.*
song *n.* cân *f.*
son-in-law *n.* mab yng nghyfraith *m.*
soon *adv.* yn fuan
sore *adj.* dolurus
sorrow *n.* galar *m.*
sorry *adj.* blin; **I'm** ~ mae'n flin gen i
sound *n.* sain *f.*; *adj.* cadarn
soup *n.* cawl *m.*
sour *adj.* sur
south *n.* de *m.*
souvenir *n.* cofrodd *f.*
space *n.* gofod *m.*
Spain *n.* Sbaen *f.*
Spaniard *n.* Sbaenwr *m.*; Sbaenes *f.*
Spanish *n.* Sbaeneg *f.* (*language*); *adj.* Sbaenaidd
spare part *n.* darn sbâr *m.*
speak *v.* siarad
special *adj.* arbennig
specialty *n.* arbenigrwydd *m.*

spectator *n.* gwyliwr *m.*
speech *n.* araith *f.*
speed *n.* cyflymder *m.*
spell *v.* sillafu
spend *v.* gwario (*money*), treulio (*time*)
spider *n.* pryf cop *m.*
spine *n.* asgwrn cefn *m.*
spit *v.* poeri
spoil *v.* sbwylio, difetha
sponge *n.* sbwng *m.*
spoon *n.* llwy *f.*; **tea ~** llwy de; **table ~** llwy fwrdd
sport *n.* chwaraeon *pl.*
spring *n.* sbring *m.*
square *n.* sgwâr *m.*
stadium *n.* stadiwm *m.*
stage *n.* llwyfan *mf.*
stain *n.* staen *m.*
stairs *n.* grisiau *pl.*
stamp *n.* stamp *m.*
star *n.* seren *f.*
start *v.* dechrau, cychwyn
starve *v.* llwgu
state *n.* cyflwr *m.* (*condition*), gwladwriaeth *f.* (*country*)
station *n.* gorsaf *f.*
statue *n.* cerflun *m.*
stay *v.* aros
steady *adj.* cyson (*regular*), cadarn (*strong*)
steak *n.* stecen *f.*
steal *v.* dwyn, lladrata
steam *n.* ager *m.*
step *n.* gris *m.*; *v.* camu
stepfather *n.* llystad *m.*
stepmother *n.* llysfam *f.*
still *adv.* o hyd; *adj.* llonydd
sting *v.* pigo
stink *v.* drewi
stitch *n.* pwyth *m.*
stocking *n.* hosan *f.*
stomach *n.* stumog *f.*
stone *n.* carreg *f.*

stool *n.* stôl *f.*
stop *v.* aros
store *n.* siop *f.*
storm *n.* storm *f.*
story *n.* stori *f.*
stove *n.* ffwrn *f.*
straight *adj.* syth
strange *adj.* rhyfedd
stranger *n.* dieithryn *m.*
straw *n.* gwelltyn *m.*
stream *n.* nant *f.*
street *n.* stryd *f.*
strength *n.* cryfder *m.*
stress *n.* straen *m.*
string *n.* llinyn *m.*
stroke *n.* ergyd *f.* (*shot*), cur calon *m.* (*heart*)
strong *adj.* cryf
student *n.* myfyriwr *m.*
study *v.* astudio; *n.* astudiaeth *f.*
stuff *n.* defnydd *m.*; *v.* stwffio
stupid *adj.* ffôl
stylish *adj.* coeth
subject *n.* pwnc *m.*
subtitle *n.* is-deitl *m.*
subtract *v.* tynnu
suburb *n.* maestref *f.*
subway *n.* isffordd *f.*
success *n.* llwyddiant *m.*
such *adj.* o'r math
suck *v.* sugno
suffer *v.* dioddef
sugar *n.* siwgr. *m.*
suicide *n.* hunanladdiad *m.*
suit *n.* siwt *f.*; *v.* siwtio
suitcase *n.* cês *m.*
sum *n.* swm *m.*
summary *n.* crynodeb *m.*
summer *n.* haf *m.*
sun *n.* haul *m.*
Sunday *n.* Sul *m.*

sunflower *n.* blodyn haul *m.*
sunglasses *n.* sbectol haul *f.*
sunny *adj.* heulog
sunrise *n.* codiad haul *m.*
sunscreen *n.* sgrin haul *f.*
sunset *n.* machlud *m.*
sunstroke *n.* trawiad haul *m.*
supermarket *n.* archfarchnad *f.*
supper *n.* swper *m.*
sure *adj.* siŵr
surgeon *n.* llawfeddyg *m.*
surgery *n.* meddygfa *f.*
surroundings *n.* cynefin *m.*
survive *v.* goroesi
suspect *v.* drwgdybio, amau
swallow *v.* llyncu
swamp *n.* cors *f.*
swear *v.* rhegi, tyngu (*oath*)
sweat *n.* chwys *m.*; *v.* chwysu
sweater *n.* siwmper *f.*
sweep *v.* ysgubo
sweet *adj.* melys
swell *v.* chwyddo; *adj.* swanc
swim *v.* nofio
swimming pool *n.* pwll nofio *m.*
swimsuit *n.* siwt nofio *f.*
swing *n.* siglen *f.*; *v.* siglo
Swiss *n.* Swisiad *m.* (*person*)
switch *v.* newid; *n.* swits *f.*
Switzerland *n.* Y Swistir *f.*
symptom *n.* symptom *m.*
synagogue *n.* synagog *m.*
syringe *n.* chwistrell *m.*

T

table *n.* bwrdd *m.*, tabl *m.* (*figures*)
tablecloth *n.* lliain bwrdd *m.*
tablespoon *n.* llwy fwrdd *f.*

tailor *n.* teiliwr

take *v.* cymryd, mynd â +*S.M.*; **~ care** cymerwch ofal;
   ~ off diosg (*clothes*), codi (*airplane*)

talk *v.* siarad

tall *adj.* tal

tampon *n.* tywel mislif

tan *n.* lliw haul *m.*

tap *n.* tap *m.*; *n.* **~ water** dŵr tap *m.*

target *n.* targed *m.*

taste *n.* blas *m.*; *v.* blasu

tasteful *adj.* chwaethus

tasty *adj.* blasus

tattoo *n.* tatŵ *m.*

tax *n.* treth *f.*; *v.* trethu

taxi *n.* tacsi *m.*

tea *n.* te *m.*

teach *v.* dysgu

teacher *n.* athro *m.*, athrawes *f.*

team *n.* tîm *m.*

teapot *n.* tebot *m.*

tear *n.* deigryn *m.*; *v.* rhwygo

tease *v.* poeni

teaspoon *n.* llwy de *f.*

teenager *n.* arddegwr *m.*

teleconference *v.* telegynadledda

telephone *n.* teleffôn *m.*; ffôn *m.*; **~ book** llyfr ffôn;
   ~ number rhif ffôn; *v.* ffonio

television *n.* teledu *m.*

tell *v.* dweud; **to ~ someone** dweud wrth rywun

temper *n.* tymer *f.*

temperature *n.* tymheredd *m.*, gwres *m.* (*fever*)

temple *n.* teml *f.*

temporary *adj.* dros dro

ten *num.* deg

tenant *n.* tenant *m.*

tennis *n.* tennis *m.*

tent *n.* pabell *f.*; **~ pole** polyn pabell

tepid *adj.* claear

terrace *n.* teras *m.*

terrible *adj.* ofnadwy

text *n.* testun

textbook *n.* llyfr gosod *m.*

textile *n.* tecstil *m.*

than *conj.* na + *SP.M.*

thank *v.* diolch; ~ **you** diolch i chi ~ **you very much** diolch yn fawr

thankful *n.* diolchgar

that *rel.pron.* bod (*with long forms of verbs*), a + *S.M.* (*with short forms of verbs*); *adj.* hwnnw, honno

thaw *v.* meirioli, toddi, dadlaith

the *art.* y, yr, 'r

theater *n.* theatr *f.*

theft *n.* lladrad *m.*

them *pron.* nhw

then *adv.* yna, wedyn

there *adv.* yno

thermometer *n.* thermomedr *m.*

they *pron.* nhw

thick *adj.* trwchus

thickness *n.* trwch *m.*

thief *n.* lleidr *m.*

thigh *n.* clun *m.*

thin *adj.* tenau

thing *n.* peth *m.*

think *v.* meddwl

third *num.* trydydd

thirst *n.* syched *m.*

thirsty *adj.* sychedig

this *pron.* hwn *m.,* hon *f.*

thought *n.* syniad *m.*

thousand *num.* mil *f.*

threat *n.* bygythiad *m.*

threaten *v.* bygwth

three *num.* tri *m.,* tair *f.*

throat *n.* llwnc *m.*

through *prep.* trwy + *S.M.*

throw *v.* taflu

thumb *n.* bawd *mf.*

thunder *n.* taran *f.*

thunderstorm *n.* storm daranau *f.*

Thursday *n.* Iau *m.*

ticket *n.* tocyn *m.*

tickle *v.* cosi

tide *n.* llanw *m.*

tie *v.* clymu

time *n.* amser *m.*

tire *v.* blino

tired *adj.* wedi blino

title *n.* teitl *m.*

to *prep.* i +*S.M.*

tobacco *n.* baco *m.*

today *adv.* heddiw

toe *n.* bys troed *m.*

together *adv.* gyda'i gilydd

toilet *n.* tŷ bach *m.*, toiled *m.*; ~ **paper** papur tŷ bach

toll *n.* toll *f.*

tomb *n.* bedd *m.*

tombstone *n.* carreg fedd *f.*

tomorrow *adv.* yfory

tongue *n.* tafod *m.*

tonight *adv.* heno

tonsils *n.* tonsil *m.*

too *adv.* hefyd

tool *n.* offeryn *m.*

tooth *n.* dant *m.*

toothache *n.* dannodd *f.*

toothbrush *n.* brwsh dannedd *m.*

toothpaste *n.* past dannedd *m.*

top *adj.* prif (*chief*); *n.* pen *m.*

toss *v.* taflu

total *n.* cyfanswm *m.*

touch *v.* cyffwrdd

tough *adj.* gwydn

tour *n.* taith *f.*

tourism *n.* twristiaeth *f.*

tourist *n.* twrist *m.*

tourist office *n.* swyddfa dwristiaid *f*, swyddfa groeso *f.*

tournament *n.* pencampwriaeth *f.*

tow *v.* tynnu

toward *prep.* tuag at +*S.M.*

towel *n.* tywel *m.*

tower *n.* tŵr *m.*

town *n.* tref *f.*

toy *n.* tegan *m.*

track *n.* llwybr *m.*

trade *n.* masnach *f.*; *v.* masnachu

tradition *n.* traddodiad *m.*

traffic *n.* traffig *m.*, trafnidiaeth *f.*

trail *n.* llwybr *m.*

trailer *n.* carafán *f.*

train *n.* trên *m.*

transfer *v.* trosglwyddo

translate *v.* cyfieithu

translation *n.* cyfieithiad *m.*

translator *n.* cyfieithydd *m.*

transport *n.* cludiant *m.*

trash *n.* sbwriel *m.*

trash can *n.* bin sbwriel *m.*

travel *v.* teithio

traveler *n.* teithiwr *m.*

traveler's check *n.* siec deithio *f.*

tray *n.* hambwrdd *m.*

treasure *n.* trysor *m.*

tree *n.* coeden *f.*

trial *n.* achos *m.* (*law*), arbrawf *m.* (*experiment*)

tribe *n.* llwyth *m.*

tribute *n.* teyrnged *f.*

trouble *n.* trafferth *m.*

truck *n.* lorri *f.*

true *adj.* gwir

trunk *n.* cist *f.*

trust *n.* ymddiriedaeth *f.*, ymddiriedolaeth *f.* (*organization*)

truth *n.* gwirionedd *m.*

try *v.* ceisio; *n.* cais *mf.* (*rugby*)

Tuesday *n.* Mawrth *m.*

tuition *n.* hyfforddiant *m.*

tunnel *n.* twnnel *m.*

turn *n.* tro *m.*; *v.* troi

twice *adv.* dwywaith

twin *n.* gefell *m.*
two *num.* dau *m.*, dwy *f.*
typical *adj.* nodweddiadol

U

ugly *adj.* salw
ulcer *n.* wlser *m.*
umbrella *n.* ymbarél *m.*
unable *adj.* analluog
unauthorized *adj.* heb awdurdod
unaware *adj.* heb wybod
unbearable *adj.* annioddefol
unbelievable *adj.* anghredadwy
uncle *n.* ewythr *m.*
uncomfortable *adj.* anghysurus
unconscious *adj.* anymwybodol
under *prep.* dan +*S.M.*
underground *adj.* tanddaearol
understand *v.* deall
underwear *n.* dillad isaf *pl.*
undo *v.* datod
undress *v.* dadwisgo
uneasy *adj.* pryderus
uneven *adj.* anwastad
unfamiliar *adj.* anghyfarwydd
unforgettable *adj.* bythgofiadwy
unhappy *adj.* anhapus
unhealthy *adj.* afiach
uniform *n.* ffurfwisg *f.*
union *n.* undeb *m.*
unique *adj.* unigryw
unit *n.* uned *f.*
United States *n.* Unol Daleithiau'r America *f.*
universal *adj.* cyffredinol
universe *n.* bydysawd *m.*
university *n.* prifysgol *f.*
unknown *adj.* anhysbys

unless *conj.* oni bai
unlike *adj.* annhebyg
unlikely *adv.* yn annhebyg
unlimited *adj.* diderfyn
unload *v.* dadlwytho
unpack *v.* dadbacio
unsafe *adj.* anniogel
until *prep.* tan +*S.M.*
unusual *adj.* anarferol
up *adv.* i fyny
upper *adj.* uwch, uchaf
upset *v.* tarfu; *adj.* wedi cyffroi
upside-down *adv.* ben-i-waered
upstairs *adv.* lan llofft, i fyny'r grisiau
up-to-date *adj.* cyfoes
urban *adj.* trefol
urge *v.* annog
urgent *adj.* brys
use *v.* defnyddio
used *adj.* wedi'i ddefnyddio, ail-law
usual *adj.* arferol
usually *adv.* fel arfer
utensil *n.* offeryn *m.*
U-turn *n.* tro U bedol *m.*

V

vacancy *n.* swydd wag *f.*
vacant *adj.* gwag
vacation *n.* gwyliau *pl.*
vaccinate *v.* brechu
vacuum cleaner *n.* sugnydd llwch *m.*
valid *adj.* dilys
validity *n.* dilysrwydd *m.*
validate *v.* dilysu
valley *n.* cwm *m.*
valuables *n.* pethau gwerthfawr *pl.*
value *n.* gwerth *m.*

van *n.* fan *f.*
vanilla *n.* fanila *m.*
various *adj.* amrywiol
VCR *n.* chwaraewr fideo *m.*
vegetable *n.* llysieuyn *m.*
vegetarian *n.* llysfwytäwr *m.*
vein *n.* gwythïen *f.*
velvet *n.* melfed *m.*
venereal disease *n.* clefyd gwenerol *m.*
verb *n.* berf *f.*
verdict *n.* dyfarniad *m.*
verify *v.* gwireddu
versus *prep.* yn erbyn
very *adv.* iawn
veterinarian *n.* milfeddyg *m.*
victim *n.* dioddefwr *m.*
video camera *n.* camera fideo *m.*
view *n.* golygfa *f.*; *v.* gwylio
villa *n.* fila *m.*
village *n.* pentref *m.*
vine *n.* gwinwydden *f.*
vinegar *n.* finegr *m.*
vineyard *n.* perllan *f.*
violent *adj.* treisgar
virgin *n.* morwyn *f.*
visa *n.* fisa *m.*
visible *adj.* gweladwy
visit *v.* ymweld; *n.* ymweliad *m.*
visitor *n.* ymwelydd *m.*
vitamin *n.* fitamin *m.*
vocabulary *n.* geirfa *f.*
voice *n.* llais *m.*
void *adj.* di-rym
voltage *n.* foltedd *m.*
volunteer *n.* gwirfoddolwr *m.*
vomit *v.* cyfogi; *n.* cyfog *m.*
vote *v.* pleidleisio; *n.* pleidlais *f.*
vow *v.* addo; *n.* addewid *mf.*
vowel *n.* llafariad *f.*

W

wage *n.* cyflog *mf.*
waist *n.* gwasg *m.*
wait *v.* aros
waiter *n.* gweinydd *m.*
waiting room *n.* ystafell aros *f.*
waitress *n.* gweinyddes *f.*
wake (up) *v.* deffro, dihuno
walk *v.* cerdded
wall *n.* wal *f.*, mur *m.*
wallet *n.* waled *f.*
want *v.* eisiau *m.*; **I ~** mae eisiau … arna i, rydw i eisiau
war *n.* rhyfel *m.*
warm *adj.* cynnes, twym
warn *v.* rhybuddio
warranty *n.* gwarant *m.*
wash *v.* golchi
washing machine *n.* peiriant golchi *m.*
wasp *n.* cacynen *f.*
watch *v.* gwylio; *n.* oriawr *f.*, wats *m.*
water *n.* dŵr *m.*
waterproof *adj.* diddos
waterskiing *v.* sgio dŵr
wave *n.* ton *f.*; *v.* chwifio
wax *n.* gwêr *m.*, cŵyr *m.*
way *n.* ffordd *f.*
we *pron.* ni
weak *adj.* gwan.
weakness *n.* gwendid *m.*
weapon *n.* arf *f.*
wear *v.* gwisgo
weather *n.* tywydd *m.*
weather forecast *n.* rhagolygon y tywydd *mpl.*
website *n.* gwefan *f.*
wedding *n.* priodas *f.*
wedding ring *n.* modrwy briodas *f.*
Wednesday *n.* Mercher *m.*
week *n.* wythnos *f.*
weekday *n.* dydd gwaith *m.*

weekend *n.* penwythnos *m.*
weigh *v.* pwyso
weight *n.* pwysau *pl.*
weird *adj.* rhyfedd
welcome *v.* croesawu; *inter.* croeso
well *n.* ffynnon *f.*; *adv.* yn dda;
west *n.* gorllewin *m.*
wet *adj.* gwlyb
what *interrog.* beth
wheat *n.* gwenith *pl.*
wheel *n.* olwyn *f.*
when *interrog.* pryd
where *interrog.* ble
whether *rel.pron.* a + *S.M.*
which *interrog.* pa + *S.M.*
while *cong.* tra
white *adj.* gwyn
who *interrog.* pwy
whole *adj.* cyfan
why *interrog.* pam
wise *adj.* doeth
widow *n.* gwraig weddw *f.*
widower *n.* gŵr gweddw *m.*
wife *n.* gwraig *f.*
wig *n.* penwisg *f.*
wild *adj.* gwyllt
win *v.* ennill
wind *n.* gwynt *m.*
window *n.* ffenest *f,* ffenestr *f.*
windshield *n.* sgrin wynt *f.*
wine *n.* gwin *m.*
wing *n.* adain *f.*
winner *n.* enillydd *m.*
winter *n.* gaeaf *m.*
wipe *v.* sychu
wish *v.* dymuno; *n.* dymuniad *m.*
with *prep.* gyda +*SP.M.*
without *prep.* heb +*S.M.*
witness *n.* tyst *m.*
woman *n.* menyw *f.*, dynes *f.*

wonderful *adj.* godidog, arbennig
wood *n.* pren *m.*
wool *n.* gwlân *m.*
word *n.* gair *m.*
work *n.* gwaith *m.*; *v.* gweithio
world *n.* byd *m.*
worldwide *adj.* byd-eang
worry *v.* pryderu
worse *adj.* gwaeth
wound *n.* clwyf *m.*
wrap *v.* lapio
wreck *n.* llongddrylliad *m.*; *v.* llongddryllio
wrinkle *n.* crych *m.*
wrist *n.* arddwrn *m.*
write *v.* ysgrifennu
writer *n.* ysgrifennwr *m.*, awdur *m.*
wrong *adj.* anghywir

X

X ray *n.* pelydr X *m.*

Y

yacht *n.* cwch hwylio *m.*
yard *n.* buarth *m.*
yawn *v.* agor pen
year *n.* blwyddyn *f.*
yell *v.* bloeddio, gweiddi
yellow *adj.* melyn
yes *adv.* ie
yesterday *adv.* ddoe
yield *v.* ildio
you *pron.* chi, ti
young *adj.* ifanc
youth *n.* ieuenctid *m.*
youth hostel *n.* hostel ieuenctid *f.*

Z

zero *n.* dim *m.*, sero *m.*
zip code *n.* cod post *m.*
zipper *n.* zip *m.*
zone *n.* ardal *f.*, rhanbarth *m.*
zoo *n.* sw *m.*

PHRASEBOOK

BASICS	175
TIME	183
TRAVEL IN WALES	186
ACCOMMODATIONS	195
TRANSPORT	221
EATING OUT	238
OUT AND ABOUT	253
SHOPPING	266
AT THE DOCTOR'S OR DENTIST'S	293
MISCELLANEOUS	300

BASICS
PETHAU SYLFAENOL

Yes.	**Ie.**	*ee-eh*
No.	**Na.**	*nah*
Please.	**Os gwelwch yn dda.**	*os gooehlooch uhn dda*
Thanks/ Thank you.	**Diolch.**	*deeolch*
You're welcome.	**Croeso.**	*croeesoh*
OK.	**Iawn.**	*eeahoon*
Excuse me.	**Esgusodwch fi.**	*esgisodooch vee*
I'm sorry.	**Mae'n flin 'da fi.**	*maheen vleen da vee*
Hello.	**Helo.**	*helo*
Good-bye.	**Hwyl.**	*hooeel*
How are you?	**Shwmae?**	*shoomahee*

In Difficulty
Mewn Anhawster

All Welsh adults speak English, so you may speak English, but if you want to keep to Welsh, use these phrases.

Can you help me?
Allwch chi fy helpu i?
allooch chee vuh helpee ee

Can you translate this?
Allwch chi gyfieithu hwn?
allooch chee guhvyaythee hoon

Could you say it again?
Allech chi'i ddweud e eto?
allehch chee ddooayd eh eto

Do you speak English?
Ydych chi'n siarad Saesneg?
uhdich chee'n sharad Saheesneg

I don't know.
Wn i ddim.
oon ee ddim

I don't speak Welsh.
Dydw i ddim yn siarad Cymraeg.
duhdoo ee ddim uhn sharad kuhmraheeg

I don't understand.
Dydw i ddim yn deall.
duhdoo ee ddim uhn dehall

I'm learning Welsh.
Rydw i'n dysgu Cymraeg.
ruhdoo een duhsgee kuhmraheeg

Speak slowly.
Siaradwch yn araf.
sharadooch uhn arav

Thanks for you help.
Diolch am eich help.
deeohlch am aych help

What is … in English?
Beth yw … yn Saesneg?
beth ioo … uhn saheesnehg

What is … in Welsh?
Beth yw … yn Gymraeg?
beth ioo … uhn guhmraheeg

Greetings and Courtesy
Cyfarchion a chwrteisi

Hello!
Helo!
helo

Hi!
Shwmae!
shoomahee

Good morning!
Bore da!
boreh dah

Good afternoon!
Pnaw'n da!
pnahoon dah

Good evening!
Noswaith dda!
nosooeth ddah

How are you?
Shwd y'ch chi?; Sut ydych chi?
shood eech chee; sit uhdich chee

Very well, thanks.
Da iawn diolch.
dah yahoon deeolch

And you?
A chi?
ah chee

Nice to meet you.
Braf cwrdd â chi.
brahv koordd ah chee

Good night!
Nos da!
nohs dah

Good-bye!
Hwyl!
hooeel
Hwyl fawr!
hooeel vahoor

See you!
Gwela i chi!
gooehlah ee chee
Gwela i ti!
gooehlah ee tee

I'm …
… ydw i.
… uhdoo ee

What's your name?
Beth yw'ch enw chi?
behth iooch ehnoo chee

Here's …
Dyma …
duhma

… my daughter.
… fy merch.
… vuh mehrch

… my husband.
… 'ngŵr.
… ngoor

… my son.
… fy mab.
… vuh mahb

… my wife.
… 'ngwraig.
… vuh ngooraheeg

I'm on holiday.
Rydw i ar wyliau.
ruhdoo ee ahr ooeelyeh

I live in London.
Rydw i'n byw yn Llundain.
ruhdoo een bioo uhn Llindehn

I come …
Rydw i'n dod …
ruhdoo een dohd

… from America.
… o America.
… o amerika

… from Australia.
… o Awstralia.
… o Ahoostrahlya

… from Canada.
… o Ganada.
… o ganada

… from New York.
… o Efrog Newydd.
… o Ehvrog Nehooidd

… from the U.S.A.
… o'r Unol Daleithiau
… ohr eenohl dahlaythyeh

Basic Questions
Dechrau cwestiynau

How? **Sut?** *sit*

How do I get there?
Sut ydw i'n mynd yno?
sit uhdoo een mihnd uhno

How much? **Faint?** *vaheent*

How much does it cost?
Faint mae'n ei gostio?
vaheent maheen ee gostyo

How much is it?
Faint yw e?
vaheent ioo eh

What? **Beth?** *beth*

What is it?
Beth yw e?
beth ioo eh

What's at the cinema?
Beth sy yn y sinema?
beth see uhn uh sinema

When?   **Pryd?**   *preed*

When does it start?
Pryd mae e'n dechrau?
preed mahee ehn dechreh

Where?   **Ble?**   *bleh*

Where's the shop?
Ble mae'r siop?
bleh maheer shop

Which?   **Pa?**   *pah*

Which bus is here?
Pa fws sy yma?
pah voos see uhma

Who?   **Pwy?**   *pooee*

Who's coming?
Pwy sy'n dod?
pooee seen dohd

Who is she?
Pwy yw hi?
pooee ioo hee

Why?   **Pam?**   *pam*

Why are we waiting?
Pam rydyn ni'n aros?
pam ruhdin neen aros

Why is the hotel expensive?
Pam mae'r gwesty'n ddrud?
pam maheer gooehsteen ddreed

TIME
AMSER

What's the time?
Faint o'r gloch yw hi?
vaheent ohr glohch ioo hee

It's … o'clock.
Mae hi'n … o'r gloch.
mae heen … ohr glohch

one (1)	**un**	*een*
two (2)	**ddau**	*ddahee*
three (3)	**dri**	*dree*
four (4)	**bedwar**	*bedooahr*
five (5)	**bump**	*bimp*
six (6)	**chwe**	*chooeh*
seven (7)	**saith**	*saheeth*
eight (8)	**wyth**	*ooeeth*
nine (9)	**naw**	*nahoo*
ten (10)	**ddeg**	*ddehg*
eleven (11)	**un ar ddeg**	*een ar ddehg*
twelve (12)	**ddeuddeg**	*ddayddehg*

The numbers undergo soft mutation after *mae hi'n*
and *i*. These are the forms used:

five to	**bum munud i**	*bim minid ee*
ten to	**ddeg munud i**	*ddehg minid ee*
quarter to	**chwarter i**	*chooarter ee*
twenty to	**ugain munud i**	*eegehn minid ee*
twenty-five to	**bum munud ar hugain i**	*bim minid ar hugehn ee*

It's two o'clock.
Mae hi'n ddau o'r gloch.
mahee heen ddahee ohr glohch

It's five to ten.
Mae hi'n bum munud i ddeg.
mae heen bim minid ee ddehg

The same number forms are used after *am* ("at"):

The bus goes at three o'clock.
Mae'r bws yn mynd am dri o'r gloch.
maheer boos uhn mind am dree ohr glohch

The numbers do not mutate after *wedi* ("past"):

five past	**bum munud wedi**	*bim minid ooehdy*
ten past	**ddeng munud wedi**	*ddeng minid ooehdy*
quarter past	**chwarter wedi**	*chooarter ooehdy*
twenty past	**ugain munud wedi**	*eegehn minid ooehdy*
twenty-five past	**bum munud ar hugain wedi**	*bim minid ar heegehn ooehdy*
half past	**hanner awr wedi**	*haner ahoor ooehdy*

It's a quarter past five.
Mae hi'n bum munud wedi pump.
mahee heen bim minid ooehdy pimp

It starts at half past four.
Mae e'n dechrau am hanner awr wedi pedwar.
mahee ehn dechreh am haner aoor ooehdy pedooahr

Some Time Expressions
Rhai Ymadroddion Amser

after supper	**ar ôl swper**	*ar ohl soopehr*
after three	**ar ôl tri**	*ar ohl tree*
at midday	**ganol dydd**	*gahnol deedd*
at midnight	**ganol nos**	*gahnol nohs*
before breakfast	**cyn brecwast**	*kin brekooast*
before lunch	**cyn cinio**	*kin kinyo*
before tea	**cyn te**	*kin teh*
in an hour	**mewn awr**	*mehoon ahoor*
in half an hour	**mewn hanner awr**	*mehoon haner ahoor*
next week	**wythnos nesa'**	*ooeethnos nehsa*
next year	**y flwyddyn nesa'**	*uh vlooeeddin nehsa*
this afternoon	**prynhawn 'ma**	*pruhnhaoon ma*
this evening	**heno**	*hehno*
this morning	**bore 'ma**	*boreh ma*
this year	**eleni**	*elehny*
tomorrow morning	**bore 'yfory**	*boreh vohry*
tomorrow night	**nos yfory**	*nohs uhvory*
tomorrow	**yfory**	*uhvoree*
tonight	**heno**	*hehno*
yesterday	**ddoe**	*ddohee*
an hour ago	**awr yn ôl**	*ahoor uhn ohl*
I'm late	**dwi'n hwyr**	*dooeen hooeer*
it's late	**mae hi'n hwyr**	*mahee heen hooeer*
it's early	**mae hi'n gynnar**	*mahee heen guhnar*
we're early	**ry'n ni'n gynnar**	*reen neen guhnar*

TRAVEL IN WALES
TEITHIO YNG NGHYRMU

Arriving
Cyrraedd

If you arrive in Wales by air, you will probably arrive in Cardiff International Airport. You may see some Welsh signs here, but the personnel largely speak English.

The airport is some ten miles out of Cardiff—you will need a taxi or bus to go to the city center.

Other airports used for travel to Wales are Bristol, Birmingham, Manchester, as well as Heathrow or Gatwick in London. If your flight ends at one of these, you will then probably proceed to Wales by train or bus. Trains are quite expensive if you do not book passage at least a fortnight beforehand. Buses are far more reasonably priced.

The train stations in Wales have a bilingual policy. Announcements are made in both English and Welsh. However, the employees, particularly in southern Wales, generally speak English.

Don't be surprised, if, after studying this book, you seem to know more of the native language than many of the Welsh you'll meet.

Some signs you might see:

Bank	**Banc**	*bank*
Customs	**Tollau**	*tolleh*
Entry	**Mynedfa**	*muhnedva*

Exit	**Allanfa**	*allanva*
Information	**Gwybodaeth**	*gwibohdaheeth*
Show Your Passport	**Dangoswch eich pasbort**	*dan-gosooch aych pasbort*
Station	**Gorsaf**	*gorsav*
Taxi	**Tacsi**	*taxi*
Telephone	**Ffôn**	*phohn*
Tickets	**Tocynnau**	*tokuhneh*
Timetable	**Amserlen**	*amsehrlehn*
To the Buses	**I'r bysiau**	*eer buhsyeh*
Toilets	**Toiledau**	*toylehdeh*
Trains	**Trenau**	*trehneh*
Waiting Room	**Ystafell aros**	*uhstavell aros*
Welcome	**Croeso**	*croyso*

Questions you may ask:

| Where is/ are the …? | **Ble mae'r …?** | *bleh maheer* |

ATM machine	**peiriant arian**	*payryant ahryan*
bank	**banc**	*bank*
bar	**bar**	*bar*
bus stop	**safle bws**	*savleh boos*
buses	**bysiau**	*buhsyeh*
café	**caffe**	*kapheh*
information desk	**ddesg wybodaeth**	*ddesk ooibohdaheeth*
lockers	**loceri**	*lokehry*
lost luggage	**bagiau coll**	*bagyeh koll*
lounge	**lolfa**	*lolva*
nearest bank	**banc agosa'**	*bank agosa*
parking lot	**maes parcio**	*mahees parkyo*
train station	**gorsaf trenau**	*gorsav trehneh*

Where is the train/bus …?
Ble mae'r trên/bws …?
bleh maheer trehn/boos

to Bangor	**i Fangor**	*ee Van-gor*
to Cardiff	**i Gaerdydd**	*ee Gaheerdeedd*
to Llanelli	**i Lanelli**	*ee Lanehlly*
to London	**i Lundain**	*ee Lindaheen*
to the hotel	**i'r gwesty**	*eer gooehstee*
to the station	**i'r orsaf**	*eer orsav*
to the town center	**i ganol y dre'**	*ee ganol uh dreh*
to town	**i'r dre'**	*eer dreh*

Where can I …? **Ble galla i …?** *bleh galla ee*

buy a present	**brynu anrheg**	*bruhnee anrhehg*
catch a bus	**ddal bws**	*ddal boos*
find a toilet	**ffeindio tŷ bach**	*phindyo tee bach*
get a drink	**gael diod**	*gaheel deeod*
get a ticket	**gael tocyn**	*gaheel tokin*
get money	**gael arian**	*gaheel ahryan*
get some food	**gael bwyd**	*gaheel booeed*
leave my case	**adael fy nghes**	*adaheel vuh nghehs*
telephone	**ffonio**	*phonyo*

When does …? **Pryd mae'r …?** *preed maheer*

the bus depart	**bws yn mynd**	*boos uhn mind*
the plane land	**awyren yn glanio**	*ahoouhrehn uhn glanyo*

| the shop open | **siop yn agor** | *shop uhn agor* |
| the train leave | **trên yn gadael** | *trehn uhn gadaheel* |

Problems
Problemau

These are some useful expressions in problem situations. However, if the situation is serious, it's best to use English.

I have no money.
Does dim arian 'da fi.
dohs dim aryan da vee

I can't find my bag.
Dw i ddim yn gallu ffeindio fy mag i.
dooee ddim uhn gally ffindo vuh mag ee

Someone has stolen my wallet.
Mae rhywun wedi dwyn fy waled.
mahee rhiooin ooehdy dooeen vuh ooahled

Where is the police station?
Ble mae gorsaf yr heddlu?
bleh mahee gorsav uhr heddly

I've got nowhere to stay.
Does dim lle 'da fi i aros.
dohees dim lleh da vee ee aros

Where is the nearest doctor?
Ble mae'r meddyg agosa?
ble maheer meddig agosa

Is there a pharmacy here?
Oes fferyllydd yma?
oys fferuhllidd uhma

I'm looking for a hotel.
Dw i'n chwilio am westy.
dooeen chooilyo am ooehstee

Some Answers
Rhai Atebion

behind you	**y tu ôl i chi**	*uh tee ohl ee chee*
by the door	**wrth y drws**	*oorth uh droos*
by the entrance	**wrth y fynedfa**	*oorth uh vuhnedva*
here	**yma**	*uhma*
in front of the building	**o flaen yr adeilad**	*o vlaheen uhr adaylad*
in front of you	**o'ch blaen chi**	*ohch blaheen chee*
in the shop	**yn y siop**	*uhn uh shop*
on the left	**ar y chwith**	*ar uh chooeeth*
on the right	**ar y dde**	*ar uh ddeh*
on this floor	**ar y llawr yma**	*ar uh llahoor uhma*
outside	**tu allan**	*tee allan*
over there	**fan'na**	*vana*
'round the corner	**rownd y g ornel**	*rohoond uh gornehl*
straight ahead	**yn syth ymlaen**	*uhn seeth uhmlaheen*
upstairs	**i fyny'r grisiau**	*ee vuhneer grisyah [N.W.]*
	lan lloft	*lan lloph [S.W.]*

Travel in Wales
Teithio Yng Nghyrmu

On foot.
Ar droed.
ar droyd

Asking for directions.
Gofyn y ffordd.
govin uh phordd

Excuse me.
Esgusodwch fi.
ehsgisodooch vee

Where is the …?
Ble mae'r …?
Bleh maheer

I am looking for the …
Dw i'n chwilio am y … (yr *before vowels)*
doo een chooilyo am uh (uhr)

art gallery	**oriel gelf**	*oriehl gehlv*
beach	**traeth**	*traheeth*
bus station	**orsaf fysiau**	*orsav vuhsyeh*
castle	**castell**	*kastehll*
hotel	**gwesty**	*gooehstee*
market	**farchnad**	*varchnad*
police station	**orsaf heddlu**	*orsav hehddly*
shops	**siopau**	*shopeh*
station	**orsaf**	*orsav*

Go …	then	turn …
Ewch …	**yna**	**trowch …**
ehooch	*uhna*	*trohooch …*

to the left	**i'r chwith**	*eer chooeeth*
to the right	**i'r dde**	*eer ddeh*
straight ahead	**yn syth**	*uhn seeth*
	ymlaen	*uhmlaheen*

Names of Places in Wales
Enwau Lleoedd Cymru

Many places in Wales have both a Welsh name and an English one. The English name is often distinct from the Welsh, although in some places it is only an anglicization.

Abergavenny	**Y Fenni**
	uh veny
Barmouth	**Abermo**
	abehrmoh
Brecon	**Aberhonddu**
	abehrhonddee
Bridgend	**Pen-y-bont**
	pen uh bont
Cardiff	**Caerdydd**
	caheerdeedd
Cardigan	**Aberteifi**
	abehrtayvy
Carmarthen	**Caerfyrddin**
	caheervuhrddin
Denbigh	**Dinbych**
	dinbich
Holyhead	**Caergybi**
	caheerguhby
Milford Haven	**Aberdaugleddau**
	abehrdaeeglehddahee

Neath	**Castell-nedd**
	castehll nehdd
Newport	**Casnewydd**
	casnehooidd
Pembroke	**Penfro**
	penvro
Swansea	**Abertawe**
	abehrtaooeh
Tenby	**Dinbych y Pysgod**
	dinbich uh puhsgod
Welshpool	**Y Trallwng**
	uh trahlloong

Staying in Wales
Aros yng nghyrmu

Information
Gwybodaeth

The tourist industry in Wales is promoted by The Welsh Tourist Board (*Bwrdd Croeso Cymru*) and is to some extent regulated by it. It awards crowns for various kinds of hotels and guest houses. It can be contacted at:

Tŷ Brunel, 2 Ffordd Fitzalan, Caerdydd / Cardiff CF2 1UY.
Tel: 029 20499909
E-mail: info@tourism.wales.gov.uk.

You may ask them for brochures on Wales or various parts of Wales, which include listings of hotels, guest houses, holiday homes, farms, caravan parks, and bed & breakfast accommodations.

For detailed information on northern Wales contact North Wales Tourism at 77 Heol Conwy, Bae Colwyn, Conwy. Tel: 01492 531731.

Information on southern and western Wales is available from South and West Wales Tourism at Tŷ Penfro, Charter Court, Swansea Enterprise Park, Swansea. Tel: 01792 781212.

Information on central Wales is available from Mid Wales Tourism at Yr Orsaf/The Station, Machynlleth, Powys. Tel: 01654 702653.

ACCOMMODATIONS
LLETY

In all parts of Wales, there are large chain hotels and impressive Welsh-owned ones. Some are notable for their food, while others are distinguished by their surroundings and facilities. Excellent private hotels can be found throughout the country, many in beautiful locations.

Welsh coastal towns, such as Llandudno, Caernarfon, Aberystwyth, abound in hotels of varying sizes, as do small towns in the national parks, e.g. Beddgelert and Llanberis.

Wales, however, prides itself in the excellent quality of smaller hotels, especially in the countryside, and in accommodations available at nearby farms. Many country taverns also offer accommodations.

Bed & breakfast establishments abound in all areas. Their quality varies: beware of those which are frequented by social security, or welfare, tenants; these are usually three- or four-story row buildings. It is a good idea to ask to see your room in such accommodations before deciding to stay. Also be wary of paying too much in sub-standard bed & breakfasts, as some newcomers to Wales try to get rich quickly by running these. In the country, and in towns where WTB crowns are awarded, you should be given a clean, warm welcome, but some AA/RAC stars are years out of date.

A large cooked Welsh breakfast should be available in all establishments, and many can also provide an evening meal.

Your room in many bed & breakfast homes will be provided with facilities for making a cup of tea. Many now provide en-suite facilities of the sort that are taken for granted in hotels.

There are many holiday cottages and houses, as well as static caravans available for rental, usually on a weekly basis. Information on these are available from the appropriate tourist offices.

Electricity throughout Wales is 240 volts. Plugs are of the three-pin square variety.

Reservations should be made in advance if one is planning to visit during the high season (July-August). You will usually find a Tourist Information Centre (TIC) or Canolfan Croeso near the town centers, which can arrange last minute accommodations and give you local maps and brochures.

You can expect to be able to use Welsh in the northern and western parts of Wales. Staff at some establishments use an English/Cymraeg badge, which indicates the ability to speak both languages.

For those who wish a specifically Welsh-language holiday, contact the Welsh Language Centre at Nantgwrtheyrn, Llithfaen, Gwynedd. Tel: 01758 750334. E-mail: post@nantgwr.com

Asking for a Room
Gofyn am stafell

Have you a room for tonight?
       – Yes   – No
Oes stafell gyda chi am heno?
       – Oes   – Na / Nag oes
oys stavell guhda chee am hehno
       – oys   – nah / nag oys

Do you have a single room?
Oes stafell sengl 'da chi?
oys stavell sengl da chee

Do you have a double room?
Oes stafell ddwbl 'da chi?
oys stavell ddoobool da chee

I would like a single room for one night.
Fe hoffwn i gael stafell sengl am un noson.
veh hophoon ee gahl stavell sengl am een noson

We would like a double room for two nights.
Fe hoffen ni gael stafell ddwbl am ddwy noson.
veh hophen nee gahl stavell ddoobool am ddooee noson

  … for three nights
  … am dair noson
  … am daheer noson

  … for four nights
  … am bedair noson
  … am behdaheer noson

… for five nights
… am bum noson
… am bim noson

… for six nights
… am chwe noson
… am chooeh noson

… for a week
… am wythnos
… am ooeethnos

… for a forthnight
… am bythefnos
… am buhthevnos

I would like to see the room.
Fe hoffwn i weld y stafell.
veh hophoon ee oo-ehld uh stavell

What is the price per night?
Beth yw'r pris y noson?
beth ioor prees uh noson

£20	**ugain punt**	*eegehn pihnt*
£25	**pum punt ar hugain**	*pim pihnt ar heegehn*
£30	**deg punt ar hugain**	*dehg pihnt ar heegehn*

Does it include breakfast?   – Yes
Ydy e'n cynnwys brecwast?   – Ydy
uhdee ehn kuhnooees brekooast   – uhdy

How much is …?
Faint yw …?
vaheent ioo

---

bed and breakfast
gwely a brecwast
gooehlee a brehkooast

an extra bed for a child
gwely ychwanegol i blentyn
gooehlee uhchooangeol ee blehntin

full-board
gwely a phob pryd
gooehlee a phob preed

Can we have a spare bed for a child?
Allwn ni gael gwely sbâr i blentyn?
alloon nee gahl gooelee sbahr ee blehntin

Do you make lunch / supper?
Ydych chi'n gwneud cinio / swper?
uhdich cheen goonayd kinyo / sooper

I've gotten a room for tonight.
Dw i wedi cadw lle am heno.
doo ee ooehdy kahdoo lleh am hehno

I phoned yesterday / this morning.
Ffonies i ddoe / bore ma.
phohnyehs ee ddoh / bohreh ma

Is the room on the first floor / second floor?
Ydy'r stafell ar y llawr cyntaf / ail lawr?
uhdeer stavell ar uh llaoor kuhnta / aheel laoor

Where is the [dining] room?
Ble mae'r stafell frecwast?
bleh maheer stavell vrekooast

ACCOMMODATIONS

When is …?
Pryd mae …?
preed mahee

breakfast	**brecwast**	*brekooast*
lunch	**cinio**	*kinyo*
dinner	**bwyd nos**	*booeed nohs*

When does the …?
Pryd mae'r …?
preed maheer

bar open	**bar yn agor**	*bahr uhn agor*
bar close	**bar yn cau**	*bar uhn kahee*
restaurant open	**bwyty'n agor**	*booeeteen agor*
restaurant close	**bwyty'n cau**	*booeeteen kahee*
hotel close	**gwesty'n cau**	*gooehsteen kahee*
front door close	**drws blaen yn cau**	*droos blaheen uhn kahee*

It opens …
Mae'n agor …
maheen agor

at six	**am chwech**	*am chooehch*
at seven	**am saith**	*am saheeth*
at eight	**am wyth**	*am ooeeth*
at nine	**am naw**	*am nahoo*
at ten	**am ddeg**	*am ddehg*
at eleven	**am un ar ddeg**	*am een ar ddehg*
at twelve	**am ddeuddeg**	*am ddayddehg*

Do you have (a) …?		– Yes	– No
Oes … 'da chi?		**– Oes**	**– Na / Nag oes**
oys … da chee		*– oys*	*– nah / nag oys*

bar	**bar**	*bar*
computer for	**pwynt**	*pooeent*
e-mail	**ebost**	*ebohst*
elevator	**lifft**	*lipht*
fax machine	**peiriant ffacs**	*payryant phax*
freezer	**rhewgell**	*rheoogehll*
garage	**garej**	*gahrehj*
Internet access	**rhyngrwyd**	*rhuhngrooeed*
menu	**bwydlen**	*booeedlehn*
minibar	**minibar**	*mineebar*
parking place	**lle i barcio**	*lleh ee barkyo*
refrigerator	**oergell**	*oeergehll*
safe	**sêff**	*sehph*
sauna	**sawna**	*saoona*
swimming pool	**pwll nofio**	*pooll novyo*
telephone	**ffôn**	*phohn*
television	**teledu**	*tehlehdy*

Do we need a key?
     – Yes   – No
Oes angen (a)goriad arnon ni?
     – Oes   – Na/ Nag oes (N.W.)
oys angehn goryad arnon nee
     – oys   – nah / nag oys
Oes angen allwedd arnon ni?
     – Oes   – Na / Nag oes (S.W.)
oys angehn allooedd arnon nee
     – oys   – nah / nag oys

Where is the …?
Ble mae'r …?
bleh maheer

bathroom	**stafell ymolchi**	*stahvell uhmolchy*
lounge	**lolfa**	*lolva*
soap	**sebon**	*sehbon*
stairs	**grisiau**	*grishyeh*
toilet	**tŷ bach**	*tee bach*
towel	**tywel**	*tuhooehl*

in the …
yn y …
uhn uh

on the …
ar y …
ar uh

bathroom	**stafell ymolchi**	*stavehll uhmolchy*
bedroom	**stafell wely**	*stavehll ooehly*
first floor	**llawr cyntaf**	*llahoor kuhnta*
ground floor	**llawr gwaelod**	*llahoor gwaheelod*
outside	**y tu allan**	*uh tee allan*
restaurant	**bwyty**	*booeety*
second floor	**ail lawr**	*aeel lahoor*

Asking for Services
Gofyn am wasanaethau

May I …?	– Yes	– No
Ga i …?	**– Cewch**	**– Na / Nac chewch**
ga ee	*– kehooch*	*– nah / na chehooch*

use the phone
ddefnyddio'r ffôn
ddehvnuhddyor phohn

have breakfast early
gael brecwast yn gynnar
gaheel brehkooast uhn guhnar

have a key
agoriad (N.W.)
agoryad
allwedd (S.W.)
allooedd

see the lounge
weld y lolfa
ooehld uh lolva

have an ashtray
flwch llwch
vlooch llooch

have a brochure
daflen
davlen

have another pillow
glustog arall
glistog arall

see a newspaper
weld papur newydd
ooehld papir nehooidd

leave my money in the safe
adael fy arian yn y sêff
adaheel vuh aryan uhn uh sehph

use my computer
ddefnyddio fy nghyfrifadur
ddevnuhddyo vuh nghuhvrivyadir

smoke
smygu
smuhgee

have a drink
gael diod
gaheel deeod

use a credit card
ddefnyddio cerdyn credyd
ddehvnuhddyo kehrdin krehdid

pay by check
dalu â siec
dahlee ah shek

Would you …?
Allwch chi …?
allooch chee

wake me at 7
fy neffro i am saith
vuh nephro ee am saheeth

put another blanket on the bed
roi blanced arall ar y gwely
roy blanked arall ar uh gooehly

turn the heating on
troi'r gwres ymlaen
troyr goorehw uhmlaheen

turn the heating off
troi'r gwres i ffwrdd
troyr goorehs ee phoordd

give me another towel
roi tywel arall i fi
roy tuhooehl arall ee vee

give me the bill, please
roi'r bil i fi, os gwelwch yn dda
royr bill ee vee os gooehlooch uhn ddah

give me a receipt
roi derbynneb i fi
roy dehrbuhnehb ee vee

phone for me, please
ffonio droso i, os gwelwch yn dda
phonyo droso ee os gooehlooch uhn ddah

recommend a good restaurant
argymell bwyty da
arguhmell booeety dah

I would like …
Dw i eisiau …
dooee eesheh / dooee eesho [N.W.]

toilet paper
papur tŷ bach
papir tee bach

breakfast at at eight
brecwast am wyth
brehkooast am ooeeth

a plug for my razor
plwg i eillio
ploog ee ayllyo

some paper
papur
papir

some soap
sebon
sehbon

shampoo
siampŵ
shampoo

some stamps
stampiau
stampyeh

to use the fax machine
defnyddio'r peiriant ffacs
devnuhddyor payryant phax

to stay another night
aros noson arall
aros noson arall

find the train station
ffeindio'r orsaf
phayndyor orsav

batteries
batris
batrees

Questions You'll Be Asked
Cwestiynau a gaiff eu gofyn i chi

When …?
Pryd …?
preed

do you want breakfast
ydych chi am gael brecwast
uhdich chee am gaheel brehkooast

do you want to get up
ydych chi am godi
uhdich chee am gohdy

do you want supper
ydych chi am gael swper
uhdich chee am gaheel soopehr

do you want to pay
ydych chi eisiau talu
uhdich chee eesheh tahly

Do you want …?	– Yes	– Na
ydych chi eisiau …?	**– Ydw**	**– Na / Na'dw**
uhdich chee eesheh	*– uhdoo*	*– nah / nahdoo*

milk in your tea
llefrith yn eich te (N.W.)
llevrith uhn aych teh
llaeth yn eich te (S.W.)
llaheeth uhn aych teh

sugar in your coffee
siwgr yn eich coffi
shoogoor uhn aych kophy

to get up early
codi'n gynnar
kohdy'n guhnar

more blankets
mwy o flancedi
mooee oh vlankehdy

a full Welsh breakfast
brecwast Cymreig llawn
brekooast Kuhmrayg llahoon

another piece of toast
darn arall o dost
dahrn arall oh dohst

more milk
mwy o lefrith (N.W.)
mooe oh levrith
mwy o laeth (S.W.)
mooee oh laheeth

anything else
rhywbeth arall
rhioobeth arall

to pay now
talu'n awr
taleen ahoor

Complaints
Cwyno

… is the …
Mae'r …
maheer

> room is cold
> **stafell yn oer**
> *stavell uhn oheer*

> bed is dirty
> **gwely'n frwnt**
> *gooehleen vroont*

> food is cold
> **bwyd yn oer**
> *booeed uhn oheer*

> room is too noisy
> **stafell yn rhy swnllyd**
> *stavell uhn rhee soonllid*

> water is too cold
> **dŵr yn rhy oer**
> *door uhn rhee oheer*

There is no … / There are no …
Does dim …
dohs dim

> hot water
> **dŵr poeth**
> *door poheeth*

> key in the door
> **agoriad yn y drws (N.W.)**
> *agoryad uhn uh droos*
> **allwedd yn y drws (S.W.)**
> *allooehdd uhn uh droos*

> plug in the bathtub
> **plwg yn y sinc**
> *ploog uhn uh sink*

> towel in the bathroom
> **tywel yn y stafell ymolchi**
> *tuhooehl uhn uh stavell uhmolchy*

> light in the room
> **golau yn y stafell**
> *goleh uhn uh stavell*

> curtains on the window
> **llenni ar y ffenest**
> *llehny ar uh phenest*

The … is not working.
Dyw'r … ddim yn gweithio.
dioor ddim uhn gooeethyo

heating	**gwres**	*goorehs*
key	**agoriad (N.W.)**	*agoryad*
	allwedd (S.W.)	*allooehdd*
light	**golau**	*gohleh*
tap	**tap**	*tap*

May I speak to the manager?
Ga i siarad â'r rheolwr?
ga ee sharad ahr rheholoor

Where is the manager?
Ble mae'r rheolwr?
bleh maheer rheholoor

Upon Leaving
Wrth adael

I would like to pay.
Fe hoffwn i dalu.
Veh hophoon ee dahly

It has been very pleasant.
Mae hi wedi bod yn ddymunol iawn.
mahee he ooehdy bohd uh dduhmeenol yahoon

When do we have to check out of the room?
Pryd mae rhaid i ni adael y stafell?
preed mahee rhaheed ee nee ahdehl uh stavell

May I leave my suitcase here?
Ga i adael fy nghes yma?
ga ee ahdehl vuh nghehs uhma

Can you call a taxi?
Allwch chi alw tacsi?
allooch chee ahloo taxi

May I have the bill, please?
Ga i'r bil os gwelwch yn dda?
ga eer bil os gooehloolch uhn ddah

We are leaving tomorrow.
Ry'n ni'n gadael yfory.
Reen neen gahdehl uhvohry

Can we stay another night?
Allwn ni aros noson arall?
Alloon nee ahros noson ahrall

We will come here again.
Byddwn ni'n dod yma eto.
Buhddoon neen dohd uhma eto

Are you sure the bill is correct?
Ydych chi'n siŵr bod y bil yn iawn?
Uhdich cheen shoor bohd uh bil uhn yahoon

Renting Property
Rhentu eiddo

The buying of property for use as vacation homes has been an issue in Wales for many years. It has drastically altered the way of life in a number of coastal villages. Property costs have increased beyond the reach of many locals' incomes, and younger people often cannot afford to buy a home in their own communities. This has had a detrimental effect on the communities and on the Welsh language. In many traditionally Welsh-speaking rural areas, it is now common to find that up to 50% of the population has been born outside Wales, and English has taken over from Welsh as the *lingua franca* of many communities.

Visitors who show a willingness to speak Welsh are made very welcome. Houses, cottages, and caravans are available for rental throughout the year. Some buildings on local farms have been converted into rental homes by farmers looking to increase their income. Many of these are in attractive locations and offer insight into the local way of life. Rental addresses are available through local TIC centers and the regional offices of the WTB.

We would like to rent …
Rydyn ni am logi …
Ruhdin nee am lohgy

a cottage	**bwthyn**	*boothin*
a farmhouse	**ffermdy**	*phehrmdy*
a flat	**fflat**	*phlat*
a house	**tŷ**	*tee*

… for …
… am …
… ahm …

a few days	**rai dyddiau**	*rahee duhddyeh*
a fortnight	**bythefnos**	*buthevnos*
a month	**fis**	*vees*
a week	**wythnos**	*ooeethnos*
a weekend	**benwythnos**	*benooeethnos*

We have booked this house.
Rydyn ni wedi cadw'r tŷ 'ma.
ruhdin nee ooehdy kadoor tee ma

Are you the owner?
Chi yw'r perchennog?
chee ioor pehrchehnog

The … don't/doesn't work.
Dyw'r … ddim yn gweithio.
dioor … ddim uhn gooeheethyoh [N.W.]
gooeeethoh [S.W.]

heating	**gwres**	*grehs*
hot water	**dŵr poeth**	*door poheeth*
keys	**agoriadau (N.W)**	*agoryada*
	allweddi (S.W.)	*allooehddy*
lights	**goleuadau**	*golayadeh*
oven	**ffwrn**	*phoorn*
tap	**tap**	*tap*
toilet	**tŷ bach**	*tee bach*

Is the house cleaned every day?
Gaiff y tŷ ei lanhau bob dydd?
gaheeph uh tee ay lanhahee bob deedd

Are there more blankets?
Oes rhagor o flancedi?
oys rhagor oh vlankehdy

Where is/are the …?
Ble mae'r …?
bleh maheer

fuse box	**blwch ffiwsys**	*blooch phioosis*
nearest shops	**siopau agosa**	*shopeh agosa*
trash can	**bin sbwriel**	*bin sbooryehl*

In the House
Yn y tŷ

bathroom	**stafell ymolchi**	*stafell uhmolchy*
bath	**bath**	*bath*
bathtub	**basn ymolchi**	*bahsn uhmolchy*
shower	**cawod**	*kahoo-od*
soap	**sebon**	*sehbon*
towel	**tywel**	*tuhooehl*
bedroom	**stafell wely**	*stafell ooehly*
alarm clock	**cloc larwm**	*klok lahroom*
bed	**gwely**	*goo-ehly*
blankets	**blancedi**	*blankedy*
cushion	**clustog**	*klistog*
mirror	**drych**	*dreech*
garden	**gardd**	*gahrdd*
flowers	**blodau**	*blodeh*
lawn	**lawnt**	*lahoont*
path	**llwybr**	*lloo-eebr*
pool	**pwll**	*pooll*
shade	**cysgod**	*kuhsgod*
tree	**coeden**	*koydehn*
the kitchen	**y gegin**	*uh gegin*
chair	**cadair**	*kadehr*
cups	**cwpanau`**	*koopahneh*
dishes	**llestri**	*llehstry*

dishwasher	**golchwr llestri**	*golchoor llehstry*
freezer	**rhewgell**	*rhehoogehll*
refrigerator	**oergell**	*oheergehll*
glasses	**gwydrau**	*goo-idreh*
grill	**gril**	*gril*
microwave	**microdon**	*meekrodon*
oven	**ffwrn**	*phoorn*
plates	**platiau**	*plahtyeh*
saucers	**soseri**	*sosehry*
sink	**sinc**	*sink*
table	**bwrdd**	*boordd*
toaster	**tostwr**	*tostoor*
lounge/ living room	**lolfa**	*lolva*
armchair	**cadair freichiau**	*kadehr vraychyeh*
carpet	**carped**	*karpehd*
radio	**radio**	*rahdyo*
sofa	**soffa**	*sopha*
television	**teledu**	*telehdy*
toilet	**tŷ bach**	*tee bach*
bowl	**padell**	*pahdell*
seat	**sedd**	*sehdd*
toilet paper	**papur tŷ bach**	*papir tee bach*

Camping
Gwersylla

There are campsites in all parts of Wales, but the facilities vary greatly. Some are large, modern, and well-run, while others offer only the most basic services. Those on farms offer a particularly friendly environment, but the facilities can be very limited. Remember that, as most campsites are only open during the summer months, they tend to have fewer facilities than is typical elsewhere in Europe, where the camping season tends to be longer. It is best to carefully scrutinize campsites to ensure they suit your requirements and taste.

Many campsites accommodate unreserved tents and touring caravans, although others do not. With those that do not, accommodations must usually be booked beforehand.

Youth hostels

There are many youth hostels in Wales that cater to young people, families, and older adults. Accomodations are usually barracks-style, although there are usually individual rooms available for families or groups. Breakfast, a packed lunch, and an evening meal may be provided for visitors, and there are often cooking facilities available. Those considering staying in one of these facilities should be members of an equivalent youth hostel organization in their own country or the IYHF (International Youth Hostel Organisation). Membership is also available from the Youth Hostel Organisation in Wales and other parts of the UK.

Have you got room for a tent / caravan?
Oes lle gyda chi i babell / garafán?
oys lle guhda chee ee bahbell / garavan

We are a family of three / four / five / six.
Ry'n ni'n deulu o dri / bedwar / pump / chwech.
reen neen dayly o dree / behdooar / pimp / chooehch

We have a small / large tent.
Mae papell fach / fawr gyda ni.
mahee pabell vach / vahoor guhda nee

We would like to stay for a night.
Hoffen ni aros am noson.
hophen nee ahros am noson

We want to stay for three nights.
Ry'n ni am aros am dair noson.
reen nee am ahros am daheer noson

Is there a … here?
Oes … yma?
oys … uhma

electricity	**trydan**	*truhdan*
restaurant	**bwyty**	*booeetee*
a shower	**cawod**	*kahoo-od*
a swimming pool	**pwll nofio**	*pooll novyo*
a washing machine	**peiriant golchi**	*payryant golchee*

What does it cost per night?
Beth yw'r gost y noson?
beth ioor gost uh noson

Here is my card.
Dyma fy ngherdyn.
duhma vuh nghehrdin

Is the camp quiet?
Ydy'r gwersyll yn dawel?
uhdeer gooersill uhn dahooel

When does the camp close at night?
Pryd mae'r gwersyll yn cau yn y nos?
preed maheer gooehrsill yn kahee uhn uh nohs

When do you close at night?
Pryd ydych chi'n cau yn y nos?
preed uhdich cheen kahee uhn uh nohs

Have you got a key?
Oes allwedd gyda chi? (S.W.)
oys allooedd guhda chee
Oes gynnoch chi agoriad? (N.W.)
oys guhnoch chee agoryad

Where can I park the car?
Ble galla i barcio'r car?
bleh galla ee barkyor car

The caravan is dirty.
Mae'r garafán yn frwnt.
maheer garavan uhn vroont

Is the water drinkable?
Ydy'r dŵr yn yfadwy?
uhdeer door uhn uhvadooee

Do you provide meals?
Ydych chi'n gwneud bwyd?
uhdich cheen goonayd booeed

Around the camp / caravan site
O gwmpas y gwersyll / safle carafanau

bottle opener	**agorwr poteli**	*agoroor potehly*
candle	**cannwyll**	*kanooeell*
fire	**tân**	*tahn*
frying pan	**padell ffrio**	*pahdell phreeoh*
gate	**gât**	*gaht*
ground	**ddaear**	*ddahyahr*
lamp	**lamp**	*lamp*
matches	**matsys**	*matshis*
pegs	**pegs**	*pegs*
pocketknife	**cyllell boced**	*kuhllell bokehd*
rope	**rhaff**	*rhahph*
saucepan	**sosban**	*sosban*
shelter	**cysgod**	*kuhsgod*
tent	**pabell**	*pahbell*
torch	**torts**	*tortsh*

TRANSPORT
CLUDIANT

It is best to buy train tickets at least two weeks ahead of time, as prices are less than those for tickets bought a week beforehand or on the day of the trip. Tickets can be bought through the station ticket office, but they are also available through the conductors on the trains. The primary rail lines run along the northern and southern coasts. Other services are available in central Wales, but there is nothing linking the northern and southern lines that does not require travel through England. The rail lines are privately owned and transfers can be a bit challenging to work out. It should be noted that, as of 2005, there are no trains running between Cardiff International Airport and the Cardiff city center.

Buses are more reasonably priced. They are available in all towns and run daily between northern and southern Wales. Service is less available in rural areas. Tickets are usually purchased upon boarding, although weekly tickets are available in some areas. Retirees travel free, although documentation showing proof of age may be required to take advantage of this. Bus service is available from Cardiff International Airport to the City Center.

Automobile rentals are available in most towns and may be the best bargain for families. Prices vary between rental services, so it is recommended that one check with a few to compare prices before making a decision.

Buying Tickets
Prynu tocyn

May I have a one way ticket to …, please?
Ga i docyn un ffordd i … os gwelwch yn dda?
ga ee dokin een phordd ee … os gooehlooch uhn ddah

A return ticket for three adults, please.
Tocyn dychwel i dri oedolyn os gwelwch yn dda.
tokin duhchooehl ee dree oydolin os gooehlooch uhn ddah

One adult and one child.
Un oedolyn ac un plentyn.
een oydohlin ak een plehntin

Two adults.
Dau oedolyn.
dahee oydolin

Two children.
Dau blentyn.
dahee blentin

Does the bus go to …?
Ydy'r bws yn mynd i …?
uhdeer boos uhn mihnd ee

Does the train stop at …?
Ydy'r trên yn aros yn …?
uhdeer trehn uhn aros uhn

When does the train leave?
Pryd mae'r trên yn gadael?
preed maheer trehn uhn gadaheel

When does the bus go?
Pryd mae'r bws yn mynd?
preed maheer boos uhn mihnd

From what platform does the train leave?
O ba blatfform mae'r trên yn gadael?
oh bah blatphorm maheer trehn uhn gadayl

Where is the bus stop?
Ble mae'r safle bws?
bleh maheer savleh boos

Will we have to change trains?
Fydd rhaid i ni newid trên?
veedd rhaheed ee nee nehooid trehn

Where do we have to transfer?
Ble mae rhaid i ni newid?
bleh mahee rhaheed ee nee nehooid

When does the train arrive?
Pryd mae'r trên yn cyrraedd?
preed maheer trehn uhn kuhraheedd

Is there a bus to …?
Oes bws i …?
oys boos ee

I would like to reserve a seat.
Fe hoffwn i gadw sedd.
veh hophoon ee gahdoo sehdd

Second class or first class?
Ail ddosbarth neu ddosbarth cyntaf?
aheel ddosbarth nay ddosbarth kuhnta

On the Bus and Train
Ar y bws / trên

Is there someone sitting here?
Oes rhywun yn eistedd fan hyn?
oys rhiooin uhn aystedd van hin

I have booked this seat.
Dw i wedi cadw'r sedd yma.
doo ee ooehdy kadoor sehdd uhma

May I open the window?
Ga i agor y ffenest?
ga ee agor uh phenest

Where is the restaurant car?
Ble mae'r cerbyd bwyd?
bleh maheer kerbid booeed

Can you please tell me when to get off?
Allwch chi ddweud wrtho i pryd i fynd allan?
allooch chee ddooayd wrtho ee preed ee vihnd allan

I can't find my ticket.
Dw i ddim yn gallu ffeindio fy nhocyn i.
doo ee ddim uhn gallee pheyndyo vuh nhokin ee

Where is the toilet?
Ble mae'r tŷ bach?
ble maheer tee bach

When is the last bus?
Pryd mae'r bws olaf?
preed maheer boos ola

By Taxi
Gyda'r tacsi

Where can I get a taxi?
Ble galla i gael tacsi?
bleh galla ee gahl taxi

Can a taxi come in an hour?
All tacsi ddod mewn awr?
all taxi ddod mehoon ahoor

at six o'clock
am chwech o'r gloch
am chooehch or glohch

I want to go to …
Dw i am fynd i …
doo ee am vihnd ee

About how much will it cost?
Tua faint fydd y gost?
teeah vaheent veedd uh gost

I am in a hurry.
Mae brys arna i.
mahee brees arna ee

Keep the change.
Cadwch y newid.
kadooch uh nehooid

To the station, please.
I'r orsaf os gwelwch yn dda.
eer orsav os gooehlooch uhn ddah

I have two suitcases.
Mae dau ges 'da fi.
mahee dahee gehs da vee

The suitcase is heavy.
Mae'r ces yn drwm.
maheer kehs uhn droom

Stop here, please.
Stopiwch fan hyn os gwelwch yn dda.
stopyooch van hin os gooehlooch uhn ddah

Driving
Gyrru

Drive on the left. You have right of way on main roads, but yield to traffic entering a roundabout on your right. If a pedestrian starts to walk on a zebra crossing, you must stop.

Keep to the speed limits, as they may be strictly enforced, and many speed cameras are ready to catch those who exceed the limits. The speed limit on motorways is 70 mph. On main roads it is 60 mph, and 30 mph in urban areas. Other limits are shown in red circular signs.

The only motorway in Wales runs along the south from east to west, and goes past Newport, Cardiff, Bridgend, Neath and Swansea. It comes to an end before Carmarthen, but there is a two-lane road west of Carmarthen. There is also a two-lane road along the northern Welsh coast.

The A470 to Cardiff is the main road between northern and southern Wales, but remember that road quality is highly variable. The other main roads, called A roads, lack two lanes and are often winding, but they offer beautiful views of the countryside. The secondary, or B, roads are often just as good, but they are also winding and generally very narrow (usually no more than two car widths). The minor roads, which typically appear on maps in yellow, are also narrow, but many can accommodate cars traveling in either direction.

There are no tolls on motorways, but there are toll bridges in Pembrokeshire and Meirionydd. There is a substantial toll for travelling into Wales on either of the Severn bridges.

Road signs are bilingual, with both the English and Welsh names for towns indicated, e.g.

| Swansea | **Abertawe** |

Warning and information signs are also bilingual, e.g.

Beach	**Traeth**
Danger	**Perygl**
Dangerous bend	**Tro peryglus**
Dip in road	**Pant**
Go to your lane	**Ewch i'ch lôn**
Heavy vehicles	**Cerbydau trwm**
Hospital	**Ysbyty**
Junction	**Croesffordd**
Low bridge	**Pont isel**
No hard shoulder	**Dim llain galed**
No waiting	**Dim aros**

One way	**Un ffordd**
School	**Ysgol**
Services	**Gwasanaethau**
Slow	**Araf**
Town center	**Canol y dref**
Yield	**Ildiwch**

On signs and maps, distances are measured in miles rather than kilometers. Five miles is approximately 8 kilometers.

Good road atlases for the UK can be bought in all motorway service stations and bookstores. There are also good tourist maps of Wales available. For detailed maps of parts of Wales, there are a number of excellent OS maps available.

Parking in the cities and towns can be difficult. In Cardiff, one can park on the street if the vehicle displays a parking token, which can be bought at newsstands and other outlets. Most towns have parking lots that use coin machines for payment. Multi-story parking garages are also available; they usually charge for parking when one leaves. If a street has parking restrictions, these are indicated by street signs. Some streets only allow parking by residents.

The RAC and AA are the two main companies offering road service for motorists. When purchasing insurance, it is highly recommended that coverage includes service from these or similar companies.

If your are involved in an accident, the police must be told if someone is injured. Otherwise, you should exchange names, addresses, and insurance information with the other driver. Do not admit responsibility, as this will be dealt with by the respective insurance companies after they have received the accident reports.

There are numerous filling stations on motorways and other roads, but gasoline often costs more at motorway garages and in rural areas.

Roadside assistance is readily available on motorways. There are telephones at regular intervals: park your car on the hard shoulder, make the necessary calls, and wait for assistance. In rural areas, phone a local garage. If you do not know the number, inquire through the phone directory. There are several numbers that offer assistance, e.g. 118 500 and 118 888.

If your are stopped by the police, and asked to show your driver's license and insurance certificate, you are, if you do not have them on you, usually allowed four days to show these at a police station. In an emergency, remember that all police officers speak English. An emergency is not the best opportunity to practice your Welsh.

Driving under the influence of alcohol or drugs is forbidden. One's blood alcohol level cannot exceed the equivalent of having ingested two pints of beer or four small glasses of wine. If the police stop you, they may require a breath test and, in some circumstances, a blood test.

Some Welsh words for car parts are widely known, e.g. *olwyn* – wheel; *corff* – body; *batri* – battery; *gwregys* – seat belt; *teiar* – tyre. All car parts have

Welsh names, but many mechanics have only passing familiarity with them. It is quite common for the English words to used in a Welsh sentence, so don't be afraid to mimic this tendency.

Automobiles
Ceir

I want to rent a car …
Dw i eisiau rhentu car …
doo ee eesheh rhentee car …

> … for a day
> **… am un diwrnod**
> *… am een dioornod*

> … for two days
> **… am ddau ddiwrnod**
> *… am ddahee ddioornod*

> … for three days
> **… am dri diwrnod**
> *… am dree dioornod*

> … for a week
> **… am wythnos**
> *… am ooeethnos*

How much does it cost?
Beth yw'r gost?
behth ioor gost

Is insurance included?
Oes yswiriant wedi'i gynnwys?
oys uhsooiryant ooehdy guhnooees

Can I leave the car in …?
Alla i adael y car yn …?
alla ee adehl uh kar uhn

May I see your license? – Yes, here it is.
Ga i weld eich trwydded? – Cewch, dyma hi.
ga ee ooehld uch trooeedded – kehooch, duhma hee

Is there a charge per mile?
Oes tâl y filltir?
oys tahl uh villtir

I would like …
Fe hoffwn i gael …
veh hophoon ee gaheel

> a large car
> **car mawr**
> *kar mahoor*

> a small car
> **car bach**
> *kar bach*

What kind of gas does it use?
Pa fath o betrol mae e'n 'ddefnyddio?
pa vath o betrol mahee ehn ddevnuhddyo

> … lead-free
> **… di-blwm**
> *… dee bloom*

Where is the …?
Ble mae …?
bleh mahee

   … headlight switch
   … swits y goleuadau
   … sooitsh uh golayadeh

   … windshield wiper switch
   … switsh y sychwyr
   … sooitsh uh suhchooir

How do the windows open?
Sut mae'r ffenestri'n agor?
sit maheer phenstryn agor

How does/do the … work?
Sur mae'r … yn gweithio?
sit maheer … uhn gooaythyo

   … gears
   … gêr
   … gehr

   … lights
   … goleuadau
   … golayadeh

   … lock
   … clo
   … kloh

   … seat belt
   … gwregys
   … goorehgis

At the Service Station
Yn y garej

Fill the tank, please.
Llanwch y tanc, os gwelwch yhn dda.
llanooch uh tank os gooehlooch uhn ddah

Twenty pounds' worth of gasoline.
Gwerth ugain punt o betrol.
gooerth eegaheen pihnt o betrol

20 liters, please.
Dau ddeg litr os gwelwch yn dda.
dahee ddeg litr os gooehlooch uhn dda

Can you check the oil and water?
Allwch chi edrych ar yr olew a'r dŵr?
allooch chee edrich ar uhr olehoo ahr door

Can you put air in the tires?
Allwch chi roi awyr yn y teiars?
allooch chee roy ahooir uhn uh tayars

The … is/are broken.
Mae'r … wedi torri.
maheer … ooehdy tohry

battery	**batri**	*batry*
cable	**cebl**	*kehbl*
clock	**cloc**	*klok*
exhaust	**egsost**	*egsohst*
heater	**gwresogydd**	*gooresogidd*
key	**(a)goriad (N.W.)**	*goryad*
	allwedd (S.W.)	*allooehdd*
switch	**swits**	*sooitsh*
window	**ffenest**	*phenest*

Is there a garage nearby?
Oes garej yn agos?
oys garej uhn agos

Can you repair it?
Allwch chi'i drwsio fe?
allooch chee droosho veh

When can you do the work?
Pryd gallwch chi wneud y gwaith?
preed gallooch chee oonayd uh gooaheeth

The tire is flat.
Mae'r teiar yn fflat.
maheer tayar uhn phlat

On the Road
Ar yr heol

I'm lost.
Dw i ar goll.
doo ee ar goll

I'm looking for the road to …
Dw i'n chwilio am yr heol i …
doo een chooilyo am uhr hehol ee

Is it far to …?
Ydy hi'n bell i …?
uhdee heen bell ee

Is the road closed?
Ydy'r heol ar gau?
uhdeer hehol ar gahee

There is a traffic jam on the bridge.
Mae tagfa ar y bont.
mahee tagva ar uh bont

When is the rush hour?
Pryd mae'r awr brysur?
preed maheer aoor bruhsir

Where can I park?
Ble galla i barcio?
bleh galla ee barkyo

Where can I buy a parking token?
Ble galla i brynu tocyn parcio?
bleh galla ee bruhnee tokin parkyo

May I park here?
Alla i barcio fan hyn?
alla ee barkyo van hin

Police
Heddlu

What's your name?
Beth yw'ch enw chi?
behth iooch ehnoo chee

What's your address?
Beth yw eich cyfeiriad chi?
beth ioo aych kuhvayryad chee

May I see your insurance certificate?
Ga i weld eich papur yswiriant?
ga ee ooehld uhch papir uhsooiryahnt

Here is my license.
Dyma fy nhrwydded.
duhma vuh nhrooeeddehd

Here is my certificate.
Dyma fy nhystysgrif.
duhma vuh nhistuhsgriv

I haven't had anything to drink.
Dydw i ddim wedi yfed dim.
duhdoo ee ddim ooehdy uhved dim

I have only drunk one pint.
Dim ond un peint yfes i.
dim ond een paynt uhves ee

In an Accident
Mewn damwain

I'm sorry, I am a visitor.
Mae'n flin 'da fi, ymwelydd ydw i.
maheen vleen da vee, uhmooehlidd uhdoo ee

I did not see the sign.
Welais i mo'r arwydd.
ooehlehs ee mor arooeedd

The car was moving too fast.
Roedd y car yn symud yn rhy gyflym.
roeedd uh kar uhn suhmid uhn rhee guhvlim

It stopped suddenly.
Stopiodd e'n sydyn.
stopyodd ehn suhdin

You stopped suddenly.
Stopioch chi'n sydyn.
stopyoch cheen suhdin

You did not give a signal.
Wnaethoch chi ddim rhoi arwydd.
oonaheethoch chee ddim rhoy arooeedd

We should phone an ambulance.
Dylen ni ffonio am ambiwlans.
duhlehn nee phonyo am ambioolans

EATING OUT
BWYTA ALLAN

Wales has a wide variety of cafés and restaurants. There are, of course, the American fast food chains, but one can find healthier eating elsewhere. If one is looking for fast food, the fish-and-chip shops are recommended.

There are many cafés that offer locally made cakes and a wide variety of restaurants and taverns that offer fresh-cooked meals. Many public house chains offer meals, but the food is often microwaved.

Breakfast can include toast, marmalade, cereal, tea, and an orange. The "full Welsh breakfast" includes fried eggs, sausage, bacon, and a tomato. As for other meals, one usually has a cup of tea with cake at 11 A.M. Lunch is usually eaten around 1 P.M. There is another tea at 4 P.M., often served with cake or sandwiches. One usually eats supper at 7 P.M. or later.

Prices vary according to quality and locality. Meals in public houses are usually less expensive than in restaurants. Small local cafés can be more interesting. Lunchtime meals, consisting of the same fare as evening meals, are usually much less expensive.

Some cafés offer a bilingual menu, or *bwydlen*, but most will supply you with an English version.

The best establishments serve fresh fish and meat and vegetables from local farms. Welsh lamb and beef is highly recommended. Welsh seafood, including laver bread and cockles, is also very worthwhile.

Local pastries include currant loaf (*bara brith*), flat currant cake (*teislen lap*), and Welsh cakes (*pice ar y mân*), which are small round cakes with currants. Apple tarts (*tarten afalau* or *paste fale*) are a Welsh specialty.

There are an increasing number of varieties of Welsh cheese. Caerffili and cheddar are particularly recommended, especially when flavored with herbs and spices.

Welsh vineyards produce wines that are highly regarded in some quarters. However, they generally do not compare favorably with wines from southern Europe. The amount of sunshine in Wales is considered a contributing factor.

At lunch or supper, a three-course meal is commonplace. The meal begins with a starter dish, followed by the main course and then dessert. A cheese plate may be served after dessert. One is not expected to eat all three courses; the main course is usually sufficient.

Meal Reservations
Cadw lle

Have you got a table for …?
Oes bwrdd gyda chi i …?
oys boordd guhda chee ee …

> … two
> **… ddau**
> *… ddahee*

… three
… dri
… dree

… four
… bedwar
… behdooar

… five
… bump
… bimp

I would like to book a table for tonight / tomorrow night.
Fe hoffwn i gadw bwrdd am heno / nos yfory.
veh hophoon ee gahdoo boordd am hehno / nos uhvory

Have you got a table for …?
Oes bwrdd gyda chi am …?
oys boordd guhda chee am

… seven o'clock
… saith o'r gloch
… saheeth o'r gloch

… eight o'clock
… wyth o'r gloch
… ooeeth or gloch

… nine o'clock
… naw o'r gloch
… nahoo or gloch

May we have a table by the window?
Allwn ni gael bwrdd wrth y ffenest?
alloon nee gahl boordd oorth uh phenest

What is your name, please?
Beth yw'ch enw chi, os gwelwch yn dda?
behth iooch ehnoo chee, os gooehlooch uhn ddah

Have you made a reservation?   – Yes.
Ydych chi wedi cadw lle?   **– Ydw.**
uhdich chee ooehdy kadoo lle   *– uhdoo*

General Questions
Cwestiynau cyffredinol

May we have the menu, please?
Allwn ni gael y fwydlen, os gwelwch yn dda?
alloon nee gahl uh vooeedlehn os gooehlooch uhn ddah

Can you recommend anything?
Allwch chi argymell rhywbeth?
allooch chee arguhmell rhioobeth

Do you have a local dish?
Oes bwyd lleol gyda chi?
oys booeed llehol guhda chee

Will we have to wait a while?
Fydd rhaid i ni aros tipyn?
veedd rhaheed ee nee aros tipin

Is there a non-smoking area?
Oes ardal dim ysmygu?
oys ardal dim uhsmuhgee

Where can we put our coats?
Ble gallwn ni roi ein cotiau?
bleh galloon nee roy uhn kotyeh

Is there a *plat du jour*?
Oes pryd y dydd?
oys preed uh deedd

Ordering
Archebu

May I have …?
Alla i gael …?
alla ee gahl

… melon	**melon**	*mehlon*
… prawns	**corgimwch**	*korgeemooch*
… ribs	**asennau**	*asehneh*
… soup	**cawl**	*kahool*

… then as a main course …
… yna yn brif gwrs …
… uhna uhn breev goors …

… beef	**cig eidion**	*keeg aydyon*
… chicken	**cyw**	*kioo*
… fish	**pysgodyn**	*puhsgodin*
… lamb	**cig oen**	*keeg oheen*
… an omelette	**omled**	*omlehd*
… pasta	**pasta**	*pasta*
… pie	**pei**	*pay*
… pizza	**pizza**	*peetsa*
… pork	**porc**	*pork*
… sausages	**selsig**	*sehlsig*

… with …
… gyda …
… guhda …

... salad	**salad**	*salad*
... vegetables	**llysiau**	*lluhsyeh*
... potatoes	**thatws**	*thatoos*
... chips	**sglodion**	*sglodyon*

I would like to have the meat well-cooked.
Hoffwn i gael y cig wedi'i goginio'n dda.
hophoon ee gahl uh keeg ooehdy goginyon dda

I don't want too many potatoes.
Dw i ddim eisiau gormod o datws.
doo ee ddim eesheh gormod o datoos

May we have some bread?
Allwn ni gael bara?
alloon nee gahl bara

May I have more gravy?
Ga i fwy o grefi?
ga ee vooee o grehvy

May we have more wine?
Gawn ni ragor o win?
gahoon nee ragor o ooeen

May we have another bottle of water?
Gawn ni botelaid arall o ddŵr?
gahoon nee botehlehd arall o ddoor

I would like to have ...
Fe hoffwn i gael ...
veh hophoon ee gaheel

    ... a bottle of beer
    ... potelaid o gwrw
    ... potehlehd o gooroo

EATING OUT

… half a pint of beer
… hanner peint o gwrw
… hanehr paynt o gooroo

… a pint of beer
… peint o gwrw
… paynt o gooroo

… a pint of lager beer
… peint o lager
… paynt o lager

… a cup of coffee
… cwpaned o goffi
… koopahnehd o gophee

… four coffees
… pedwar coffi
… pehdooar kophee

… fruit juice
… sudd ffrwythau
… seedd phrooeetheh

… a glass of lemonade
… gwydraid o lemwnêd
… gooidrehd o lemoonehd

… mineral water
… dŵr mwynol
… door mooeenol

… a cup of tea
… cwpaned o de
… koopanehd o deh

... a glass of water
... gwydraid o ddŵr
... gooidrehd o ddoor

... a jug of water
... jwged o ddŵr
... joogehd o ddoor

... a bottle of red wine
... potelaid o win coch
... potehlehd o ooeen kohch

... a bottle of white wine
... potelaid o win gwyn
... potehlehd o ooeen gooin

... a glass of red wine
... gwydraid o win coch
... gooidrehd o ooeen kohch

... a glass of white wine
... gwydraid o win gwyn
... gooidrehd o ooeen gooin

... with cream
... gyda hufen
... guhda heevehn

... with milk (N.W.)	(S.W.)
... gyda llefrith	**gyda llaeth**
... guhda llevrith	*guhda llaheeth*

... without milk (N.W.)	(S.W.)
... heb lefrith	**heb laeth**
... hehb llevrith	*hehb laheeth*

… with sugar
… gyda siwgr
… guhda shoogoor

Do you have a vegetarian meal?
Oes pryd llysieuol gyda chi?
oys preed lluhsyayol guhda chee

May we have …?
Allwn ni gael …?
alloon nee gaheel

… biscuits	**a bisgedi**	*ah bisgehdy*
… cake	**teisen**	*tayshehn*
… cheese	**caws**	*kahoos*
… cream	**hufen**	*heevehn*
… fruit	**ffrwythau**	*phrooeetheh*
… ice cream	**hufen iâ**	*heevehn yah*
… tart	**tarten**	*tartehn*

Is everything alright?
Ydy popeth yn iawn?
uhdee popehth uhn yahoon

Yes, thanks.
Ydy, diolch.
uhdy, deeolch

The … is very good.
Mae'r … yn dda iawn.
maheer … uhn ddah yahoon

… food	**bwyd**	*booeed*
… meal	**pryd**	*preed*
… wine	**gwin**	*goo-een*

Complaints
Cwyno

The food is cold.
Mae'r bwyd yn oer.
maheer booeed uhn oheer

We've been waiting for half an hour.
Ry'n ni wedi bod yn aros am hanner awr.
reen nee ooehdy bod uhn aros am hanehr ahoor

I didn't order this.
Wnes i ddim archebu hyn.
oonehs ee ddim archehby hin

There is a draft coming from the door.
Mae drafft yn dod o'r drws.
mahee drapht uhn dod ohr droos

The meat is too well-done.
Mae'r cig wedi coginio gormod.
maheer keeg ooehdy koginyo gormod

The potatoes are cold.
Mae'r tatws yn oer.
maheer tatoos uhn oheer

The fork is dirty.
Mae'r fforc yn frwnt.
maheer phork uhn vroont

The … is not clean.
Dyw'r … ddim yn lân.
dioor … ddim uhn lahn

| … fork | **fforc** | *phork* |
| … glass | **gwydryn** | *gooidrin* |

... knife	**gyllell**	*guhllell*
... plate	**plât**	*plaht*
... spoon	**llwy**	*llooee*
... table	**bwrdd**	*boordd*
... tablecloth	**lliain**	*llyehn*

Paying
Talu

May I have the bill, please?
Ga i'r bil os gwelwch yn dda?
ga eer bil os gooehlooch uhn ddah

The bill is not correct.
Dyw'r bil ddim yn iawn.
dihoor bil ddim uhn yahoon

Is the tip included?
Ydy'r cildwrn wedi'i gynnwys?
uhdeer kildoorn ooehdy guhnooees

Keep the change.
Cadwch y newid.
kadooch uh nehooid

May I use my credit card?
Alla i ddefnyddio fy ngherdyn?
alla ee ddehvnuhddyo vuh ngherdin

Will you accept a check?
Ydych chi'n derbyn siec?
uhdich cheen dehrbin shek

We'll see you again.
Fe welwn ni chi eto.
veh ooehloon nee chee eto

Good-bye.
Pob hwyl.
pob hooeel

On the Menu
Ar y fwydlen

apple	**afal**	*aval*
beans	**ffa**	*pha*
runner beans	**ffa dringo**	*pha dringo*
beef	**eidion**	*aydyon*
beetroot	**betys**	*behtis*
bread	**bara**	*bara*
laver bread	**bara lawr**	*bara lahoor*
butter	**menyn**	*mehnin*
cabbage	**bresych**	*brehsich*
cake	**teisen**	*tayshehn*
carrots	**moron**	*mohron*
cauliflower	**blodfresych**	*blodvrehsich*
cheese	**caws**	*kahoos*
chicken	**cyw iâr**	*kioo yahr*
chips	**sglodion**	*sglodyon*
cockles	**cocos**	*kokos*
cucumber	**cwcwmeren**	*kookoomehrehn*
curry	**cyri**	*kuhry*
deer	**carw**	*karoo*
dessert	**pwdin**	*poodin*
duck	**hwyaden**	*hooeeahdehn*
egg	**wy**	*ooee*
boiled egg	**wy wedi'i ferwi**	*ooee ooehdy verooy*
fried egg	**wy wedi'i ffrio**	*ooee ooehdy phryo*
fish	**pysgodyn**	*puhsgodin*
cod	**penfras**	*pehnvras*
plaice	**lleden**	*llehdehn*

salmon	**eog**	*ehog*
trout	**brithyll**	*brithill*
fruit	**ffrwythau**	*phrooeetheh*
goose	**gwydd**	*gooeedd*
grapes	**grawnwin**	*grahoonooin*
ham	**ham**	*ham*
ice cream	**hufen iâ**	*heevehn yah*
lamb	**oen**	*oyn*
leek	**cennin**	*kehnin*
lemon	**lemwn**	*lehmoon*
lettuce	**letys**	*lehtis*
lobster	**cimwch**	*keemooch*
meat	**cig**	*keeg*
melon	**melon**	*mehlon*
omelette	**omled**	*ohmlehd*
onion	**wynwyn**	*ooinooin*
orange	**oren**	*ohren*
oyster	**wystrys**	*ooistris*
parsnips	**panas**	*pahnas*
peas	**pys**	*pees*
pepper	**pupur**	*pipir*
pineapple	**pinafal**	*peenaval*
pork	**porc**	*pork*
potatoes	**tatws**	*tatoos*
baked potatoes	**tatws pob**	*tatoos pohb*
prawn	**corgimwch**	*korgeemooch*
rice	**reis**	*rays*
salad	**salad**	*salad*
salt	**halen**	*hahlehn*
sauce	**saws**	*sahoos*
sausage	**selsig**	*sehlsig*
soup	**cawl**	*kahool*
tart	**tarten**	*tahrtehn*
toast	**tost**	*tost*
tomato	**tomato**	*tomato*

vegetables	**llysiau**	*lluhsyeh*
vinegar	**finegr**	*vinehgr*
wine	**gwin**	*goo-een*
yogurt	**iogwrt**	*yogoort*

Drinks
Diodydd

beer	**cwrw**	*kooroo*
bitter beer	**cwrw**	*kooroo*
	chwerw	*chooehroo*
dark beer	**cwrw melyn**	*kooroo mehlin*
lager	**lager**	*lager*
brandy	**brandi**	*brandy*
coffee	**coffi**	*kophy*
black coffee	**coffi du**	*kophy dee*
gin	**jin**	*jin*
juice	**sudd**	*seedd*
apple juice	**sudd afal**	*seedd aval*
grapefruit	**sudd**	*seed*
juice	**granffrwyth**	*grahoonphrooeeth*
orange juice	**sudd oren**	*seedd orehn*
lemonade	**lemwnêd**	*lehmoonehd*
milk (N.W.)	**llefrith**	*llevrith*
(S.W.)	**llaeth**	*llaheeth*

| tea | **te** | *teh* |

w/ milk and sugar (N.W.)
te a llefrith a siwgr
teh ah llevrith ah shoogoor

w/ milk and sugar (S.W.)
te a llaeth a siwgr
teh ah llaheeth ah shoogoor

w/o milk (N.W.)
te heb lefrith
teh hehb levrith

w/o milk (S.W.)
te heb laeth
teh hehb laheeth

water	**dŵr**	*door*
whiskey	**whisgi**	*hooisgy*
wine	**gwin**	*gooeen*
dry wine	**gwin sych**	*gooeen seech*
red wine	**gwin coch**	*gooeen kohch*
sherry	**sieri**	*shehry*
sweet wine	**gwin melys**	*gooeen mehlis*
white wine	**gwin gwyn**	*gooeen gooin*
a bottle of …	**potelaid o …**	*potehlehd o*
a cup of …	**cwpaned o …**	*koopanehd o*
a glass of …	**gwydraid o …**	*gooidrehd o*
non-alcoholic	**dialcohol**	*deealkohol*

OUT AND ABOUT
O GWMPAS Y WLAD

Weather
Tywydd

The weather's fine.
Mae'r tywydd yn braf.
maheer tuhooidd uhn brahv

It's …
Mae hi'n …
mahee heen

… cloudy	**gymylog**	*guhmuhlog*
… cold	**oer**	*oheer*
… very cold	**oer iawn**	*oheer yahoon*
… fine	**braf**	*brahv*
… hot	**boeth**	*boheeth*
… raining	**bwrw glaw**	*booroo glahoo*
… snowing	**bwrw eira**	*booroo ayrah*
… sunny	**heulog**	*haylog*
… wet	**wlyb**	*ooleeb*
… windy	**wyntog**	*oointog*

	Yes.	No.
Is it going to be fine?		
Fydd hi'n braf?	**Bydd.**	**Na.**
veedd heen brahv	*beedd*	*nah*

	Yes.	No.
Will the weather get better?		
Fydd y tywydd yn gwella?	**Bydd.**	**Na.**
veedd uh tuhooidd uhn gooehlla	*beedd*	*nah*

	Yes.	No.
Do I need to take a coat?		
Oes angen i fi fynd â chot?	**Oes.**	**Na.**
oys angehn ee vee vind ah chot	*oys*	*nah*

It's going to …
Mae hi'n mynd i …
mahee heen mihnd i

… be fine	**fod yn braf**	*vohd uhn brav*
… be dry	**fod yn sych**	*vohd uhn seech*
… rain	**fwrw glaw**	*vooroo glahoo*

It's been very nice.
Mae hi wedi bod yn braf iawn.
mahee hee ooehdy bod uhn brahv yahoon

In the Pub
Yn y dafarn

Wales has many fine pubs and taverns, especially in villages and rural areas. Pub chains dominate the city centers, and although some of these offer decent food, they do not compare in atmosphere to the numerous smaller, privately run pubs.

May I have a pint please?
Ga i beint os gwelwch yn dda?
ga ee baynt os gooehlooch uhn ddah

A pint of beer and a glass of wine.
Peint o gwrw a gwydraid o win.
paynt o gooroo a gooidrehd o ooeen

Half a pint of lager.
Hanner peint o lager.
hahner paynt o lahger

Do you make food?
Ydych chi'n gwneud bwyd?
uhdich cheen goonayd booeed

It's my round.
Fy rownd i yw hi.
vuh rohoond ee ioo hee

May we smoke?
Gawn ni smygu?
gahoon nee smuhgee

Is there a non-smoking area?
Oes ardal dim ysgmygu?
oys ahrdal dim uhsmuhgee

Do you have a beer garden?
Oes gardd gwrw gyda chi?
oys gardd gooroo guhda chee

bar	**bar**	*bahr*
lounge	**lolfa**	*lolva*
toilet	**tŷ bach**	*tee bach*
gentlemen	**dynion**	*duhnyon*
ladies	**merched**	*mehrchehd*

Beaches
Ar y traeth

There are many fine beaches along the coasts of Wales. Most have fine yellow sand and clear blue water. Beaches that are particularly notable for clean water are awarded the Blue Flag.

Most beaches are safe for swimming. One should, however, be careful of the undertow created by tides and the flow of rivers into the sea. Lifeguards are on duty during the day in most locations.

Surfing is best on beaches which directly face the Atlantic Ocean.

Where is the best beach?
Ble mae'r traeth gorau?
bleh maheer traheeth gohreh

Is it safe to swim?
Ydy hi'n ddiogel nofio?
uhdee heen ddyogehl novyo

Where can we park?
Ble gallwn ni barcio?
bleh galloon nee barkyo

When is high tide?
Pryd mae'r llanw i mewn?
preed maheer llanoo ee mehoon

Is the sea warm enough to swim?
Ydy'r môr yn ddigon twym i nofio?
uhdeer mohr uhn ddeegon tooeem ee novyo

Is there a café near the beach?
Oes caffe wrth y traeth?
oys kapheh oorth uh traheeth

Is the sea clean?
Ydy'r môr yn lân?
uhdeer mohr uhn lahn

Is it possible to …?
Ydy hi'n bosibl …?
uhdee heen bosibl

rent a boat	**llogi cwch**	*llogee kooch*
sail	**hwylio**	*hooeelyo*

surfboard	**syrffio**	*suhrphyo*
swim	**nofio**	*novyo*
waterski	**sgïo dŵr**	*sgeeo door*
windsurf	**hwylfyrddio**	*hooeelvuhrddyo*

The cliffs are beautiful.
Mae'r clogwyni'n brydferth.
maheer clogooeeneen bruhdvehrth

The cliffs are dangerous.
Mae'r clogwyni'n beryglus.
maheer clogooeeneen behruhglis

Sports
Chwaraeon

Wales has many sports facilities. There are fine golf courses in all parts of the country. Tennis facilities and swimming pools are available in most towns.

Popular spectator sports include rugby and football in winter, and cricket in summer. The major rugby teams are in Llanelli, Swansea/Neath, Cardiff, and Newport in southern Wales. Football (soccer) teams can be found in most towns, but the major ones are in Swansea, Cardiff, and Wrexham. Little or no American football is played.

Where can we play …?
Ble gallwn ni chwarae …?
bleh galloon nee chooahreh

| golf | **golff** | *golph* |
| tennis | **tennis** | *tehnis* |

Where is the nearest swimming pool?
Ble mae'r pwll nofio agosaf?
bleh maheer pooll novyo agosa

Swimming for two adults, please.
Nofio i ddau oedolyn, os gwelwch yn dda.
novyo ee ddahee oydolin, os gooehlooch uhn dda

Where is the changing room?
Ble mae'r stafell newid?
bleh maheer stavehll nehooid

Are there clothes lockers?
Oes loceri dillad?
oys lokehry dillad

Is there a gym in the hotel?
Oes campfa yn y gwesty?
oys kampva uhn uh gooehstee

Where can we see a … game?
Ble gallwn ni weld gêm …?
ble galloon nee ooehld gehm

cricket	**criced**	*krikehd*
football	**pêl-droed**	*pehl droyd*
rugby	**rygbi**	*rughby*

It is possible to …
Ydy hi'n bosibl …
uhdee heen bosibl

| fish | **pysgota** | *puhsgota* |
| go riding | **marchogaeth** | *marchohgaheeth* |

Useful terms

goal	**gôl**	*gohl*
half-time	**hanner amser**	*hanehr amsehr*
try	**cais**	*kahees*

Who is winning?
Pwy sy'n ennill?
pooee seen ehnill

Entertainment
Adloniant

Special Welsh festivals, called *eisteddfod*, are cultural competitions, involving poetry, singing, instrument playing, dancing, and other artforms. The *eisteddfodau* are special Welsh festivals featuring competitions in many artforms, including poetry, music, and dancing. Some are held locally, whereas others are national or international events.

The Youth National Eisteddfod (*Eisteddfod yr Urdd*) is held for a week in a different location each year. The location alternates between northern and southern Wales. It is held during the schools' half-term holiday at the end of May andor beginning of June. This is Europe's biggest youth cultural festival. All activities are conducted in Welsh.

The National Eisteddfod of Wales (*Eisteddfod Genedlaethol Cymru*) is also held for a week every year, again at alternate locations in northern and southern Wales. Held during the first full week of August, this is Wales' most important cultural event. Welsh is the sole language of competition.

This *eisteddfod* maintains traditions established at *eisteddfods* dating from those held by the Lord Rhys at Cardigan in the 12th century. A chair is given to the winning poet writing in the Welsh strict meters (*cynghanedd*), the crown is given for a poem in free verse, and a prose medal is given for prose writing. Prizes are also awarded to singers, choirs, bands, artists, dramatists, novelists, and others. Information on the national *Eisteddfod* is available from the Eisteddfod Office, 40 Parc Tŷ Glas, Llanishen, Cardiff, CF4 5WU.

The annual International Musical Eisteddfod is held in July at Llangollen.

Wales has many cinemas and theaters. The National Opera Company of Wales performs in Swansea and Llandudno and is based at the 1,900 seat performance hall at the Millennium Centre, Cardiff, which opened in 2004. There are nightclubs in all towns. Although much of the entertainment is in English, following Anglo-American trends, Welsh medium evenings, (evenings in which Welsh is spoken), are commonplace in western and northern Wales. Special Welsh medium (language) events are held in all parts of Wales. To find out details of these, the best way is to ask at Welsh bookstores, which can be found in most medium-sized towns. Other places to look are post offices and other shops.

Is there a good nightclub here?
Oes clwb nos da yma?
oys kloob nohs dah uhma

What's showing at the theater?
Beth sy yn y theatr?
behth see uhn uh thehahtr

When does the film start?
Pryd mae'r ffilm yn dechrau?
preed maheer philm uhn dehchreh

Is there a movie theater nearby?
Oes sinema yn agos?
oys sinehma uhn agos

What is the entrance fee?
Beth yw'r tâl mynediad?
behth ioor tahl muhnehdyad

Two tickets, please.
Dau docyn os gwelwch yn dda.
dahee dokin os gooehlooch uhn ddah

One adult and one child.
Un oedolyn ac un plentyn.
een oydolin ak een plehntin

Is it suitable for children?
Ydy e'n addas i blant?
uhdee ehn addas ee blant

When does the evening show start?
Pryd mae'r noson yn dechrau?
preed maheer noson uhn dehchreh

May I buy tickets here?
Alla i brynu tocynnau fan hyn?
alla ee bruhnee tokuhneh van hin

Who's performing?
Pwy sy'n perfformio?
poee seen pehrphormyo

Are they a good band?
Ydyn nhw'n fand da?
uhdin nhoon vand da

When does the evening show end?
Pryd mae'r noson yn gorffen?
preed maheer noson uhn gorphen

Castles and Museums
Cestyll, amgueddfeydd ac ati

Public museums currently offer free admission. These museums include the national museums of Wales, the national museum of Welsh life at St. Fagan's, and many local public galleries. Castles and monuments in the care of Cadw, the Welsh Heritage Body, are open throughout the year, but they charge an entrance fee. Houses and mansions in the care of the National Trust also charge a fee, and many do not open until 11 A.M. Many museums are closed on Monday.

Many Welsh castles date from the 13th century, when Wales was conquered by both the Anglos and Normans. There are, however, many ruins, including those from the Roman period. The most notable are at Caernarfon in northern Wales and Caerleon in southern Wales. The ruins of the inland castles of Welsh princes and kings are open to visitors.

Other tourist attractions include the Roman gold mines at Dolaucothi, near Llandeilo There are also the underground coal mines in the Rhondda valley and in Blaenafon, Gwent. One can also visit the underground slate quarries at Blaenau Ffestiniog and the surrounding areas.

Where is the museum?
Ble mae'r amgueddfa?
Bleh maheer amgee-ehddva

Is the castle open?
Ydy'r castell ar agor?
uhdeer kastehll ar agor

What is the entrance fee?
Beth yw'r tâl mynediad?
behth ioor tahl muhnedyad

Can we take photographs?
Allwn ni dynnu lluniau?
alloon nee duhny llinyeh

What time does the gallery open?
Pryd mae'r oriel yn agor?
preed maheer oryel uhn agor

Is it open on Monday?
Ydy e ar agor ddydd Llun?
uhdee eh ar agor ddeedd lleen

What is this place's history?
Beth yw hanes y lle 'ma?
behth ioo hanehs uh lle ma

Can I buy a brochure?
Alla i brynu llyfryn?
alla ee bruhny lluhvrin

Have you got postcards?
Oes cardiau post gyda chi?
oys kardyeh post guhda chee

Is there a good view?
Oes golygfa dda?
oys goluhgva ddah

When was this built?
Pryd cafodd hwn ei adeiladu?
preed kavodd hoon ay adaylahdy

The castle was built by the Normans.
Y Normaniaid adeiladodd y castell.
uh normanyaheed adayladodd uh kastell

Were the Romans here?
Oedd y Rhufeiniaid yma?
oedd uh rhivaynyaheed uhma

Can we buy a season ticket?
Allwn ni brynu tocyn tymor?
alloon nee bruhny tokin tuhmor

Do you sell calendars?
Ydych chi'n gwerthu calendrau?
uhdich cheen gooehrthy kalehndreh

How much does it cost?
Beth yw'r gost?
behth ioor gost

Going to Chapel
Mynd i'r capel

There are many chapels in Wales. Going to chapel on Sunday morning—services usually start around 10:30 and last an hour—is a good way of hearing Welsh spoken, and hearing the singing of Welsh hymns.

Where is the chapel?
Ble mae'r capel?
bleh maheer kapehl

Is there a Welsh service on Sunday?
Oes gwasanaeth Cymraeg ddydd Sul?
oys gooasanaheeth kuhmraheeg ddeedd seel

Who is the minister?
Pwy yw'r gweinidog?
pooee ioor gooayneedog

What time is the service?
Pryd mae'r gwasanaeth?
preed maheer gooasanaheeth

Useful terms

Baptists	**Bedyddwyr**	
	behuhddooir	
Church in Wales	**yr Eglwys yng Nghymru**	
	uhr eglooees uhng nghuhmry	
collection	**casgliad**	
	kasglyad	
Independents	**Annibynwyr**	
	anibuhnooir	
Methodists	**Methodistiaid**	
	methodistyaheed	

SHOPPING
SIOPA

The main shopping areas are in the town centers, and also in a growing number of out-of-town shopping malls. There are a few factory shopping centers (the equivalent of such American chains as Wal-Mart) where designer goods are more inexpensive. Gifts for tourists are best found in the town centers and village shops, which have ample stocks of locally produced crafts.

Welsh bookstores are a good source of Welsh- and English-language books on Wales, and many also sell Welsh crafts. Chain bookstores also stock many Welsh-language books, as well as titles of local interest.

Objects made from Welsh slate, coal, or wood make excellent gifts. The love spoons carved by local craftsmen are especially notable. Wool goods are also popular, as are the items produced by local glass and pottery artisans

One should never underestimate the feast offered by Welsh produce, the many varieties of Welsh cheese, and the growing variety of Welsh wine, whiskey, and other spirits.

The markets in Welsh towns are always an attraction, with a variety of stalls selling such items as fresh food, crafts, and other items.

Do you sell …?
Ydych chi'n gwerthu …?
uhdich cheen gooehrthy

Do you have …?
Oes … gyda chi?
oys … guhda chee

I would like to have …
Fe hoffwn i gael …
veh hophoon ee gaheel

May I see another one?
Alla i weld un arall?
alla ee ooehld een arall

I'm just looking.
Dim ond edrych rydw i.
dim ond edrich ruhdoo ee

Where are the …?
Ble mae'r …?
bleh maheer

Where is the main street for shopping?
Ble mae'r brif stryd siopa?
bleh maheer breev streed shopa

Is there a supermarket here?
Oes archfarchnad yma?
oys archvarchnad uhma

Where is a Welsh bookstore?
Ble mae'r siop llyfrau Cymraeg?
bleh maheer shop lluhvreh kuhmraheeg

Where can I buy …?
Ble galla i brynu …?
bleh galla ee bruhny

I like this one.
Rwy'n hoffi hwn.
rooeen hophy hoona

I like that one.
Rwy'n hoffi hwn'na.
rooeen hophy hoona

Do you have one that is less expensive?
Oes un llai drud 'da chi?
oys een llahee dreed da chee

This is rather expensive.
Mae hwn braidd yn ddrud.
mahee hoon braheedd uhn ddreed

This is too big.
Mae hwn yn rhy fawr.
mahee hoon uhn rhee vahoor

This is too small.
Mae hwn yn rhy fach.
mahee hoon uhn rhee vach

Do you have anything else?
Oes rhywbeth arall 'da chi?
oys rhioobeth arall da chee

How much does it cost?
Beth yw'r pris?
behth ioor prees

How much is it?
Faint yw e?
vaheent ioo eh

May I have a pound of …?
Ga i bwys o …?
ga ee booees o

Half a pound of … please.
Hanner pwys o … os gwelwch yn dda.
hanehr pooees o … os gooehlooch uhn ddah

Four ounces of …
Pedair owns o …
pehdaheer ohoons o

Will you accept a check?
Ydych chi'n derbyn siec?
uhdich cheen dehrbin shek

May I pay with a credit card?
Alla i dalu â cherdyn?
alla ee dahly ah chehrdin

Can you pack it?
Allwch chi'i bacio fe?
allooch chee bahkyo veh

I am looking for a …
Rwy'n chwilio am …
rooeen chooilyo am

I don't like that one.
Dw i ddim yn hoffi hwn'na.
doo ee ddim uhn hophy hoona

Welsh Bookstores
Siopau llyfrau Cymraeg

There are Welsh bookstores in most towns. They sell Welsh language books, English language books on Wales, and Welsh music and videos. One may also find crafts for sale. As Welsh literature and history go back 1,500 years or so, there is a wealth of material awaiting those who look. There are numerous books intended for those looking to learn Welsh, as well as many titles for children and young people.

Welsh music prides itself on its singers. The baritone Bryn Terfel is Wales' latest star on the world stage. Choirs abound throughout the island, as do folk groups. Welsh folk music is available on CDs. Dafydd Iwan has been a leading folk singer for more than a generation. Bob Delyn (Twm Morys) is an exponent of Welsh/Celtic folk music.

Do you have a dictionary?
Oes geiriadur gyda chi?
oys gayryadir guhda chee

I'm looking for a book on Wales.
Rwy'n chwilio am lyfr ar Gymru.
rooeen chooilyo am luhvir ar guhmry

Is it bilingual?
Ydy e'n ddwyieithog?
uhdee ehn ddooee-yaythog

Do you have a map of Wales?
Oes map o Gymru gyda chi?
oys map o guhmry guhda chee

Do you sell love spoons?
Ydych chi'n gwerthu llwyau caru?
uhdich cheen gooehrthy llooee-eh kahry

Do you have CDs in Welsh?
Oes CDs Cymraeg 'da chi?
oys seedees kuhmraheeg guhda chee

Do you have children's books?
Oes llyfrau plant 'da chi?
oys lluhvreh plant da chee

Do you have a Welsh calendar?
Oes calendr Cymreig 'da chi?
oys kalendr kuhmrayg da chee

I'm looking for a book with pictures of Wales.
Rwy'n chwilio am lyfr gyda lluniau o Gymru.
rooeen chooilyo am luhvir guhda llinyeh o guhmry

Do you sell postcards?
Ydych chi'n gwerthu cardiau post?
uhdich cheen gooehrthy kardyeh post

Do you sell stamps?
Ydych chi'n gwerthu stampiau?
uhdich cheen gooehrthy stampyeh

How much are stamps to the USA?
Faint yw stampiau i'r Unol Daleithiau?
vaheent ioo stampyeh eer eenol dahlaythyeh

Do you have a good book on Welsh literature?
Oes llyfr da 'da chi ar lenyddiaeth Gymraeg?
*oys lluhvir dah da chee ar lenuhddyaheeth
    guhmraheeg*

I'm looking for a book on Welsh history.
Rwy'n chwilio am lyfr ar hanes Cymru.
rooeen chooilyo am luhvr ar hanehs kuhmry

Can you send it to me at home?
Allwch chi'i anfon e ata i gartref?
allooch chee anvon eh ata ee gartreh

Can I order it?
Alla i'i archebu e?
alla ee archebee eh

Useful words

book	**llyfr**	*lluhvr*
calendar	**calendr**	*kalehndr*
CD	**CD**	*see-dee*
history	**hanes**	*hanehs*
literature	**llenyddiaeth**	*llenuhddyaheeth*
novel	**nofel**	*novel*
poetry	**barddoniaeth**	*barddonyaheeth*
postcard	**cerdyn post**	*kerdin post*
record	**record**	*rekord*
stamp	**stamp**	*stamp*
video	**fideo**	*vidyo*

Markets and Supermarkets
Marchnadoedd ac Archfarchnadoedd

Be on the lookout for local produce, including cheese, meat and fish, and bakery products. Cockles and laver bread are available at the Swansea market. Most Welsh towns have an indoor market, with many individual stalls selling a variety of goods.

Where is/are the …?
Ble mae'r …?
bleh maheer

apples	**afalau**	*avaleh*
beef	**eidion**	*aydyon*
bread	**bara**	*bara*
cakes	**teisennau**	*taysehneh*
carrots	**moron**	*mohron*
cereals	**grawnfwyd**	*grahoonvooeed*
chicken	**cyw iâr**	*kioo yahr*
eggs	**wyau**	*ooee-eh*
fish	**pysgod**	*puhsgod*
frozen food	**bwyd rhew**	*booeed rhehoo*
fruit	**ffrwythau**	*phrooeetheh*
ice cream	**hufen iâ**	*heevehn yah*
jam	**jam**	*jam*
juices	**suddoedd**	*seeddoydd*
lamb	**oen**	*oyn*
meat	**cig**	*keeg*
milk (N.W.)	**llefrith**	*llevrith*
milk (S.W.)	**llaeth**	*llaheeth*
newspapers	**papurau newydd**	*papireh nehooidd*
oil	**olew**	*ohlehoo*
oranges	**orenau**	*orehneh*
pork	**porc**	*pork*
potatoes	**tatws**	*tatoos*
rice	**reis**	*rays*
salt	**halen**	*hahlehn*
soap	**sebon**	*sehbon*
sugar	**siwgr**	*shoogoor*
tins	**tuniau**	*tinyeh*
toilet paper	**papur tŷ bach**	*papir tee bach*
turkey	**twrci**	*toorky*
vegetables	**llysiau**	*lluhsyeh*

washing	**powdr**	*pohoodoor*
powder	**golchi**	*golchy*
wines	**gwinoedd**	*gooeenoydd*
yogurt	**iogwrt**	*yogoort*

I can't find the …
Dw i ddim yn gallu ffeindio'r …
doo ee ddim uhn gally phayndyor

Do you have change?
Oes newid gyda chi?
oys nehooid guhda chee

I'm looking for the …
Rwy'n chwilio am y …
rooeen chooilyo am uh

Six eggs, please.
Chwech o wyau os gwelwch yn dda.
chooehch o ooee-eh os gooehlooch uhn ddah

Half a pound of butter.
Hanner pwys o fenyn.
hanehr pooees o venin

A box of matches.
Blwch o fatsys.
blooch o vatshis

Half a kilo of apples.
Hanner cilo o afalau.
hanehr keelo o avaleh

Four oranges.
Pedair oren.
pedaheer orehn

A pint of milk.
Peint o laeth.
paynt o laheeth

Three slices of ham.
Tair tafell o ham.
taheer tavehll o ham

A bar of chocolate.
Bar o siocled.
bar o shoklehd

A packet of crisps.
Pecyn o greision.
pehkin o graysyon

A packet of biscuits.
Pecyn o fisgedi.
pekin o visgehdy

A pound of cheese.
Pwys o gaws.
pooees o gahoos

A tin of soup.
Tun o gawl.
tin o gahool

A bottle of wine.
Potelaid o win.
potehlehd o oo-een

A packet of sugar.
Pecyn o siwgr.
pekin o shoogoor

Can I help you?
Alla i'ch helpu chi?
alla eech hehlpy chee

Do you want anything else?
Ydych chi eisiau rhywbeth arall?
uhdich chi eesheh rhioobeth arall

Newsstands
Y siop bapur

A newspaper, please.
Papur newydd, os gwelwch yn dda.
papir nehooidd, os gooehlooch uhn ddah

Do you have a local newspaper for sale?
Ydych chi'n gwerthu papur lleol?
uhdich cheen gooehrthy papir llehol

Do you sell Welsh magazines?
Ydych chi'n gwerthu cylchgronau Cymraeg?
udich cheen gooehrthy kuhlchgroneh kymraheeg

Do you have postcards?
Oes cardiau post gyda chi?
oys kardyeh post guhda chee

Do you sell stamps?
Ydych chi'n gwerthu stampiau?
uhdich cheen gooehrthy stampyeh

Do you have a ballpoint pen?
Oes beiro gyda chi?
oys bayro guhda chee

I would like some envelopes.
Rwy eisiau rhai amlenni.
rooee eesheh rhahee amlehny

Do you sell writing paper?
Ydych chi'n gwerthu papur sgrifennu?
uhdich cheen gooehrthy papir sgriveny

Do you have a map of the town?
Oes map o'r dre gyda chi?
oys map or dreh guhda chee

A packet of cigarettes, please.
Pecyn o sigarets, os gwelwch yn dda.
pehkin o sigarehts, os gooelooch uhn ddah

Can I add minutes to my cell phone here?
Alla i roi arian i'm ffôn symudol i fan hyn?
alla ee roy aryan eem phohn suhmeedol ee van hin

Do you sell cell phone cards?
Ydych chi'n gwerthu cardiau ffôn symudol?
uhdich cheen gooerthy kardyeh phohn suhmeedol

Do you sell film?
Ydych chi'n gwerthu ffilmiau?
uhdich cheen gooehrthy philmyeh

A box of chocolates, please.
Blwch o siocledi, os gwelwch yn dda.
blooch o shoklehdy, os gooehlooch uhn dda

At the Pharmacist
Gyda'r fferyllydd

Pharmacies and drugstores are called chemist shops in Wales and can be found in every town. The stores are either independently owned or part of a larger chain. Pharmacists are called chemists or *fferyllydd* (pronounced pheruhllidd) in Wales. They are well trained and can help you in most instances of minor illness. Anything serious, however, should be treated by a doctor, as a number of medicines, e.g. antibiotics, are available only through prescription. It's quite common for Welsh speakers to use the English word for necessities such as shaving cream in a Welsh sentence.

Do you have something for …?
Oes rhywbeth gyda chi ar gyfer …?
oys rhioobeth guhda chee ar guhver

backache	**cefn tost**	*kevn tost*
a cold	**annwyd**	*anooid*
constipation	**rhwymedd**	*rhooeemedd*
a cough	**peswch**	*pesooch*
diarrhea	**dolur rhydd**	*dolir rheedd*
fever	**gwres**	*goorehs*
a headache (N.W.)	**cur pen**	*keer pen*
(S.W.)	**pen tost**	*pen tost*
pain	**poen**	*poyn*
a sore throat (N.W.)	**dolur gwddf**	*dolir gooddv*
(S.W.)	**llwnc tost**	*lloonk tost*
a stomachache	**stumog tost**	*stimog tost*

Is it safe for children?
Ydy e'n ddiogel i blant?
uhdee ehn ddyogehl ee blant

How often should I take it?
Pa mor aml dylwn i'i gymryd e?
pa mor aml duhloon ee guhmryd eh

I would like …
Rydw i eisiau …
ruhdw ee eesheh

a bandage	**rhwymyn**	*rhooeemin*
disinfectant	**diheintydd**	*deehayntidd*
hair spray	**chwistrell gwallt**	*chooistrehll gooallt*
hand cream	**hufen dwylo**	*heevehn dooeelo*
ointment	**eli**	*ehly*
pain killer	**lladdwr poen**	*lladdoor poyn*
razor blades	**llafnau eillio**	*llavneh ayllyo*
sanitary towels	**tywelion mislif**	*tuhooehlyon misliv*
shampoo	**siampŵ**	*shampoo*
shaving cream	**hufen eillio**	*heevehn ayllyo*
soap	**sebon**	*sebon*
sun cream	**hufen haul**	*heevehn haheel*
suntan lotion	**hylif haul**	*huhliv haheel*
toothpaste	**past dannedd**	*past danedd*
towels	**tywelion**	*tuhooelyon*

Photography
Ffotograffiaeth

Film is available at most newsstands and drugstores, as well as photography shops. It can be developed at newsstands, drugstores, photography shops, and special film development stores. The drugstores and film developing stores often have one-hour service available. All stores that offer film developing should have overnight service, which includes printing pictures taken with digital cameras.

I want to buy a roll of … film.
Dw i eisiau prynu ffilm …
doo ee eesheh pruhny philm

> black-and-white
> **du a gwyn**
> *dee ah goohin*

> color
> **lliw**
> *llihoo*

> slide
> **sleidiau**
> *slaydyahee*

> 24-exposure
> **dau ddeg pedwar llun**
> *dahee ddehg pedooar lleen*

> 36-exposure
> **tri deg chwe llun**
> *tree dehg chooeh lleen*

I would like a tape for a camcorder.
Dw i eisiau tâp i'r camera fideo.
doo ee eesheh tahp eer kamera video

Do you have a disposable camera?
Oes camera un tro gyda chi?
oys kamera een tro guhda chee

Can you look at my camera?
Allwch chi edrych ar fy nghamera?
allooch chee edrich ar vuh nghamera

Something is wrong.
Mae rhywbeth yn bod.
mahee rhioobeth uhn bod

Can you put the film in?
Allwch chi roi'r ffilm i mewn?
alloch chee royr philm ee mehoon

Can you take the film out?
Allwch chi gymryd y ffilm allan?
alloch chee guhmrid uh philm allan

I would like a battery for the camera.
Dw i eisiau bateri i'r camera.
doo ee eesheh batery eer kamera

Can you develop a roll of film …?
Allwch chi ddatblygu ffilm …?
allooch chee ddatbluhgy philm …

in an hour	**mewn awr**	*mehoon ahoor*
in a day	**mewn diwrnod**	*mehoon dioornod*
in three days	**mewn tri dydd**	*mehoon tree deedd*

When will the photos be ready?
Pryd bydd y lluniau'n barod?
preed beedd uh llihnyehn barod

At the Hairdresser's
Yn y Siop trin gwallt

Do you have a opening in the schedule today?
Oes apwyntiad rhydd gyda chi heddiw?
oys apooeentyad rheedd guhda chee hehddioo

I would like a haircut.
Dw i eisiau torri fy ngwallt.
doo ee eesheh tohry vuh ngooallt

A trim all around, please.
Ychydig i ffwrdd o bob man, os gwelwch yn dda.
uhchuhdig ee phoordd o bob man, os gooehlooch uhn ddah

Please cut my hair short.
Torrwch fy ngwallt yn fyr, os gwelwch yn dda.
torooch vuh ngwallt uhn vihr, os gooehlooch uhn ddah

I would like a …
Hoffwn i gael …
hophoon ee gaheel

   … a blow-dry
   … chwyth-sychu
   … cooeeth suhchy

   … a hair-spray
   … chwistrell gwallt
   … chooistrell gooallt

   … highlights
   … darnau golau
   … darneh goleh

   … a perm
   … perm
   … pehrm

   … a shampoo and set
   … siampŵ a set
   … shampoo a set

… a shampoo
… siampŵ
… shampoo

A little shorter.
Ychydig yn fyrrach.
uhchuhdig uhn virach

A little longer.
Ychydig yn hirach.
uchudig uhn hirach

In the front.
Yn y blaen.
uhn uh blahn

In the back.
Yn y cefn.
uhn uh kevn

On top.
Ar y pen.
ar uh pen

On the sides.
Ar yr ochrau.
ar uhr ochreh

Not too long.
Ddim yn rhy hir.
ddim uhn rhee heer

Not too short.
Ddim yn rhy fyr.
ddim uhn rhee vir

How much does a perm cost?
Beth yw pris perm?
behth ioo prees perm?

Laundry
Londri

Can I leave my clothes here?
Alla i adael fy nillad yma?
alla ee adehl vuh nillad uhma

Can you wash these clothes?
Allwch chi olchi'r dillad yma?
allooch chee olchyr dillad uhma

When should I call back?
Pryd dylwn i alw'n ôl?
preed duhloon ee aloon ohl

When will they be ready?
Pryd byddan nhw'n barod?
preed buhddan nhoon barod

Do you dry-clean clothes?
Ydych chi'n sychlanhau dillad?
uhdich cheen seechlanhahee dillad

Can you wash and press these …?
Allwch chi olchi a smwddio'r … yma?
allooch chee olchy a smooddyo'r … uhma

| … blouses | **… blowsys** | *blohoosis* |
| … clothes | **… dillad** | *dillad* |

| ... dresses | **... gwisgoedd** | *gooisgoydd* |
| ... shirts | **... crysau** | *kruhseh* |

There is a(n) ... stain on it.
Mae staen ... arno fe.
mahee staheen ... arno veh

... grass	**... glaswellt**	*glasooehllt*
... ink	**... inc**	*ink*
... oil	**... olew**	*olehoo*
... wine	**... gwin**	*gooeen*

In a Clothing Store
Mewn siop ddillad

Clothing sizes:

Women

American	UK (Wales)	European
8	10	36
10	12	38
12	14	40
14	16	42
16	18	44
18	20	46

Men

Suits, coats and shirts are the same in the U.K. as in U.S.

Shoes:

American	UK	European
6	5	38
7	6	39
7½	7	40
8	8	41
8½	9	42
9	10	43
10	11	44
11	12	45

I'm looking for a …
Rwy'n chwilio am …
rooen chooilyo am

jacket	**siaced**	*shakehd*
jeans	**jîns**	*jeens*
jumper	**siwmper**	*shoompehr*
sandals	**sandalau**	*sandahleh*
scarf	**sgarff**	*sgarph*
shoes	**sgidiau**	*sgidyeh*
skirt	**sgert**	*sgehrt*
socks	**sanau**	*saneh*
suit	**siwt**	*sihoot*

I would like …
Rydw i eisiau …
ruhdoo ee eesheh

a belt	**gwregys**	*goorehgis*
a blouse	**blows**	*blohoosa*
a bra	**bronglwm**	*brongloom*
clothes	**dillad**	*dillad*
a coat	**cot**	*cot*
pants	**trowsus**	*trohoosis*

a raincoat	**cot law**	*cot lahoo*
a shirt	**crys**	*crees*
shorts	**siorts**	*shorts*
a swimsuit	**siwt nofio**	*sioot novyo*

What size would you like?
Pa faint ry'ch chi eisiau?
pa vaheent reech chee eesheh

Does this fit?
Ydy hwn yn ffitio?
uhdee hoon uhn phityo

Which color would you like?
Pa liw ry'ch chi eisiau?
pa lioo reeh chee eesheh

blue	**glas**	*glahs*
brown	**brown**	*bro-oon*
green	**gwyrdd**	*gooirdd*
gray	**llwyd**	*llooeed*
orange	**oren**	*orehn*
red	**coch**	*kohch*
white	**gwyn**	*gooin*
yellow	**melyn**	*mehlin*

May I try this on?
Alla i wisgo hwn?
alla ee ooisgoh hoon

Where can I try this on?
Ble galla i wisgo hwn?
bleh galla ee ooisgo hoon

Do you have another size?
Oes maint arall gyda chi?
oys maheent arall guhda chee

Can I exchange it if it doesn't fit?
Alla i'i newid e os bydd e ddim yn ffitio?
alla ee nehooid eh os beedd eh ddim uhn phityo

Can I bring it back?
Alla i ddod ag e nôl?
alla ee ddod ag eh nohl

Do you have a smaller one?
Oes un llai 'da chi?
oys een llahee da chee

Do you have a bigger one?
Oes un mwy 'da chi?
oys een mooee da chee

Where can I pay?
Ble galla i dalu?
bleh galla ee dahly

At the Post Office
Yn Swyddfa'r Post

There are two classes of stamps for letters sent inland. Letters and cards sent by first-class post should arrive the next day. Second-class letters should arrive within three days. Postal codes should ensure that letters are delivered promptly. When sending posts abroad, ask for an air mail sticker.

I would like to mail a letter to the U.S.A.
Rydw i eisiau postio llythyr i'r Unol Daleithiau.
*ruhdoo ee eesheh postyo lllythir eer eenol
    dalaythyeh*

What is the price of a stamp to the U.S.A.?
Beth yw pris stamp i'r Unol Daleithiau?
beth ioo prees stamp i'r eenol dalaythyeh

May I have an air mail sticker?
Ga i sticer post awyr?
ga ee stikehr post aooir

Five stamps, please.
Pum stamp os gwelwch yn dda.
pim stamp os gooelooch uhn ddah

I would like to send these postcards to …
Rydw i eisiau anfon y cardiau post yma i …
ruhdoo ee aysheh anvon uh kardieh post uhma ee

A telephone card, please.
Cerdyn ffôn os gwelwch yn dda.
kerdin phohn os gooelooch uhn ddah

Can I cash a check here?
Alla i newid siec yma?
alla ee neooid shek uhma

I would like to send a parcel to …
Rydw i eisiau anfon parsel i …
ruhoo ee eesheh anvon parsel ee

A first-class stamp please.
Stamp dosbarth cyntaf os gwelwch yn dda.
stamp dosbarth kuhntav os gooelooch uhn ddah

Three second-class stamps.
Tri stamp ail ddosbarth.
tree stamp aheel ddosbarth

Using the Internet
Defnyddio'r rhyngrwyd

May I use the Internet, please?
Alla i ddefnyddio'r rhyngrwyd os gwelwch yn dda?
alla ee ddevnuhddyor rhuhngrooeed os gooelooch uhn ddah

May I send an e-mail?
Ga i anfon ebost?
ga ee anvon ebost

How much does it cost for half an hour?
Beth yw'r gost am hanner awr?
beth ioor gost am hanehr ahoor

Do you have an Internet connection?
Oes cysylltiad rhyngrwyd 'da chi?
oys kuhsuhlltyad rhuhngrooeed da chee

Can I check my e-mail here?
Alla i edrych ar fy ebost i yma?
alla ee edrich ar vuh ebost ee uhma

What is your e-mail address?
Beth yw eich cyfeiriad ebost?
beth ioo aych kuhvayryad ebost?

Using the Telephone
Defnyddio'r ffôn

Public phones take coins, credit cards, and telephone cards. (Coins come in denominations of 10p, 20p, 50p, and £1.) To telephone abroad, start with "00" then the number of the country, e.g. USA – 1; Germany –

49. Drop the initial "0" from the local number. To phone a number in Wales or England, use the area code, e.g. Cardiff – 02920; Aberystwyth – 01970; Swansea – 01792, followed by the house or business number.

May I speak to …?
Ga i siarad â …?
ga ee sharad ah

I'm …
… ydw i
… uhdoo ee

I would like to speak to …
Rydw i eisiau siarad â …
ruhdoo ee eesheh sharad ah

What is the code for …?
Beth yw'r cod am …?
beth ioor kohd am

Can you call me back?
Allwch chi fy ffonio i nôl?
allooch chee vuh phonyo i nohl

My number is …
Fy rhif yw …
vuh rheev ioo

At the Bank
Yn y Banc

I would like to exchange some money.
Rydw i eisiau newid arian.
ruhdoo ee eesheh neooid ahryan

Here is my passport.
Dyma fy mhasbort.
duhma vuh mhasbort

Do you charge a commission?
Ydych chi'n codi comisiwn?
uhdich cheen kody komishoon

May I cash a check?
Alla i newid siec?
alla ee neooid shek

May I cash these traveler's checks?
Alla i newid y sieciau teithio 'ma?
alla ee nehooid uh shekyeh taythyo ma

Can I use my credit card to get money?
Alla i ddefnyddio fy ngherdyn i gael arian?
alla ee ddevnuhddyo vyh ngherdin ee gaehl ahryan

I've forgotten my PIN number.
Rydw i wedi anghofio fy rhif PIN.
ruhdoo ee ooehdy anghovyo vuh rheev pin

AT THE DOCTOR'S OR DENTIST'S
GYDA'R MEDDYG NEU'R DEINTYDD

Most doctors work in health centers or private offices. Opening times vary, but most are on or before 8:30 A.M. An appointment may be required, and the nearest health center should be called beforehand to ask for details. If the matter is urgent, after-hours services are available at central health centers and some doctors make housecalls. If emergency service is needed, dial 999.

Health coverage should be obtained before visting Wales and brought on the trip, because, thanks to government arrangements, it will be honored by Welsh health providers. Prescriptions for retirees and children are filled free of charge. Free medical coverage became available throughout Wales in 1997.

If you have had an accident, emergency treatment is available in the Accident and Emergency departments of hospitals—drive there or take a taxi, and give your name and details at the reception desk. You will be seen by the appropriate doctors and nurses.

What exactly is wrong with you?
Beth sy'n bod arnoch chi?
behth seen bod arnoch chee

Do you have a fever?
Oes gwres arnoch chi?
oys goorehs arnoch chee

AT THE DOCTOR'S OR DENTIST'S

Where is the pain?
Ble mae'r boen?
ble maheer boyn

When did you become sick?
Ers pryd rydych chi'n sâl? (N.W.)
ehrs preed uhdich cheen sahl
Ers pryd rydych chi'n dost? (S.W.)
ehrs preed uhdich cheen dost

Do you feel weak?
Ydych chi'n teimlo'n wan?
uhdich cheen taymlon wan

Do you have a toothache?
Ydy'r ddannodd arnoch chi?
uhdeer ddanodd arnoch chee

I have a toothache.
Mae'r ddannodd arna i.
maheer ddanodd arna ee

I'm not feeling well.
Dydw i ddim yn teimlo'n dda.
duhdoo ee ddim uhn taymlon ddah

May I see a doctor?
Ga i weld meddyg?
ga ee ooehld meddig

I would like to see a dentist.
Rydw i eisiau gweld deintydd.
ruhdoo ee eesheh gooehld dayntidd

May I make an appointment?
Ga i wneud apwyntiad?
ga ee oonayd apooeetyad

Can you give me a prescription?
Allwch chi roi papur meddyg i fi?
allooch chee roy papir meddig ee vee

Where is the nearest chemist's [pharmacy]?
Ble mae'r fferyllydd agosa?
bleh maheer pheruhllidd agosa

I have a sore …
Mae … tost 'da fi.
mahee … tost da vee

back	**cefn**	*kevn*
finger	**bys**	*bees*
head	**pen**	*pen*
throat	**llwnc**	*lloonk*
tooth	**dant**	*dant*

I have a sore …
Mae … dost 'da fi.
mahee … dost da vee

arm	**braich**	*braheech*
foot	**troed**	*troyd*
hand	**llaw**	*llahoo*
leg	**coes**	*koys*

I have broken my …
Rwy wedi torri fy …
rooee ooehdy tory vuh

arm	**mraich**	*mraheech*
finger	**mys**	*mees*
foot	**nhroed**	*nhroyd*
hand	**llaw**	*llahoo*
leg	**nghoes**	*nghohees*
rib	**asen**	*asehn*

I am pregnant.
Rwy'n feichiog.
rooeen vaychyog

I'm on the pill.
Rwy ar y bilsen.
rooee ar uh bilsen

I'm diabetic.
Rwy'n ddiabetig.
rooeen ddyahbetig

I'm taking …
Rwy'n cymryd …
rooeen kuhmrid

Would you take my blood pressure?
Allwch chi gymryd fy ngwasgedd gwaed?
allooch chee guhmrid vuh ngooasgedd gooaheed

Would you take a blood test?
Allwch chi wneud prawf gwaed?
allooch chee ooneheed prahoov gooaheed

I need an ambulance.
Mae angen ambiwlans arna i.
mahee angen ambioolans arna ee

Will I have to stay in the hospital?
Fydd rhaid i fi aros yn yr ysbyty?
veedd rhaheed ee vee aros uhn uhr uhsbuhty

Will I be able to go out?
Fydda i'n gallu mynd allan?
vuhdda een gally mind allan

Will I need an operation?
Fydd angen triniaeth arna i?
veedd angen trinyaheeth arna ee

My mouth hurts.
Mae 'ngheg i'n boenus.
mahee nghehg een boynis

I have dentures.
Mae dannedd gosod gyda fi.
mahee danedd gosod guhda vee

The filling has come out.
Mae'r llenwad wedi dod allan.
maheer llenooad ooehdy dod allan

My tooth is broken.
Mae 'nant i wedi torri.
mahee nant ee ooehdy tohry

That hurts.
Mae hynny'n brifo.
mahee huhnyn breevo

Other parts of the body:

ankle	**migwrn**	*meegoorn*
back	**cefn**	*kevn*
bone	**asgwrn**	*asgoorn*
breast	**bron**	*bron*
chest	**brest**	*brest*
ear	**clust**	*clist*
elbow	**penelin**	*penelin*
eye	**llygad**	*lluhgad*
face	**wyneb**	*ooeeneb*
finger	**bys**	*bees*

foot	**troed**	*troyd*
hand	**llaw**	*llahoo*
heart	**calon**	*kalon*
kidney	**aren**	*arehn*
knee	**pen-lin**	*penleen*
liver	**afu**	*avee*
lungs	**ysgyfaint**	*uhsguhvaheent*
mouth	**ceg**	*kehg*
muscle	**cyhyr**	*kuhhir*
neck	**gwddf**	*gooddv*
nose	**trwyn**	*trooeen*
skin	**croen**	*kroyn*
throat	**llwnc**	*lloonk*
wrist	**arddwrn**	*arddoorn*

Emergencies
Gwasanaethau argyfwng

Emergency services are all reached by telephoning 999.

ambulance	**ambiwlans**	*ambioolans*
fire brigade	**brigâd dân**	*brigahd dahn*
help	**help**	*help*
police	**heddlu**	*heddly*

There is a fire.
Mae tân.
mahee tahn

I'm at …
Rydw i yn …
ruhdoo ee uhn

There has been an accident.
Mae damwain wedi bod.
mahee damooaheen ooehdy bod

We need an ambulance.
Mae angen ambiwlans arnon ni.
mahee angen ambioolans arnon nee

We need the fire brigade.
Mae angen y frigâd dân arnon ni.
mahee angen uh vrigahd dahn arnon nee

We need the police.
Mae angen yr heddlu arnon ni.
mahee angen uhr heddly arnon nee

Someone is injured.
Mae rhywun wedi'i anafu.
mahee rhiooin ooehdy anavee

Someone has been killed.
Mae rhywun wedi'i ladd.
mahee rhiooin ooehdy ladd

Someone is drowning.
Mae rhywun yn boddi.
mahee rhiooin uhn boddy

NUMBERS
RHIFAU

1	**un**	*een*
2	**dau**	*dahee*
3	**tri**	*tree*
4	**pedwar**	*pedooar*
5	**pump**	*pimp*
6	**chwech**	*cooehch*
7	**saith**	*saheeth*
8	**wyth**	*ooeeth*
9	**naw**	*nahoo*
10	**deg**	*dehg*
11	**un deg un**	*een dehg een*
12	**un deg dau**	*een dehg dahee*
13	**un deg tri**	*een dehg tree*
14	**un deg pedwar**	*een dehg pedooar*
15	**un deg pump**	*een dehg pimp*
16	**un deg chwech**	*een dehg chooehch*
17	**un deg saith**	*een dehg saheeth*
18	**un deg wyth**	*een dehg ooeeth*
19	**un deg naw**	*een dehg nahoo*
20	**dau ddeg**	*dahee ddehg*
21	**dau ddeg un**	*dahee ddehg een*
22	**dau ddeg dau**	*dahee ddehg dahee*
23	**dau ddeg tri**	*dahee ddehg tree*
30	**tri deg**	*tree dehg*
31	**tri deg un**	*tree dehg een*
40	**pedwar deg**	*pedooar dehg*
41	**pedwar deg un**	*pedooar dehg een*
50	**pum deg**	*pim dehg*
60	**chwe deg**	*chooeh dehg*
70	**saith deg**	*saheeth dehg*
80	**wyth deg**	*ooeeth dehg*

90	**naw deg**	*nahoo dehg*
100	**cant**	*kant*
101	**cant ac un**	*kant ak een*
102	**cant a dau**	*kant a dahee*
110	**cant a deg**	*kant a dehg*
111	**cant un deg un**	*kant een dehg een*
120	**cant dau ddeg**	*kant dahee ddehg*
200	**dau gant**	*dahee gant*
300	**tri chant**	*tree chant*
400	**pedwar cant**	*pedooar kant*
500	**pum cant**	*pim kant*
600	**chwe chant**	*chooeh chant*
700	**saith cant**	*saheeth kant*
800	**wyth cant**	*ooeeth kant*
900	**naw cant**	*nahoo kant*
1000	**mil**	*meel*
2000	**dwy fil**	*doee veel*
3000	**tair mil**	*taheer meel*
4000	**pedair mil**	*pedaheer meel*
1000 000	**miliwn**	*milyoon*

Ordinal Numbers
Trefnolion

1st	**cyntaf**	*kuhntav*
2nd	**ail**	*aheel*
3rd	**trydydd**	*truhdidd*
4th	**pedwerydd**	*pedooehridd*
5th	**pumed**	*pimehd*
6th	**chweched**	*chooehchehd*
7th	**seithfed**	*saythvehd*
8th	**wythfed**	*ooeethvehd*
9th	**nawfed**	*nahoovehd*
10th	**degfed**	*degvehd*

12ᵗʰ	**deuddegfed**	*deheeddegvehd*
15ᵗʰ	**pymthegfed**	*puhmthegvehd*
18ᵗʰ	**deunawfed**	*deheenahoovehd*
20ᵗʰ	**ugeinfed**	*eegeheenvehd*
100ᵗʰ	**canfed**	*kanvehd*

Fractions and Percentages
Ffracsiynau a chanrannau

five percent	**pump y cant**	*pimp uh kant*
double	**dwbl**	*doobl*
half	**hanner**	*hanehr*
quarter	**chwarter**	*chooarter*
third	**traean**	*traheean*
two thirds	**deuparth**	*dayparth*
two fifths	**dwy ran o bump**	*dooee ran o bimp*

Measures
Mesuriadau

Distances on roads are given in miles. One mile is equivalent to approximately 1.6 kilometers. Schools use centimeters, but many people, particular older ones, use inches. One inch is equivalent to approximately 2.5 centimeters.

1 centimeter	=	0.39 inches
1 foot	=	30.5 cm.
1 inch	=	2.54 cm.
1 meter	=	39.37 inches
1 yard	=	0.91 m.

centimeter	**centimetr**	*kentimetr*
foot	**troedfedd**	*troydvedd*
inch	**modfedd**	*modvedd*
kilometer	**cilometr**	*kilometr*
meter	**metr**	*metr*
mile	**milltir**	*milltir*
yard	**llathen**	*llathehn*

Gasoline, called petrol in Wales, is sold in liters. Food should be sold by the kilogram, but many stores still use pounds and ounces. Drinks are sold by the liter, although beer is available in pints and half-pints, and pints of milk are still delivered to doorsteps.

Fluid measures

1 U.S. gallon is equivalent to around 3.8 litres.
1 U.K. gallon is equivalent to around 4.5 litres.
1 U.S. quart = 0.95 litres.
1 U.K. quart = 1.14 litres.

Weights

1 pound is equivalent to around 0.45 kg.
1 kg. is equivanlent to around 2.2 lb.
1 oz. = 28.35 g
1 lb. = 453.6 g

ounce	**owns**	*ohoons*
pint	**peint**	*peheent*
gallon	**galwyn**	*galooeen*
liter	**litr**	*leetr*

Centimeters and inches

To convert centimeters into inches, multiply by 0.39.
To convert inches into centimeters, multiply by 2.54.

Temperatures

To convert centigrade, or Celsius, into degrees Fahrenheit, multiply the degrees centigrade by 1.8 and add 32.

To convert degrees Farhenheit into centigrade, subtract 32 from the degrees Fahrenheit and divide by 18.

Easy to remember degrees:
$16°C = 61°F$
$28°C = 82°F$

Kilometers into miles

To convert kilometers into miles, multiply by 0.62.

50 kilometers = 31 miles
80 kilometers = 50 miles

To convert miles into kilometers, mulitply by 1.6.

Days
Dyddiau

| Monday | **Dydd Llun** | *deedd lleen* |
| Tuesday | **Dydd Mawrth** | *deedd mahoorth* |

Wednesday	**Dydd Mercher**	*deedd mercher*
Thursday	**Dydd Iau**	*deedd iahee*
Friday	**Dydd Gwener**	*deedd gooehner*
Saturday	**Dydd Sadwrn**	*deedd sadoorn*
Sunday	**Dydd Sul**	*deedd seel*

Months
Misoedd

January	**Ionawr**	*yonahoor*
February	**Chwefror**	*chooevror*
March	**Mawrth**	*mahoorth*
April	**Ebrill**	*ebrill*
May	**Mai**	*mahee*
June	**Mehefin**	*mehevin*
July	**Gorffennaf**	*gorphenav*
August	**Awst**	*ahoost*
September	**Medi**	*medee*
October	**Hydref**	*huhdrev*
November	**Tachwedd**	*tachooedd*
December	**Rhagfyr**	*rhagvir*

The months, when spoken in Welsh, are often preceded by the word *mis* ("month"), e.g.

in March
ym mis Mawrth
uhm mees Mahoorth

Seasons
Tymhorau

| Spring | **gwanwyn** | *gooanooin* |
| Summer | **haf** | *hav* |

Autumn	**hydref**	*huhdrev*
Winter	**gaeaf**	*gaheeav*

in spring
yn y gwanwyn
uhn uh gooanooin

in summer
yn yr haf
uhn uhr hav

Holidays
Gwyliau

Bank holiday	**Gŵyl banc**
	gooeel bank
New Year	**Y flwyddyn newydd**
	uh vlooeeddin nehooidd
New Year's Day	**Dydd Calan**
	deedd kalan
Easter	**Y Pasg**
	uh pasg
Easter Monday	**Llun y Pasg**
	lleen uh pasg
May Day	**Calan Mai**
	kalan mahee
Whitsun	**Y Sulgwyn**
	uh silgooin
Boxing Day	**Dydd San Steffan**
	deedd san stephan
Christmas	**Y Nadolig**
	uh nadolig
Christmas Day	**Dydd Nadolig**
	deedd nadolig

Colors
Lliwiau

black	**du**	*dee*
blue	**glas**	*glas*
brown	**brown**	*brohoon*
gold	**aur**	*aheer*
gray	**llwyd**	*llooeed*
orange	**oren**	*orehn*
pink	**pinc**	*pink*
purple	**porffor**	*porphor*
red	**coch**	*kohch*
silver	**arian**	*aryahn*
white	**gwyn**	*gooin*
yellow	**melyn**	*melin*

Animals and Birds
Anifeiliaid ac adar

cat	**cath**	*kahth*
cow	**buwch**.	*biooch*
dog	**ci**.	*kee*
horse	**ceffyl**	*kephil*
kite	**barcut**.	*barkit*
mouse	**llygoden**.	*lluhgodehn*
seagull	**gwylan**	*gooeelan*
sheep	**dafad**	*davad*
sparrow	**aderyn y to**	*adehrin uh toh*
squirrel	**gwiwer**	*gooiooehr*
starling	**drudwy**	*dridooee*
swallow	**gwennol**.	*gooehnol*

Signs
Arwyddion

bank	**banc**	*bank*
beach	**traeth**	*traheeth*
bed & breakfast	**gwely a brecwast**	*gooehly a brekooast*
bridge	**pont**	*pont*
bus station	**gorsaf bysiau**	*gorsav buhsyahee*
café	**caffe**	*kapheh*
castle	**castell**	*kastell*
closed	**ar gau**	*ar gahee*
college	**coleg**	*kolehg*
danger	**perygl**	*perigl*
for sale	**ar werth**	*ar ooerth*
full	**llawn**	*llahoon*
garden	**gardd**	*gardd*
gentlemen	**dynion**	*duhnyon*
hospital	**ysbyty**	*uhsbuhty*
hotel	**gwesty**	*gooehstee*
ladies	**merched**	*merched*
library	**llyfrgell**	*lluhvrgell*
manager	**rheowr**	*rheoloor*
museum	**amgueddfa**	*amgee-eddva*
no smoking	**dim ysmygu**	*dim uhsmuhgee*
open	**ar agor**	*ar agor*
opening hours	**oriau agor**	*orieh agor*
post office	**swyddfa'r post**	*sooeeddvar post*
school	**ysgol**	*uhsgol*
slow	**araf**	*arav*
station	**gorsaf**	*gorsav*
taxi	**tacsi**	*taxi*
theater	**theatr**	*the-ahtr*

town center	**canol y dref**	*kanol uh drev*
town hall	**neuadd y dref**	*neheeadd uh drev*
university	**prifysgol**	*preevuhsgol*

Other Regional Interest Titles from Hippocrene Books

Wales: An Illustrated History
170 pages • 5 x 7 • $12.95pb • 0-7818-0936-3 • (418)

Beginner's Welsh
210 pages • 5½ x 8½ • 0-7818-0589-9 • (712)

Welsh-English/English-Welsh Practical Dictionary
20,000 entries • 252 pages • 4 x 6 • 0-7818-0781-6 • (566)

Welsh-English/English-Welsh Standard Dictionary
50,000 entries • 620 pages • 5¼ x 8½ • 0-7818-0136-2 • (116)

Companion Guide to Britain, England, Scotland & Wales
318 pages • 5½ x 8½ • $14.95pb • 0-7818-0147-8 • (15)

The Celtic World: An Illustrated History
191 pages • 5 x 7 • $12.95pb • 0-7818-1005-1 • (478)

The Scottish-Irish Pub and Hearth Cookbook
Recipes and Lore from Celtic Kitchens
272 pages • 5¾ x 8¾ • $24.95hc • 0-7818-0741-7 • (164)

Classic English Love Poems
143 pages • 6 x 9 • $12.95pb • 0-7818-0895-2 • (283)
143 pages • 6¼ x 9¼ • $17.50hc • 0-7818-0572-4 • (671)

British-American/American-British Dictionary & Phrasebook
1,400 entries • 3¾ x 7 • $11.95pb • 0-7818-0450-7 • (247)

Ireland: An Illustrated History
166 pages • 5¼ x 7¼ • $11.95hc • 0-7818-0693-3 • (782)

Treasury of Irish Love: Poems, Proverbs & Triads
153 pages • 5¼ x 7¼ • $11.95pb • 0-7818-0644-5 • (732)

Feasting Galore Irish-Style
Recipes and Food Lore from the Emerald Isle
144 pages • 5½ x 8½ • $14.95pb • 0-7818-0869-3 • (94)

Companion Guide to Ireland
Second Edition
300 pages • 5½ x 8½ • $14.95pb • 0-7818-0170-2 • (60)

St. Patrick's Secrets
101 Little-Known Truths & Tales of Ireland
150 pages • 5½ x 8½ • $12.95pb • 0-7818-0898-7 • (325)

Beginner's Irish with Audio CD
1 80-minute Audio CD • 150 pages • 5½ x 8½ • $19.95pb •
0-7818-1099-X • (121)

Hippocrene Children's Illustrated Irish Dictionary
English-Irish/Irish-English
500 entries • 94 pages • 8½ x 11 • $14.95hc • 0-7818-0713-1 • (798)

Irish-English/English-Irish Dictionary & Phrasebook
1,400 entries • 3¾ x 7 • $9.95pb • 0-87052-110-1 • (385)

Irish-English/English-Irish Practical Dictionary
20,000 entries • 4 x 6 • $12.95pb • 0-7818-0777-8 • (39)

Irish Love Poems: Dánta Grá
146 pages • 6¼ x 9¼ • $17.50hc • 0-7818-0396-9 • (70)

Irish Grammar: A Basic Handbook
100 pages • 5 x 7 • $9.95pb • 0-7818-0667-4 • (759)

**Hippocrene Children's Illustrated
Scottish Gaelic Dictionary**
English-Scottish Gaelic/Scottish Gaelic-English
500 entries • 94 pages • 8½ x 11 • $14.95hc • 0-7818-021-2 • (224)

Scottish Love Poems: A Personal Anthology
253 pages • 6 x 9 • $14.95pb • 0-7818-0406-X • (482)

Scottish Proverbs
112 pages • 5½ x 8½ • $14.95hc • 0-7818-0648-8 • (719)

Scottish Tartan Weddings
A Practical Guidebook
200 pages • 5½ x 8½ • $22.50hc • 0-7818-0754-9 • (353)

Gaelic-English/English-Gaelic Practical Dictionary
15,000 entries • 252 pages • 4 x 6 • $12.95 •
0-7818-0789-1 • (245)

Scottish Gaelic-English/English-Scottish Gaelic Dictionary
8,500 entries • 162 pages • 4 x 6 • $8.95pb • 0-7818-0316-0 • (285)

Etymological Dictionary of Scottish Gaelic
6,800 entries • 416 pages • 4½ x 7 • $14.95pb •
0-7818-0632-1 • (710)

Beginner's Gaelic
232 pages • 5½ x 8½ • $14.95pb • 0-7818-0726-3 • (255)

Prices subject to change without prior notice. **To purchase Hippocrene Books** contact your local bookstore, call (718) 454-2366, or write to: HIPPOCRENE BOOKS, 171 Madison Avenue, New York, NY 10016. Please enclose check or money order, adding $5.00 shipping (UPS) for the first book, and $.50 for each additional book.